THE PEWTER COLLECTOR

UNIFORM WITH THIS VOLUME
THE CHINA COLLECTOR
THE FURNITURE COLLECTOR
THE GLASS COLLECTOR
THE EARTHENWARE COLLECTOR
THE SILVER & SHEFFIELD PLATE COLLECTOR
THE STAMP COLLECTOR
THE MEDAL COLLECTOR
THE MINIATURE COLLECTOR

PLATE I.

Two dishes, temp. Charles I, with boss in centre of gilding metal
containing the Royal Arms in enamel.
The plain dish is in the possession of Wadham College, Oxford.

THE PEWTER COLLECTOR

A GUIDE TO ENGLISH PEWTER WITH SOME REFERENCE TO FOREIGN WORK ✿ ✿ ✿ ✿ BY H. J. L. J. MASSÉ, M.A. WITH NUMEROUS ILLUSTRATIONS INCLUDING THE TOUCHES FROM FOUR OF THE TOUCH PLATES IN THE POSSESSION OF THE PEWTERERS' COMPANY

NEW YORK
DODD MEAD AND COMPANY
1921

The Mayflower Press, Plymouth, England   William Brendon & Son Ltd.

PREFACE

IT is usual in a preface to express a hope that the book may fill a long-felt want. One may hope that it may, and that is all; but one cannot say that it will.

There is a difficulty in writing from the point of view of the collector because there is now so little good pewter generally available which is fit to collect, and that little is being sold at such ridiculously fancy prices that the average collector cannot hope to enter the lists and compete.

The main interest in pewter must be historical and archæological, for its metallurgical side can be dismissed in a few sentences and will not interest the ordinary reader.

The writer, in 1885, saw a round dish lying in the gutter in Bruges near a stall in the market-place, and as the dish had a crack in it, and its rim was rather badly battered, the writer became the owner of it by handing over to the dealer the sum of five francs.

This was the genesis of his interest in pewter. He cleaned it and many years later—for in 1885 he did not know how to do it—repaired it. Two years later, merely because he was the only one present at a committee meeting who owned a piece of pewter, he was constituted a sub-committee of one, with power to add to his number, to arrange for " Pewter " as a subject for discussion by what was then a small Society of Artists, and to find someone to read a paper on the subject. He failed to find this someone, and his own notes made the basis of a contribution to the evening's discussion. That evening meeting, however, bore fruit—he was told that two friends who had begun to collect information on the subject had been forced by other work to give up any idea of going on with it, and would gladly hand on their notes and sketches to him.

The usphot of this was that after some years' work at the subject "Pewter Plate" was published by Messrs. Bell in a very sumptuous edition in 1904. The same year the writer organized an Exhibition of Pewter in Clifford's Inn Hall, followed by another in 1908.

All this may or may not be of interest to the reader, but it may just be worth noting as the record of the genesis of the writer's interest in the subject.

A preface, however, is the only place in which I can thank all the friends who for many years have contributed any new marks or touches that they met with or acquired. They are contributed here to the common benefit of all collectors, and if the fact of the mark or the name being recorded here for the first time helps a collector to identify and date his piece or pieces, the work involved has not been wasted.

Anyone may parade his new knowledge acquired from my laboriously compiled lists, but if he has merely a rudimentary notion of honour (and even thieves are said to have that) he may surely take the pains to acknowledge the source of his indebtedness. After all, working with scissors and paste is not so laborious that it leaves no time for a due acknowledgment.

Here the writer may plead guilty to an absorbing interest in the marks and touches, especially those which are as yet unassigned to any known pewterer, either because they have initials only, and are so common in their combination that they may be those of half a dozen or more pewterers, or because they are in part or wholly illegible or indecipherable. He has received hundreds of marks, and though he may not expect to write another book on pewter he would be glad to receive rubbings of, and information as to, new discovered marks and touches so that he may leave his own copy with many additions for the next generation of pewter lovers. His collection (he has none) is on the shelves and dressers of his friends.

Another word of thanks is due to all who sent me at various times photographs of collections in whole or in

PREFACE

part of special pieces, and especially Dr. Young. Some of them I have used in spite of the fact that I cannot now identify the sender. It is easier to remember touches than photographs, and if I have unwittingly offended by using them I must ask for forgiveness beforehand, and in justification or, better perhaps, in extenuation, say that as I never thought I should ever require to use them I made no special record of them.

Lastly, too, a preface is the best place to make a humble bow and ask to be excused if the little word " I " comes in too much. In any account that is personal, it is difficult to keep it out, but it may be excused if there be humility rather than egotism in the background. There is no room for theories in a book like this, and one can only write from personal experiment and knowledge and from practical experience.

My special thanks are due to the Worshipful Company of Pewterers for permission to use my verbal descriptions of the touches from the 2nd edition of " Pewter Plate," 1910, and for permission to include drawings by Miss Sheila McEwan of all the legible touches, and also to Mr. Howard H. Cotterell, F.R.H.S., and Mr. M. S. Dudley Westropp for very kind permission to check and augment my imperfect lists of Irish pewterers from their joint article on the subject in the " Journal of the Proceedings of the R.S.A., Ireland," June, 1917, Vol. VII, Series VI.

(Signed)   H. J. L. J. MASSÉ.

CONTENTS

		PAGE
	PREFACE	v
CHAPTER		
I.	ON COLLECTING	15
II.	RUBBINGS	29
III.	DISPLAYING PEWTER	31
IV.	AS TO THE CLEANING AND REPAIRING OF PEWTER	35
V.	A FEW DON'TS	49
VI.	THE CRAFT OF THE PEWTERER	53
VII.	THE STANDARDS OF PEWTER	77
VIII.	THE ORNAMENTATION AND DECORATION OF PEWTER	83
IX.	PEWTER IN THE HOME	93
X.	CHURCH PEWTER	115
XI.	PEWTER MARKS	133
XII.	LIST OF THE NAMES OF PEWTERERS	145
XIII.	THE TOUCH PLATES	221
XIV.	PRICES	297
	GLOSSARY	300
	THE REFERENCE LITERATURE OF PEWTER	305
	INDEX	311

ILLUSTRATIONS

PLATE
I. . . . . *Frontispiece*

Two dishes, temp. Charles I, with boss in centre of gilding metal containing the Royal Arms in enamel.

TO FACE PAGE

II. 24

½ mutchkin measure (Scots). Gill thistle measure (Glasgow district). ½ mutchkin tappit-hen. ½ pint (old English wine measure = 8 fluid ozs.), hammer-head thumb-piece. ½ mutchkin measure (Scots). (Embryo shell thumb-piece.) ½ pint Imperial Scotch.

Quart, pint, ½ pint, gill, and ½ gill Imperial measure (Scotch).

Channel Islands jug or measure by I.D.S.X. Tappit hen (1 pint Scots). Gallon baluster measure. ½ gallon lidless tappit-hen from Aberdeenshire. Pot-belly measure (1 pint Scots).

III. 32

1 pint pear-shaped measure, by W. Scott, Edinburgh (Edinburgh type). 1 pint pear-shaped measure, but with flat lid by Ramage, Edinburgh (1826). 1 pint pear-shaped measure (Glasgow type).

IV. 40

Harvester measures (Irish): Quart, pint, ½ pint, and gill.

Pot-belly measures from Aberdeenshire: Pint (Scots), chopin, mutchkin, and gill. Pint (Scots).

Noggin measures (Irish?): ½ pint, gill, ½ gill, and ¼ gill.

V. 48

(*a*) Channel Islands jug and 4 measures. Pint (tappit-hen) (Scots). ¼ gallon Imperial (Aberdeenshire). 1 pint pot-belly (lidded). 1 pint pot-belly (unlidded).

(b) ½ pint bud thumb-piece measure (old English wine measure = 8 fluid ozs.). ¼ pint hammer-head old English wine measure (= 8 fluid ozs.). ½ pint Imperial (Scotch). Ball thumb-piece. ½ pint Imperial.

(c) Scots measures. Chopin, mutchkin, ½ mutchkin = 7½ fluid ozs. Gill, ½ gill, and ¼ gill.

(d) Imperial English measures (double volute thumb-pieces). Quart, pint, ½ pint, gill, and ½ gill.

Plate		To face page
VI.	Two flagons.	56
VII.	Two inkstands: 1. With pin-hinges and cup-feet; 2. With drawer.	64
VIII.	Thumb-pieces and lids of Stuart tankards. Thumb-pieces and lids of various tankards: Early Georgian or Queen Anne. Late Georgian. Scotch. Stuart. Early Georgian. Stuart.	72
IX.	Various spoons (left to right of page): (a) Hexagonal stem, *temp.* Henry VIII. Maker's mark N. E., with cardinal's hat. (b) Elizabethan spoon, found in crypt of Gloucester Cathedral. (c) Slip-top spoon, found in the Thames. Date 1679. (d) Pied-de-biche, rat-tail. W. L., 1668. (e) Pied-de-biche, rat-tail. I. N., with fleur-de-lys and date 1678. (f) Rat-tailed spoon. (g) Rat-tailed spoon. Maker's mark T. P. in small beaded shield. Found in Chester. (h) Rat-tailed spoon, with quality mark. Maker's mark B. T. G. with a crown, a fleur-de-lys, rose below. (i) *Temp.* William IV.	80
X.	Two large dishes: 1. Reeded rim. 20¼ diam. Made by Pettit, 1685. 2. Flat-beaded rim. Arms dated 1677.	88
XI.	1. Various measures and a teapot. 2. Two measures, showing different ways of fixing handles to the body.	96

ILLUSTRATIONS

PLATE TO FACE PAGE

XII. 104

Two old measures, with photograph of the lid stamped rather unusually in five places.

XIII. 112

Stuart tankards: 1. Height, 5 in.; base, 4⅝ in. 2. Height, 6 in.; base, 5 in. 3. Height, 7½ in.; base, 5¼ in. 4. Height, 6 in.; base, 4½ in. 5. Height, 5 in.; base, 4½ in. Sizes are from top of lid to base. Capacity of No. 3 is smaller than 2 and 4, as base is raised up.

XIV. 120

1. Chalice. Dated Assoc. Congreg. Edin., 1794. 2. Flagon. Scotch. Relief Kirk, Musselburgh, 1786. 3. Early chalice. No marks. 4. Early chalice (No. 22 in Touch Plates) (C. S. and rose). 5. Flagon or laver. Scotch. No marks.

Two flagons and paten from Somersetshire.

XV. 128

Two Scottish Episcopal Church flagons and a christening bowl.

XVI. 136

German flagon (right). Flemish measure (left).

THE PEWTER COLLECTOR

CHAPTER I

ON COLLECTING

WHY does anybody want to collect pewter? This is the question which seems to be in the minds of the people who light upon any collection of pewter, either in a friend's house or in a properly organized museum.

What possible interest, say they, is there in stuff that looks like lead, and that requires perpetual cleaning to keep it in good condition.

These two questions depend upon one another, and the answer to both is in the word—interest. It should be interesting to any thoughtful person to study and try to learn more about a material which has been in use from the first ages in which tin was alloyed with lead to make it more workable, and incidentally to render it more profitable to the maker.

It is not possible to divide the art of the pewterer into sharply defined periods, or according to any improved method or process. There is no "Spode" pewter, no "Wedgwood," no "Battersea"—but only pewter: pewter always made in the same way and of the same ingredients or nearly so. We may divide the history into Mediæval, Elizabethan, Stuart, and *late* if we like, but the marks are the real guide to the dates.

The control of the pewterers working in England was at first rigidly enforced by the Pewterers' Company in London, and when in the eighteenth century the right of control was dropped (because it was felt that it could not be enforced), the trade and the art both began to decline. This is an epitome of the whole history of pewter.

Pewter differs from other wares affected by collectors in that it came in as a substitute—more or less plausible—for more precious metal, and also formed a rather important link in the long chain of development of domestic table and other ware from wood to china. Pewter plates seem to have been in existence concurrently with "treene" or platters of wood. Then pewter took the place of wood altogether in better-class houses, and was later superseded by foreign china. This foreign china was later on ousted by home-produced wares, which gave place eventually to the various kinds of earthenware and china which are with us to-day.

In vessels for water or beer carrying we have the series of wood, leather, pewter, each overlapping the other. Earthenware and china both with pewter mounts. Britannia metal—zinc—enamelled iron or steel—and lastly aluminium either pure or in the form of an alloy.

English pewter developed on rather different lines from the pewter of the Low Countries and of France and Germany. In England the quality was the thing that was aimed at beyond all others—the shapes remained simple and remarkably free from all added ornament. Abroad the quality was neglected as compared with our makers' high standard, the shapes often developed into eccentricities and very often there was too much ornament.

There is nothing in England to correspond with the Hanaps or Guild-cups of Germany or the Netherlands: nor have we any elaborate altar candlesticks to compare with those of foreign make. Our pewter was domestic in style rather than ecclesiastical, but what was made for church use was extremely good, severe and dignified.

The keynote in the history of the pewterer's art has been imitation, and as a rule imitation of the work done by the goldsmiths and silversmiths. Church and domestic plate were made in pewter on the lines of similar plate made in silver. It was allowed in the case of Church plate when poverty was the reason, and it was done in the case of domestic ware because there was no authority to stop it, or even to hinder its production.

Two glaring instances will make it clear. The fine solid silver candlesticks of Charles I and Charles II were frankly copied by the pewterers even though the design was not suited for the baser metal. The same happened in the case of the tankards—every detail in the pewter copies the details of those made in silver—whether the tankards were of temp. Charles I or of William and Mary.

In the case of spoons we find that the same thing happened. Every change of silver fashion was copied by the workers in pewter and in latten, which was more durable than pewter.

It is this copying that gives rise to a feeling rather of disgust at the pewterers' poverty of invention. It would have been quite possible for them to work out shapes for candlesticks and tankards on their own lines suited for the metal, and the different method of construction required for the softer metal.

It is probable, however, that the cry of the public for pewter made " to look like silver " was too strong for the pewterers to resist. They gave way in Germany and they gave way in France. The clamour of the people for silver-looking spoons was perhaps stronger, and one pewterer found himself in trouble in 1652 for making spoons which he called by the suspicious name of SILVORUM.

The pewterers, however, as a rule knew the limitations of their material, and produced work which was beautiful because of its simplicity, and its good quality. There is nothing to compare with the beauty of our hand-made pewter plates of two hundred years ago when the maker kept himself away from the temptation of using either too much antimony or possibly antimony that was not chemically pure.

Pewter is the name given to an alloy in which the chief ingredients are tin and antimony, or tin and lead. Bismuth is occasionally added for the same reason as antimony, viz. to harden the alloy. The more tin there is in the alloy the better the pewter.

As tin, though not a precious metal, has always been relatively costly it was found advisable to reduce the standard of pewter by adding lead when the metal was required for trade purposes such as large wine measures, organ pipes, candle-moulds, etc.

Fine pewter has no lead in it at all but consists of tin with nearly 25 per cent. of copper.

Various alloys are here given in tabular form:—

Alloy.	Tin.	Lead.	Antimony.	Copper.	Bismuth.
Fine pewter (old)	112	—	—	26	—
Tin and temper	100	—	1·6	—	—
Plate pewter 1	100	—	8	4	4
,, ,, 2	112	—	8	—	—
,, ,, 3	90	—	6·7	2	—
,, ,, 4	89·3	—	7·1	1·8	—
Superior pewter	100	—	17	—	—
Better ,, 1	84	—	7	4	—
,, ,, 2	89	—	7	2	—
,, ,, 3	56	—	8	6	—
Hard metal	96	—	8	2	—
Trifle	83	—	17	—	—
,,	82	—	18	—	—
Ley	80	20	—	—	—
Pipe metal (organs)	60	40	—	—	—
Queen's metal	100	—	8	4	1
Good Britannia metal	150	—	10	3	—
Fioravanti (dishes and porringers)	88	12	—	—	—
Limoges pewterers	100	4	—	—	—
Montpellier pewterers (dishes)	96	4	—	—	—
Montpellier pewterers (ewers)	90	10	—	—	—
Spoons	97	1·65	—	1·42	—
,,	95·6	3·64	—	1·06	—

Pewter is made to-day as it has ever been, either by casting in moulds, or by hammering the metal from a previously prepared sheet. The moulds are generally made of gun-metal (other materials such as plaster of Paris, sand, stone, may be used when only a small number of articles are required) and for complicated vessels, e.g. for a standing cup, a ewer, are in several pieces.

Pewter is now comparatively scarce, as it was never looked upon as a thing to be treated with reverence or handled with care, and more than that it was constitutionally unfit to stand continued hard usage, if not bad treatment, at the hands of servants.

Countless plates have been destroyed in part by being carelessly overheated too near a flame, and countless candlesticks have been ruined by the socket ends being thoughtlessly thrust between the bars of a kitchen fire. The same thing has no doubt happened in the case of teapots and posset cups, and to them destruction was bound to come if they were left empty on a hob.

The advice generally given to a collector about to interest himself in pewter is that he must specialize. Quite good advice, but not easy to follow, for the genuine pewter in which to specialize is becoming year by year more difficult to find.

No one would for a moment think of collecting candlesticks or beer mugs of the nineteenth century. The only interest that can possibly attach to the latter lies in the fact that the mugs may have belonged to alehouses that have long since been improved out of existence, but the engraved name is no certain guarantee of the fact.

Pepper cruets and mustard pots again will hardly appeal to collectors. Some of the mustard pots, however, may be found to have rather graceful handles of an earlier type.

Beer mugs by good makers of the eighteenth century, even if they are battered or incomplete are useful purchases, as the metal of which they are made can be turned to good account in repairing other more important but damaged pieces.

Saltcellars are more interesting, and the earlier they are the better. Many of these on feet are Britannia metal. Snuff-boxes too are of surprising interest. The metal is good, the workmanship is careful and some of the designs are excellent. It is a curious thing with reference to these small articles that they bear no marks of identification and very rarely the name of a maker. They do not give the impression that they were made by any ordinary workman in pewter, they rather give the impression that they were made by a silversmith, or at any rate a professed box or locket-maker. It requires a skilled workman to make a metal box, locket or watch shut properly, easily and securely. Inkstands again may be worth collecting. The makers copied the patterns of the silversmiths to a great extent, but the workmanship as a rule is good. The weak point in many types was the insertion of a drawer, and the consequent weakening of the side where the drawer was fitted.

Tankards and beakers may occasionally be met with at reasonable prices, especially if slightly imperfect. A defect is no real occasion for refusing a chance of adding a good specimen. No one would refuse to buy Elizabethan silver or other early work merely because of some slight imperfection caused by hard usage or by accident.

Plates are interesting and the earlier the better. The broad flat plain rims are difficult to find, but they have a dignity that is hard to equal. Reeded rims are never so interesting, though on small plates in daily use they give a modicum of strength where it is wanted most.

Eccentricities in pewter may be left alone. They are not found in English so much as in German work. Flagons and tankards with twisted flutings, octagonalized bodies on circular bases, are all very well in a German museum, but they are merely passing fashions and warnings of what to leave undone in pewter work. Milk jugs in the form of a cow can never have been common, pepper castors after the model of bull-dogs must have soon become an eyesore.

It is not often that anything new is discovered in the way of a pint-pot, but a novelty of this kind was encountered the other day among the items of a small collection; it was a heavy pot and an ugly one too, with a very uninteresting handle and a massive base. Being very much tarnished from neglect, it seemed to be very much like the other pots and jugs on the shelf; but it turned out to be a Britannia metal casing to a cast-iron core. The core had been left quite rough except round the bottom and the top rim, and the very thin casing or lining had been soldered into its place. Some moisture, however, had found its way in through a hole or crevice and had caused the iron to rust, and this rust had burst the thin Britannia metal casing and so ruined the pint-pot.

Unfortunately the maker's name was on the bottom, which was fragmentary, and was almost illegible except that the word LONDON was quite plain. The whole was hollow and very much battered: structurally it was too weak for the pot when empty, and much too weak for the pot when full.

This faked pewter is mentioned here because if there is one there may be others, and however interesting it may be there is no need for anyone to pay a pewter price for a Britannia metal pot with a cast-iron core. One expects to find a cast-iron core in the silver candlesticks that often figure in the lists of wedding presents, for how else could ware made of silver $\frac{1}{120}$ of an inch in thickness be expected to stand upright, and one expects to find sheet lead in plenty at the back of the so-called massive silver hand-mirrors.

Another eccentricity in pewter, of which a rubbing was sent to the writer by the Curator of the Metropolitan Museum at New York, was a platter—quite flat from the description, about 14 in. in diameter and covered with ornament. Besides this the edge was alternately scalloped with ordinary pointed scallops. It must have been so difficult to pick it up from a table that one conjectures it was meant to be hung from a wall.

There is a large class of objects made in pewter that no collector could bring himself to put in a collection, unless he were so ill advised as to try to collect a specimen of everything that had been made in pewter. Some are more or less monstrosities, some on the principle of *omne ignotum pro magnifico* have been collected as the collectors were ignorant of the use of the objects, such as bottle-holders, i.e. vessels like flower-holders with a ring, supported on three feet joined to the rim, to hold a bottle (when recently washed) and catch the drippings; or again such as inhalers, quite a common-place modern invention with nothing in it to warrant its collection.

It may sound almost heretical in a book ostensibly for collectors, but it is *bona fide* for all that—the best way to begin collecting pewter is at first to collect from the decorative point of view. Anyone who begins in this way will derive more pleasure *ab initio* than a period-bound dry-as-dust collector who will only collect Stuart candlesticks or absolutely perfect spoons. From this decorative point of view the collector will be wise to buy at first some ordinary plates of good quality. For him at first the best test will be to test them for resonance. If the plate when struck gives a pleasant sound like a gong, the quality will in all probability be right; but if it sounds dull like a cracked flower-pot he may as well leave the specimen alone. He may then aspire to some 12-in. or 15-in. dishes. These again may be tested in the same way, and approved or rejected as a result of the test. In plates there are many varieties of rims, from the wide flat plain rim to the narrow reeded or moulded kind. It is impossible to lay down a hard-and-fast rule for the vogue in rims, due no doubt to the great cost of the gun-metal mould.

An Elizabethan pewter dish of some 20 in. in diameter may have the same rim as a dish of the eighteenth century, and a Charles II dish or charger of 1660 may have a flat plain rim that one might find on a dish 150 years later. This is the reason why a study of the marks is so essential to a serious collector.

Jugs of the eighteenth century are often to be found, some with and some without lids. Candlesticks, too, of the same period may be picked up. They are often in pairs, but two good ones with varying stems and slightly different in height need not be rejected.

A couple of the hexagonal vessels which for want of a better name the writer called "food-bottles," might be added. They are sometimes much battered and worn out in the screw-threading of the lid, but the sides can be straightened out. Some of them have spouts, and some have spouts with lids. The latter must have been intended for cyder, wine or beer. Those without spouts had various uses. From the inscriptions and from the decoration it can be inferred that one often formed a present for a prospective bride or for a young married woman.

Another item the collector might be able to afford is a good specimen of inkstand, one of the kind that was a copy of the silversmiths' ware of the eighteenth century. Oblong in shape on four small feet, with two ink bottles and a sand-dredger, and two hinged compartments for pens.

The men who worked at these inkstands (and the same in the case of the maker of snuff-boxes) must have been thoroughly efficient workmen, for no bungling or haphazard work was ever tolerated in anything made of pewter. Many of these beautiful inkstands are unmarked, and there is no indication to guide one to the makers' name.

Foreign copies—and they were and are common enough—are as a rule overburdened with marks, both large and small. Cartloads, if not tons, of pewter were formerly manufactured in Germany to be unloaded on guileless tourists in important centres, poor in the quality of the metal, rough in workmanship—but always ridiculously high in price, more so when the arms of the neighbouring Schloss owner were engraved or worked in repoussé on the tankard or plate.

Landlords of wayside hotels were collectors in name, but in reality collectors for profit—i.e. dealers, who in exchange for many coins, were willing to part with one or two pieces—just to oblige.

Spoons are best left alone by the novice.

A collector of pewter must become thoroughly acquainted with the feel of the metal. He must be introduced to it, he must get to know its qualities and its limitations, and in time he will love it. It is a pity that the specimens in our museums are all under glass. So much can be learned about pewter by handling and by close examination of the ware, but of course glass cases are the only thing possible in public collections.

Access to the collection of a private collector of experience

PLATE II

½ mutchkin measure (Scots).
Gill thistle measure (Glasgow district).
½ mutchkin tappit-hen.
½ pint (old English wine measure = 8 fluid ozs.), hammer-head thumb-piece.
½ mutchkin measure (Scots). (Embryo shell thumb-piece.)
½ pint Imperial Scotch.

Quart, pint, ½ pint, gill, and ½ gill Imperial measure (Scotch).

Channel Islands jug or measure by I. D. S. X.
Tappit-hen (1 pint Scots).
Gallon baluster measure.
½ gallon lidless tappit-hen from Aberdeenshire.
Pot-belly measure (1 pint Scots).

(Dr. Young.)

PLATE II.

is also desirable, and if the budding collector has an elder brother collector, i.e. one who has been singed in the fire of his ardour for pewter, to whom he can apply for advice when required, so much the better for him. One often hears the old saying that one should buy one's experience, but in pewter collecting the buying may turn out to be very expensive and most discouraging.

As has been said above pewter is, as a rule, cast in moulds, and then the castings worked up and perfected by turning and polishing. The use of moulds made the pewterers conservative, as a new mould was an expensive item. Hence we find articles varying but little in form if we look at them from the point of view of the mould, but varying widely in details such as the rim of plates and basins. The rim was finished while the dish or plate was revolving in a lathe, and variations, in an age when micrometric measurements were unknown, were bound to occur.

A pewterer would not turn out a dozen plates with the same mechanical exactitude as the wood turner who makes draughtsmen by the gross with a tool that cannot make anything but the pattern for the making of which it was devised.

One always regrets that the English stone-pots, so often mentioned by Mr. Welch, and their lids have not come down in number to our time. For beer a stone-pot, i.e. an earthenware vessel with a lid, was just the thing. Thick enough to keep the beer cool and not too heavy to handle.

Abroad, in Germany for instance, the museums are full of them, pots of a pleasant grey colour with blue ornament, capped with a simple lid, and very often fitted with a pewter rim round the roughly finished base.

Pots of the same type are made of blue-white china in Holland, with china tops framed in pewter rim, and with pewter hinges and mountings.

In Germany there used to be many types in use by students, all with pewter lids and mounts.

German guild cups are often of great beauty, especially the early ones, while some of the late eighteenth-century specimens are ugly and commonplace beyond words. One of the finest known was formerly in the Gurney collection, and was on loan at the Victoria and Albert Museum for several years. It is now the property of Lord Swaythling. The workmanship is quite Gothic in feeling, especially in the handle and the thumb-piece, and the cup is a fine specimen of inlaid work, strap ornament in brass being carried round the body.

Perhaps the next finest is one, now in the possession of Mr. A. B. Yeates, formerly the Hanap of a Guild of Gunsmiths or Locksmiths.

Many of these cups have had ball or lion feet added to them.

There are difficulties in the way of the collector which are not likely to diminish as time goes on. It is but rarely that one comes across pre-Elizabethan pewter—Elizabethan ware is scarce enough. Roman pewter of undoubted authenticity is known to the writer who has had the handling and the repairing of it. Pewter of the time of Richard II, in perfect order with the exception of holes burned through by injudicious warming, was found in South London some years back. Pewter of the period of Henry VII, and said to bear the badge of Prince Arthur, his eldest son, was dug up when the ground for the foundation for the new buildings at Guy's Hospital was being excavated. Pewter, too, from Tobermory, salved from the Spanish ship that went down there after the flight round the north of Scotland, has been restored in the last few years and made usable after nearly four hundred years' immersion.

The chances are quite small that any collector will find bargains consisting of pewter of Elizabethan date. He may pick up occasionally a damaged tankard of the time of Charles I, more frequently a tankard of the period of William and Mary, with the characteristic floral engraved ornament, mainly conventional tulips or pinks; or possibly a battered paten or communion flagon of the end of the seventeenth century.

There is a tradition that the royalists who gave up their silver plate during the Civil War were partially compensated for the loan by being allowed to have pewter copies of the borrowed pieces, and that these copies were hall-marked as a kind of guarantee that they were to be redeemed at some future date. This seems to be nothing more than a pretty story, for not a single specimen of such hall-marked pewter has come down to us, nor has one been described in a convincing fashion.

There were, however, a certain number of rosewater dishes with central enamelled bosses bearing the arms of Charles I. Six were said to have been sent to Charles I while at York in 1642. Of these one is certainly in existence. It is a fine dish 19½ in. in diameter, 2 in. deep, and it is ornamented, a rare thing in English pewter, by means of lenticular blobs made by a repoussé worker from the back. All these are rarities, and with them one could class rosewater dishes and master-salts of the same reign.

They are never likely to be found in numbers, and they can never be common.

Another piece of rare pewter is a large charger or boar's head dish 23½ in. in diameter which has been nearly three hundred years in the family of its present owner. It is a fine dish, and it is a pleasure to handle and examine such splendid work. A similar dish, but of smaller size, was shown at the first exhibition of pewter in 1904, lent by the Corporation of Abingdon. It was not as old as the large dish just mentioned, and its surface was very little scored with knife marks. The dish, however, was much scored on the bottom and apparently had been used as a block or board for cutting up meat.

Occasionally one runs up against Roman pewter. The best known Roman pewter is that which was described by the Rev. R. G. Engleheart in Volume LVI of "Archæologia," pp. 7 *sqq*.

Its former use is quite problematical. It may, or may not, have been ecclesiastical—but as pewter of good quality it must always be of interest, though the collector as a rule may not reasonably expect to become the possessor of any such finds.

The Bateman collection contained some small bowls in pewter of excellent quality and in a very fair state of preservation. They were lent for exhibition at Clifford's Inn in 1904.

More of the same date has been in the market of late, and for its age fetched very low prices. Its condition was very fragile and needed most careful handling and extensive repairs. The analyses of Roman pewter seem to give the reason for the lasting quality of the ware. There was no antimony in the Roman formula, and hence there was none of the efflorescence caused by the decaying of the antimony. There were other impurities but they were not important.

CHAPTER II

RUBBINGS

THERE is one thing that a collector may always do, and that is take rubbings of all the pieces that come into his possession or that pass through his hands on their way elsewhere. It is better to take several rubbings of the marks, as they vary so in their perfection, and spare copies may always be sent on to other collectors.

Rubbings with heelball are all very well for church brasses, but quite out of place for tiny marks which may be no larger than a pea.

For all pewter marks fine paper such as bank post or rice paper, as used for cigarettes, is preferable, and the finer the quality of the lead pencil the better and clearer the rubbing. Copying-ink pencil is often better than blacklead and gives a better rubbing.

The ideal material, however, is thin tinfoil rubbed smooth first on a piece of glass to remove any pattern or chance scratches. The rubbing may be done with any hard rounded article such as a bone or ivory penholder; and it will be found that the underneath side of the rubbing will often reveal some detail which is not so apparent on the upper side. Tinfoil rubbings must be carefully handled and are best gummed in a book for reference, and if indexed properly require very little handling.

Very often a rubbing which seems to be hopelessly illegible can be read better if the article be warmed very carefully with the flame from a spirit lamp.

A piece of hard metal such as silver, when the design upon it has been deliberately hammered out of all recognition will, when reheated, still show the original design. In the case of the pewter there must naturally be no overheating.

Photography, too, may be called in to aid the collector, and a print on glazed P.O.P. from a good photographic negative of a mark will often give a satisfactory clue to the name that cannot be read with the unaided eye.

A Coddington lens, or a focussing eye-piece, is useful in studying the touch plates or the collotype reproductions of them, but the continued use of such a lens is very tiring to the eyes.

CHAPTER III

DISPLAYING PEWTER

THE obvious method of displaying a collection of plates and drinking vessels is to use a dresser, preferably an old one; but failing that on a modern but not too flimsy copy. Plates on a dresser have to be tilted at an angle which helps the metal to reflect any light which falls upon it. Our ancestors did not trouble themselves about the decorative effect of a garnish of pewter and more often than not turned the plates to face the wall so as to have the dust on the under side instead of on the face.

With the plates there is no objection to a few flagons, measures or tankards but the dresser must not be overcrowded. Overcrowding is unfortunately a very common fault. Nothing gives a worse impression than to see all kinds of incongruous articles massed together on the table of a dresser or on the narrow shelves.

Church plate should be kept strictly by itself, either on a shelf or in a small cabinet. If it is old and in a crumbling condition it is better to have it under glass to prevent any handling. The same applies to any delicate pieces which are of sufficient rarity, such as spoons of known authenticity.

Spoons of a common type may be kept in a rack something after the manner of a pipe-rack.

Foreign spoon-racks were evidently designed to help the housewife to check her stock of spoons with the minimum of trouble. The symmetry of the arrangement of the spoons in the rack was at once marred by the gap left by one absentee.

In our return to the simple life and the use of a living-

PLATE III

1 pint pear-shaped measure, by W. Scott, Edinburgh. (Edinburgh type).
1 pint pear-shaped measure, but with flat lid by Ramage, Edinburgh (1826).
1 pint pear-shaped measure (Glasgow type).

(Dr. Young.)

PLATE III.

room the mantelshelf and the ingle-nook both form convenient places for the display of large plates and dishes. If the ingle-nook be merely a dummy, with no chimney, the pewter will seem to be dull. The play of firelight on pewter in a real ingle-nook is a sight to gladden the heart and the eyes too.

Dishes and plates are often bought as decoration, but it seems a pity to sky good plates and dishes on a frieze in a large room where no one can touch them except the man who climbs a ladder at stated intervals to dust, or once a year to spring-clean them.

In the Nürnberg Museum there is a living-room reconstituted so as to show the latter-day folk what the rooms of their forbears were like. The idea is good, but more or less Utopian, for it is manifestly impossible to have one room of this kind historically correct in all its details. To do the thing properly there would be required a series of rooms of various centuries, and space would not allow it.

If no dresser is available a set of shelves may be contrived which will answer the purpose, but the background will have to be considered.

The effect of pewter is certainly best when it is massed together. If the room is light a dull background may be used, but if the room is dark the background must be bright. One fine collection—now housed in the Metropolitan Museum in New York—was shown in London in a dark room in a semicircular recess of which all the woodwork was enamelled white and the lining paper of the recess a brilliant pillar-box red.

In another room, also in London, all the woodwork was painted white, and the pewter which was lovingly cared for by its owner, who had begun to collect long before most of us who are alive now, were born, looked remarkably well in its surroundings, both when dull and awaiting its regular day for cleaning, and when fresh from the cleaner's, i.e. the owner's hands. The latter always maintained that the modern servant could not be safely trusted to clean either plate or pewter. Certainly the pewter soup plates cleaned by the owner rivalled the silver spoons and forks cleaned by his manservant.

c

Brown paper, if it is not of too hot a shade, looks well with pewter, so do some shades of green; but the exact shade must be experimented with on the spot and with a pattern of reasonable dimensions.

A distempered wall is the cheapest, and possibly there is more variety to be obtained in the shades of any colour by means of judicious blending.

In museums the makers of show cases seem always unable to get away from cheap blue or rusty black velveteen, both of which so soon look shabby; but perhaps the official mind prescribes these materials as being the most generally useful.

Dishes should never have holes bored in the rim in order that they may be hung from a wall. The boring depreciates the value of the dish or plate and the wire which is put through will only last a limited time (shorter than usual if gas be the illuminant) and then disaster comes when the plate falls.

A narrow shelf with a ledge to it is far safer, and with proper brackets to support it may and ought to be decorative as well. If the shelf is very narrow there should be a narrow retaining ledge to hold in the plates at the top, or at any rate a panel pin driven into the wall and bent downwards to serve as a hook.

CHAPTER IV

AS TO THE CLEANING AND REPAIRING OF PEWTER

WHEN pewter is not kept bright the surface slowly oxidizes, and assumes a very pleasing subdued tone, not the least like the hard black tarnish which discolours silver. This colour is peculiarly its own.

On some specimens of old pewter a kind of efflorescence will be found resembling rust. It is probably due to some change or decomposition in the antimony used in the pewter, as tin itself is not liable to changes of this nature. It cannot be removed by cleaning and it makes holes in the metal eventually.

To keep pewter clean in old times it was found necessary to oil it, and in 1661 the Pewterers' Company paid 19s. 6d. for a year's oiling of their pewter ware.

If pewter has to be left exposed for any length of time without being occasionally rubbed, it is a good plan to rub it over with a rag or cloth saturated with vaseline. There is no necessity to leave a thick deposit of vaseline upon the pewter, as a very thin coating is all that is required. Unlike anything in the nature of a lacquer, it only requires rubbing to remove it.

To remove the obstinate black oxide or scale that has formed on pewter that has been lying forgotten for any length of time there are two methods, the one drastic and the other slow. Care is required in the former, and it is best to proceed by having a brush with which to apply hydrochloric acid to the parts affected. If a rag is preferred it should be held in a piece of bamboo split at one end; with a rag so held more pressure can be applied than with a brush. After applying the acid its action must be watched, and as the scale softens, the part so cleaned should be wiped with a wet sponge.

The slower process consists in using paraffin oil, applied locally or as a bath in obstinate cases.

It is absolutely useless for a novice to attempt to remove the oxide by scraping, as a series of ugly scratches will be the only result.

It is sometimes thought that glass-paper and emery-cloth must never be used on pewter. The prohibition is too sweeping and too vague. The very finest glass-paper glued on to a flat piece of wood makes an excellent file for the removal of the efflorescent crust from the surface, a defect which is found occasionally even in the best pewter.

As to emery-cloth—there is emery-cloth and emery-cloth. That sold by the oil and colourman for cleaning rusty fenders and neglected fire-irons is of no use at all to the pewter collector, but emery-paper and especially oo or oooo is of the greatest use to the owner of good pewter. By its help scratches can be removed with very little trouble.

An old-fashioned cleaning nostrum for household pewter was rubbing with Calais sand and elm-leaves. The latter were probably used merely to hold the sand during the cleaning process.

Putty powder, as the oxide of tin is called, is also an excellent cleaning medium. It may be used dry.

Oxalic acid by itself, dissolved in water, or with the addition of jewellers' rouge or sifted rotten-stone, is a good cleaning medium; but it is a poison, and makes the nails rather brittle and so it requires caution in use.

Cleaning or "scouring" pewter was a branch of the trade, and it was not supposed to be done elsewhere than in the pewterers' workshops.

The regulations quoted by Bapst from Boissonnet for the cleaning of church plate, if of pewter, are very precise: "It must be washed every three months in hot soapsuds, and be rubbed with oats or other husk-bearing grain, or with broken egg-shells; then washed in clean water, dried and wiped with a clean cloth."

Pewter is often ruined by injudicious cleaning and by

CLEANING AND REPAIRING OF PEWTER

cleaning by inexperienced people. All cleaning and polishing really consists in scratching the surface in such a way that the scratches are not apparent to the naked eye. As soon as the general direction of the scratch lines changes, the scratches become painfully visible. It is quite easy to take scratches out of a gold ring with very fine emery paper and a burnisher, but the scratches would be quite visible if the direction were to be changed. It is easy to try this. Take a piece of fine emery cloth, o or oo, and rub a piece of scrap pewter or the under side of a plate several times one way only, and then follow with the same number of rubbings with the lines at right angles to the first set and the scratches will be seen at once.

It is not always easy to rub regularly in a circular direction, but it can be done in a lathe—if it is big enough—or by means of a polishing lathe. Hand cleaning, as a rule, should be enough for most of the pewter in an ordinary condition.

Cleaning is dirty work at the best of times and certainly is so with pewter; and the more lead there is in it, the dirtier the cleaning will make the hands of the cleaner.

There are many cleaning nostrums, and all are probably equally efficient as cleaners; but pewter seems to tarnish more quickly after some than after others. Much good pewter has been ruined by being cleaned with sand. Sand is right enough for scouring saucepans and for other purposes, but it is a mistake to clean pewter with it. Many tankard hinges have been ruined by sand getting in between the leaves of the hinge and into the hole of the hinge-pin.

Powdered bath-brick and oil is a good cleaner for obstinate stains, especially if the powder be sifted first; but a better one is made by mixing soft soap and rotten-stone together till it makes a dry mixture and then by moistening slightly with turpentine.

Our forefathers used to use one of the Equisetum family for cleaning their pewter. The plant probably contained some minute grains of silex and owes its efficiency as a scouring agent to that botanical fact.

Powdered infusorial earth—an ingredient which finds

its way into several cleansing nostrums—is excellent, but it is always advisable to sift it. Very fine ash, such as collects behind firebricks or in the flues in a kitchener, moistened with vinegar, is an excellent cleanser.

When the pewter is clean enough, it should be easy to keep it so by the help of regular rubbing with a soft rubber, such as an old silk handkerchief or silk stocking. The rubbing will prevent the formation of the oxide or sulphide in some cases.

The great thing in the cleaning of pewter is to avoid scratching it, for it is a soft alloy and easily damaged. In cleaning a simple thing such as a plate—it is a good plan to stand up with the pewter on a rather low table, in such a way that the hand and arm can move with a circular motion. The more the movements approximate to perfect circles, the better will be the polishing. No one sitting at a table can possibly give the necessary regular rotatory motion.

In a workshop, of course, the plate would be fixed to a chuck in a lathe and would be polished while revolving at a considerable speed, but the resulting polish lacks the effect produced by good hand polishing; it is too monotonously uniform.

Scratches, if not too deep, can be easily removed with a suitable burnisher, providing that the latter is spotlessly clean and free from any suspicion of rust and grit, and properly lubricated.

If the scratches are deep, or are in the nature of vertical cuts into the surface, as happens in the case of the plates—which are often scored on both sides—scraping is the only way to reduce the depths of the cuts. To be effective the scraping must not all be in the same direction, but continually varied so as not in itself to cause slight shallow depressions.

The crust that is often found on pewter can be removed, but the process requires great patience. It is an excellent plan to rub paraffin oil or vaseline into the whole plate or dish and let it work its way in as paraffin can do, and to give the dish an occasional warming. The oil seems to be able to get under the scale or crust, and with the aid of

CLEANING AND REPAIRING OF PEWTER

the warming to spread in all directions and assist in the final removal of the scale.

This process can be effected by a ½-in. chisel with its edge made obtuse by grinding so that the cutting edge is somewhat blunted.

A short chisel is the best, and a round ball-like handle is the easiest for holding it in the hand of the user who has to push it forward, steadily and evenly until the crust gives way.

If the crust is obstinate, warming with the flame of a blowpipe will hasten matters considerably.

Remember that it is no good at all to treat pewter violently—patience is the only thing that will succeed in the end, and do not be discouraged if the metal should be scratched here and there; these are things that can be removed—with patience.

During the process of cleaning very old pewter, especially if the piece has been long buried, it will often be found that the metal has corroded to such an extent that it is holed in many places. Where this is the case it is best to clean the front or the outside first, and then to consider if the piece will stand being cleaned on the other side or in the inside.

A valuable piece which may be too thin may be backed, or coated on the inside with gesso, and so preserved from destruction.

Portions of pieces may be set up with plaster of Paris supports, or missing pieces made good in the same material.

The question whether pewter should be cleaned regularly or not is often raised. The point may be settled quite easily in this way. If the piece is obviously a museum specimen and unfit for use, clean it, put it in a case, label it and have done with it. If, on the other hand, the piece could be used in a proper way then keep it clean enough and ready for use at a moment's notice.

Mrs. Gerald Walker—whose large collection was dispersed in the autumn of 1919—once showed me some small pieces of pewter which had been originally in a deplorable dirty condition. She had had them boiled for some hours in water containing several handfuls of hay,

PLATE IV

Harvester measures (Irish): Quart, pint, ½ pint, and gill. (By Austin, of Cork, about 1820.)

Pot-belly measures from Aberdeenshire: Pint (Scots), chopin, mutchkin, and gill.
Pint (Scots). Note different types of handles.

Noggin measures (Irish?): ½ pint, gill, ½ gill, and ¼ gill.

(Dr. Young.)

PLATE IV

CLEANING AND REPAIRING OF PEWTER

and the pewter looked exactly like new as far as brilliancy and cleanliness were concerned.

It is a method worth trying, especially with fragile and delicate pieces. It goes without saying that the pieces should be suspended by a string from a stick during the boiling. Continued vibration for hours would quite alter the shape of pewter in a hot condition.

Sometimes pewter is so thin and corroded that repairing is a matter of great difficulty. Some Roman pewter that was submitted to the writer for examination and report, previous to undergoing repair, was found to be $\frac{1}{10}$ in. thick in some places, $\frac{1}{50}$ in. others, and with many holes, especially where the pewter had been exposed to continuous moisture, while the rim was consistently thick, over $\frac{1}{4}$ in., and only superficially corroded. It is very difficult indeed to fill holes in such thin metal, the chief drawback lying in the getting of the necessary clean edge on to which the new piece may be soldered. The heat of the blowpipe, or copper bit, whichever is used—the writer prefers the blowpipe—will, unless great care be exercised, melt the thin paper-like metal very quickly. One portion of one dish had to be cut out altogether and replaced with new metal. In a second dish several portions of the flat rim and the booge had to be removed and restored by the substitution of new metal.

It is quite easy to say that Roman pewter should be left alone and under glass, but there is this to be said also—that a piece honestly restored with no attempt to make the new stuff of the twentieth century look like the old stuff of the fourth—has a much better chance of surviving than it would if left in a precarious condition with portions about as strong as sponge-cake. Both these dishes were unsafe, even to examine with care; they can now be handled with impunity and passed freely from one connoisseur to another for his criticism.

Sometimes a plate is so badly scratched and cut about that it is well to have the whole surface treated by an expert. One of Charles II date was treated in this way and the result was most gratifying to the owner. All the scratches which interfered with the ornament (all joggled work) were removed, and the plain parts were burnished by hand. All blemishes or discolorations, efflorescences were erased and where necessary made good; where there was no hole a little répoussage was enough. The result was that when finally cleaned the plate, a large and handsome circular dish, looked, not like a new dish fresh from the workman's hand, but like a dish that had been well handled and looked after with care.

Before a budding repairer of pewter tries his hand on a dish or plate, let him bore a few holes in a scrap of pewter, the more irregular the shape the better, and repair them. When he can do them so neatly that the repair is invisible he may begin on a plate or dish.

The steps are as follows: Make the hole of convenient shape, level the surface, and then cut a piece of pewter of the same quality, or as near it as may be, to fit the hole, and make it a tight fit, tight enough to stay where it is put without dropping out. Support it on a damp cloth or felt, and solder it with a blowpipe, using an easily fusible solder, *not* tinman's or plumber's solder. It is better to work from the face downwards to the back, not from the back towards the face or upper surface. Any excess of metal can easily be removed by filing or scraping.

In dealing with holes in old pewter the hole must be treated as a dentist treats a tooth. The hole must be excavated until bright metal is visible on every side, then the filling is easy enough. This may have to be done two hundred and fifty times on one small plate; this calls for patience and patience and more patience.

In the case of cracks in the booge or in the rim, it is best to saw or file out all the dirty part and then go on as above.

In replacing missing parts care must be taken to fix what is left so that the missing portion may be fitted very carefully. If the piece missing be a part of a rim and part of a booge it is better to repair the rim first and then add the booge in another piece.

In repairing a tankard rim it is best to make a mould from the rim where it is perfect and cast a piece of the size required. Plaster of Paris will do quite well to cast the

CLEANING AND REPAIRING OF PEWTER

metal in, or a piece of strawboard softened in water and pressed to the required shape, but of course dried before use. Papier mâché can be used in the same way.

Handles of tankards can be repaired in the same way or replaced.

Knobs should be cast rather larger than are required, and then turned down on a lathe to the proper size.

When a plate or dish is very badly scarred with knife-cuts a dealer who is ignorant is sure to recommend that the dish should be refaced, i.e. have the scarred surface removed by being turned down in a lathe. It is a drastic process and is certainly to be condemned. Some ware may be able to stand the thinning down from the fact that it is not likely to be used, but as a general rule it should be avoided.

Much of the character of early pewter lies in the reeded rim of the plates and dishes. These rims by age become clogged with dirt and corroded at times, but they respond as a rule to careful cleaning with a stiff brush. In places it may be necessary to restore the lines of the rim, when battered by a blow or a fall, with a graver or a scorper. Either tool demands practice first, or confusion of line may become worse confounded, and sharply made deep cuts will require a great deal of treatment in their removal.

Dents or hollows are bound to come in plates and dishes, just as they are in jugs and tankards. In the case of plates they may be removed by careful hammering, with a hammer having a polished pane, on a smooth and clean flat iron from which the sharp edge has been removed by filing or grinding. In tankards the removal is effected by the use of what is called a snarling-iron.

Pewter, as already stated, is subject to a disease of an irritating kind. The metal develops imperfections in places, and these effloresce and eventually become holes. This efflorescence seems to be due to impurities in the alloy, and is developed earlier in some cases where heating or overheating has taken place.

It occurs, however, in vessels which need not be heated at all, as in the case of rose-water dishes and Communion flagons. There is only one remedy, and that is the expert's knife or drill and the restoration of the parts cut out. The disease occurs in the most perfectly made and kept pewter. Recently a flagon was brought to me in which there were nearly sixty blow holes which had to be excavated, or rather, drilled out and then filled separately. Moreover, when some of the drilled holes were being filled the heat of the blowpipe flame caused other defective places to blow through the surface, so that in the end there were over one hundred and eighty holes to be made, filled and finished off, both in the inside and on the outside of the flagon. There was nothing else to be done; but it was a pity, for the surface patina was very fine, and that is a thing which takes years to grow again.

Pewter is a long-lived material. At the present moment I have before me two dishes dating from the time of the Roman occupation of these islands and found buried in

Cambridgeshire. They are nearly alike in section; one was ornamented with incised concentric circles obviously done in a lathe, or on a turn-table, as there were traces on the back of the method in which the dishes had been fastened at three points to the chuck or to the revolving table on which it was worked. Both are very corroded—some parts entirely missing—though the rim, which is thick, is intact in both cases. This particular pewter, though distinctly sonorous, is rather soft and more lead-like in appearance than much other Roman pewter.

The weak points in the construction are the rather heavy rim and the thinness of the dish, which is 15½ in. in diameter. It is between B and C that most of the disintegration has taken place, though corrosion is fairly general all over the surface. The whole of the original surface, top and bottom, has come off in the process of repair and subsequent cleaning, but they will never look new. The new pieces inserted enable the safe handling of what was before rather precarious and risky.

CLEANING AND REPAIRING OF PEWTER

It is not everyone who is gifted with the patience to repair a flagon or a rose-water dish with missing portions in the lid or with about two hundred holes in the total area, but small repairs are well within the capacity of anyone skilled in the use of soldering tools.

Pewter ware, though of a soft alloy, has survived some very hard treatment. One often sees candlesticks in which the tubular stem has been battened down till it touches or nearly touches the level of the base. This battering down has partly been caused by undue pressure upon the object while it was being cleaned, or by ill-usage.

The candlestick must be patiently treated if it is to be restored to its original form. It can be done, as most things in the world, with care and patience. The pewter should be kept as hot as the hands can bear to handle, and should be hammered with a boxwood mallet, or raw-hide hammer, shaped for the special purpose all over the part which has been battered in. Progress can be measured by a foot rule, and though naturally slow at first it will be found that by degrees the hammering will do what is required. The hammering must be evenly distributed all over the surface, and twenty gentle blows are far more efficacious than two hard ones.

It is quite possible that in the process a crack may develop, especially if there was a sharp angle in the part compressed by battering down. A crack can be ignored at the time, and can be filled up later when all hammering is finished.

It is not proposed to give any detailed directions here for soldering pewter. The process can be learned from many manuals of workshop practice. Success comes after much experience. The writer prefers a blowpipe worked by the mouth, as in that case the flame is always under perfect control, and occasionally uses a small copper-bit heated by gas.

Soldering pewter is very risky, therefore most fascinating. Just as joy and tears, love and hate, are intimately connected, so success and failure are separated by but a hair's breadth. One puff more with a blowpipe than is necessary may make a hole ten times bigger than the original rent that was to be repaired.

Cleanliness, i.e. chemical cleanliness, is essential, and either a piece of good pewter as a solder, or some solder flowing at a low point, should be used.

Experience may be gained on some old plate or tankard, using one of the various paste fluxes now obtainable. It is possible to join two pieces of pewter with pewter without any solder or flux, by the aid of a blowpipe, if every part of the metal to be joined is absolutely clean.

It is not a bad plan to experiment with repairing the little Japanese trays and trinket boxes made of what is called antimony metal. When the repairer can repair these he may venture to try his hand on pewter of good quality.

Pewter is sometimes in such a decayed state that the question of what is to be done with it becomes rather a difficulty. A pilgrim-bottle that was dredged up somewhere was found to be corroded all along the seam, for the bottle, owing to its shape, had been cast in two pieces and then joined, quite a legitimate process. It was the solder that had corroded, so the obvious way to treat the bottle was to saw it in two, do all necessary repairs to the two halves, quite an easy thing when the piece was dismantled, and then, carefully, to join the two halves.

In another case, also a pilgrim-bottle or powder flask, it was so battered and worn that nothing would have been gained by taking it to pieces—for it would have been most difficult to join the halves together again. There were many pieces missing, and through these holes it was possible to force the battered in portions outwards. When all had been done in this way that could be done plaster of Paris was poured in to form an inner lining of about a quarter of an inch. Strapping plaster was used to cover the holes through which the plaster might have run out. After the plaster had set and the strapping plaster had been removed the plaster was tinted with water-colour—Payne's grey was the basis—to resemble pewter.

In another desperate case—a thirteenth-century paten from the tomb of an ecclesiastic of high rank who had

CLEANING AND REPAIRING OF PEWTER

been buried in one of our cathedrals—the writer made it fit to handle by coating it with many thin coats of a special white creamy cement till the back looked like a backing of porcelain. Without the backing the piece could not have been safely handled except on a piece of glass.

In the case of tankards it often happens that the part of the drum which takes the pull and the thrust of the handle is too weak structurally in proportion to the weight of the tankard even when empty. If the tankard is to be preserved the best plan is to reinforce the back from top to bottom with a strip about 2 in. wide of good pewter, soldered to the body of the tankard. It need not be unsightly and the lifetime of the tankard will be prolonged indefinitely.

Holes in dishes are not so dangerous as cracks, and the latter should always be attended to at once, as they are enlarged by any chance bending at the damaged spot by cleaning. A crack can be filled so that the repair cannot be noticed.

PLATE V

Channel Islands measure and jug.
Pint (tappit-hen) (Scots).
½ gallon Imperial (Aberdeenshire).
1 pint pot-belly (lidded).
1 pint pot-belly (unlidded).

½ pint bud thumb-piece measure (old English wine measure = 8 fluid ozs.).
½ pint hammer-head old English wine measure (=8 fluid ozs.).
½ pint Imperial (Scotch). Ball thumb-piece.
½ pint Imperial.

½ mutchkin (Scots) = 7½ fluid ozs.
Chopin, mutchkin, ½ mutchkin.
Gill, ½ gill, and ¼ gill (Scots).

Quart, pint, ½ pint, gill, and ½ gill. Imperial English measures (double volute thumb-pieces).

(Dr. Young.)

PLATE V.

CHAPTER V

A FEW DON'TS

DON'T begin to collect pewter (or anything else for that matter) because there is a craze for it. Boys at school will collect anything that anybody else is said to be collecting, and then in a short time drop the idea and collect something else. A person who is grown up should certainly find out if he (or she) is interested in the thing to be collected and studied. Without study the collecting is apt to be unintelligent and useless in consequence.

Don't attempt to secure a specimen of all the objects that have been made in pewter. Many of the later wares were badly designed and unsuitable for the metal. Cruet-stands and toast-racks and so on are best left alone. Use alone is almost too much for their constitutions, and use, with the addition of cleaning when necessary, generally proves fatal.

Don't jump at conclusions in investigating touches which seem at first indecipherable. It is a branch of the subject which is highly fascinating—the writer has given up years to it; but it is very easy to be venturesome—and to be wrong.

Don't decline a good piece of pewter merely because it has no marks upon it, or because they are indistinct. By comparison, or by reference to the analysis of the touches, a date can often be assigned to a doubtful piece.

Don't buy pewter of the sexton or other unauthorized person, nor of the clergy unless they have a faculty by which they have the power to sell granted to them. Don't be a party to this wrongful traffic in pewter.

Don't buy everything that is offered to you by a dealer.

It will cause him to be too venturesome, and you will be deceived and led to think that you are collecting.

Do not advertise for any special article in pewter; if you must, be very careful not to send a sketch of what you want. If you do so you will get an object more or less antique in appearance, but really warm from the mould or the workshop.

Do not imagine that everything that was made in silver was necessarily made in pewter. Avoid candle-snuffers, biscuit boxes, asparagus tongs, special infusers, bed-pans (even when split into their two component halves and sold as deep dishes) and as a rule the whole army of hexagonal food or wine bottles with screw tops, and those with spouts. Genuine examples are rather rare.

Do not collect pint or half-pint pots. There is very little interest attaching to them, and the names engraved on them are often later additions to enhance their value. A couple are useful as measures in the kitchen, and they make good solder if they are of good quality.

Don't think that everything sold as a tappit-hen, even if several pounds are asked as the price, is really a hen. The buyer is often a goose and pays for a converted measure from elsewhere.

Don't pay fancy prices for plates with stamped initials on them. These are often added to catch the unwary.

Do not buy Continental measures of small size under the idea that because you do not understand the metric system you have secured a rare bargain. These measures are in reality very common abroad and are not as a rule beautiful.

Do not buy oval dishes with salamanders (in so-called repoussé work) as the emblems of François I. They are being made every day somewhere in France.

Don't believe anyone who tells you that pewter cannot be repaired. It can if you will take it to an expert pewterer who knows his art, and if you are prepared to pay him for the time involved. Don't expect good work for nothing.

Don't refuse to buy a good old plate because it has a hole or holes in it. These can be repaired easily and honestly, and the plate will be the better for it.

A FEW DON'TS

Do not hesitate to buy a good piece of pewter when it is badly crushed and even broken in places. A dish with the rim off and crushed flat can be successfully restored with patience. Even a dish badly corroded by being under the sea since the time of the Armada in 1588, showing daylight through 250 odd holes, can be restored by an expert, if it is thought advisable and also worth the expense.

Do not buy a plate merely because it has armorial bearings on it. Armorial bearings on the rims of plates are usually those of the owner, but they are often added by dealers to give a fictitious value to the plates.

Don't deal with a dealer who is known to deal knowingly in faked pewter. (Don't, however, proclaim in public the fact of his so dealing.)

Don't pay silver prices for a base metal. Don't pay £16 for a small object like a pewter spoon merely to be known as a collector and to have your name advertised as the owner of the —— collection. It is not worth it. If you were a millionaire and were making a collection for the nation it might be excusable.

Don't believe anyone who tries to sell you pewter at a fancy price on the ground that it is *silver* pewter or has a high percentage of silver in it. Early pewter may be found to show traces of silver when analysed; but the silver was original, having been added (in ignorance) with the lead, if and when the lead was added, for in old times there were no patent processes for extracting the silver. Forewarned, then, is forearmed.

Don't buy pewter blindly. One dealer used to boast of his journeys to East Anglia where he bought pewter by the cask. Much of it was fit only for the solder-ladle and it was but seldom that he drew a prize. When he did the purchaser had to pay him a remunerative price.

Many of the articles thus bought at inflated prices are not worth the money, and in many cases they will supply much disappointment whether sold in the purchaser's lifetime or by his heirs, executors and assigns after his death.

Much of the pewter exposed for sale in the dealers' shops is foreign and most of it came originally from Flanders and from Germany. Occasionally some French and Swiss and, more rarely, Italian ware can be bought.

Scottish pewter is almost always of good quality; so too is Irish, but neither is met with in the ordinary way.

Don't buy a lot of tools and think you are thereby qualified to become a pewter repairer. You certainly want tools, and intelligence, but patience is the one thing that is most necessary.

Lastly, don't be discouraged when you find that you have been mistaken in a find, or taken in by anyone, even if he is your friend. Such things will always happen in collecting; they are part of the game. Play up! Carry on!

CHAPTER VI

THE CRAFT OF THE PEWTERER

THE craft of the pewterer is one of the oldest in the world and must have been practised wherever tin was an article of commerce. Our own Scilly Isles and the counties of Cornwall and Devon were *probably* the scene of the earliest attempts in this country in the art or craft, for in those days the two words were synonymous. Probably is the word to use, for there is no chance of arriving at a definite conclusion. It seems not unnatural that in the islands known all over the world as a tin-producing district, and in the Cornish lead-mining area, the art of combining the two metals—to their mutual benefit (for all alloys are the outcome of practical common sense)—should have been practised.

In any case the tin-miners of the West of England were granted charters by King John in 1201 and by Richard, king of the Romans. A century later (1305) Edward I by his words in a charter addressed to the miners of the west gives a proof of the existence of what is a regular guild organization in this country.

Though there is no official record in the possession of the Pewterers' Company earlier than 1348, there were certainly pewterers and men too who were anxious for the reputation of the craftsmen and the wares produced by them.

Pewterers did not invariably constitute a separate craft. As early as 1320 we find mentioned William the wiredrawer who lived at York and did work in pewter.

Mr. Cotterell notes that in 1344 one Walter the Goldsmith was paid for making pewter for the Prior of Holy Trinity Priory, Dublin.

In England pewterers seem to have worked in brass as

well, especially the spoon-makers. In Scotland we find craftsmen of various kinds grouped under the comprehensive title of hammermen. In Ireland too, in 1687, Mr. Cotterell mentions smiths, goldsmiths, silversmiths, cutlers, glaziers, braziers and *other hammermen who work by fire* are to take out and pay for a new charter.

Mr. Cotterell in his notes on Irish pewterers says: "The early history of the Pewterers' craft in Ireland is shrouded in almost impenetrable mystery and while one sees the Pewterers' Guilds of London, Edinburgh and York existing as flourishing institutions, governed by their own reputations and ordinances, each controlled by its own Master and wardens, yet no such guild, so far as is at present known, existed separately for the *Pewterers* of Dublin or Cork, or even of Ireland. In Dublin they formed one of the trades comprised in the Guild of Smiths, and in Cork they were one of the units embraced in the Society of Goldsmiths."[1]

These ordinances or regulations look as though they were based on the rules of the Paris Corporations described by Etienne Boileau in the early part of the thirteenth century, but it seems safer to assume that the London workmen merely had put down in writing the customs of their trade which previously had been in a floating condition, and were probably more or less identical with those of the pewterers working on the Continent.

Ordinances of the Pewterers, 22 Edw. III., A.D. 1348 (mainly from Riley, "Memorials of London," pp. 241–244, translated from the Norman French).

" In the first place—seeing that the trade of pewterers is founded upon certain matters and metals, such as copper, tin and lead, in due proportions: of which three metals they make vessels, that is to say pots, salers (salt-cellars), porringers (esquelles), platters, and other things by good folks bespoken: which works demand certain metals and certain alloys according to the manner of vessel so

---

[1] "Journ. of the Proceedings of the R.S.A., Ireland." Part I, Vol. XLVIII. Series VI (Vol. VII) half-year, June, 1917.

bespoken: the which things cannot be made without good knowledge of the pewterer, expert and cunning in the craft; seeing that many persons not knowing the right alloys, nor yet the mixtures or the right rules of the trade, do work and make vessels and other things not in due manner, to the damage of the people, and to the scandal of the trade, therefore the good folk of the trade do pray that it may be ordained that three or four of the most true and cunning in the craft be chosen to oversee the alloys and the workmanship aforesaid: and that by their examination any assay amendment may speedily be made where default has been committed. And if any one shall be found rebellious against the Wardens and Assayers, the default may be sent, with the name of the rebellious offender, unto the Mayor and Aldermen: and that by them he may be adjudged upon, in presence of the good folk of the trade, who have found such default.

"And be it understood, that all manner of vessels of pewter such as porringers, saucers, platters, charges, pi[t]chers square, and cruets squared, and chrismatories, and other things that are made square or cistils [ribbed], shall be made of fine pewter, with the proportion of *copper*[1] to the tin, as much as of its own nature, it will take. And all other things that are wrought by the trade, such as pots rounded, cruets rounded, and candlesticks and other rounded vessels ... to be wrought of tin alloyed with lead in reasonable proportions. And the proportions of the alloy are to one hundredweight of tin 22 lb.[2] of lead: and these are always called 'vessels of pewter' (*vessele desteym*).

"Also, that no person shall intermeddle with the craft aforesaid, if he be not sworn before the good folk of the craft, truly to work according to the points ordained: such as one who has been an apprentice, or otherwise a lawful workman known and tried among them. And that

[1] Probably *brass* as given in Welch.
[2] Welch, Vol. I, p. 3, gives 26 lb. of lead. Hazlitt in "Livery Companies of the City of London," says, p. 585: "We gather from some proceedings at the Guildhall in 1350, that the alloy of tin and lead, allowed and recognized by the custom of the trade, was in the proportion of 16 lb. of lead to 112 lb. of tin."

PLATE VI

Two Flagons

PLATE VI.

no one shall receive an apprentice against the usage of the City. And those who shall be admitted therein are to be enrolled according to the usage of the City.

"Also, that no person, nor stranger, shall make or bring such manner of vessel of pewter into the City for sale, or offer it for sale before that the material has been assayed, on peril of forfeiture of wares. And if the material be allowable upon assay by the Wardens made, then let the goods be sold for such as they [are], and not otherwise. And that no one of the craft shall work privily in secret places vessels of lead, or of false alloy, for to sell out of the City at fairs or markets, to the scandal of the City, and the damage and scandal of the good folk of the craft: but let the things be shown, that shall be so sent to sell without the City, to the Wardens of the trade before they go out of the same, and by them let the things be assayed.[1] And that no one shall do any work in the trade if he will not answer to his workmanship, upon the assay of his work, in whosesoever hands it be found. And if any one shall be found from henceforth carrying such wares for sale to fairs or to markets or elsewhere in the kingdom before it has been assayed, and, before the Mayor and Aldermen, shall be convicted thereof, let him have his punishment at their discretion, according to his offence, when he shall be so convicted at the suit of the good folk of his trade.

"Also, if any one shall be found doing damage to his master, whether apprentice or journeyman, privily in the way of theft, under the value of 10 pence; the first time let amends be made unto the master by him or by his surety in the craft; and if he offend a second time, let his punishment be inflicted by award of the craft; and if he offend a third time, let him be put out of the craft.

"Also, as to those of the trade who shall be found working otherwise than is before [set forth], and upon assay shall be found guilty; upon the first default let them lose the material so wrought; upon the second default let them lose the material and suffer punishment at the discretion of the Mayor and Aldermen; and if a third time

---

[1] Obviously some mark must have been necessary to show that the wares had satisfied the tests employed.

they shall be found offending, let them forswear the craft for evermore. [Welch, i. 4, " he shalbe foringed of the craft for evermore."]

" And also, the good folk of the craft have agreed that no one shall be so daring as to work at night upon articles of pewter ; seeing that they have regard among themselves to the fact that the sight is not so profitable by night,[1] or so certain, as by day,—to the common profit.

" And also, that if any one of the said craft shall be found in default in any of the points aforesaid, he shall pay 40 pence for the first default ; for the second default 6s. 8d. ; and on the third, let it be done with him at the discretion of the Mayor and the Aldermen : and of these payments let there be given one half to the Chamber, to maintain the points aforesaid, and the other half to the Wardens of the said craft, for their trouble and their expenses. And that no one of the trade, great or small, shall take away the journeyman of another man, against the assent and will of his first master, before he shall have fully served his term, according to the covenant made between them, and before the said journeyman shall have made amends to his master for the offences and misprisions committed against him (if he has in any way so offended or misprised), at the discretion of the Wardens of their craft ; and whosoever shall do to the contrary of this ordinance, let such person have his punishment at the discretion of the Mayor and Aldermen.

" Also, that no one of the said craft, great or small, shall be so daring as to receive any workman of the craft if he have been not an apprentice, or if he be not a good workman, and one who can have the testimony of his master or of good neighbours of good condition ; and can show that well and truly he has served his master for the time assigned between them."

These ordinances clearly show that a guild in some form

---

[1] It was enjoined in the " Statutes of the Streets against Annoyances," printed by Stow, No. 25, that " no hammerman, as a smith, a pewterer, a founder, and all artificers making great sound, shall work after the houre of nine in the night, nor afore the hour of foure in the morning, under pain of three shil. foure pence."

or other was in existence; without a guild there was no need for officials such as wardens, and a search would have been a farce.

These ordinances of 1348 made two qualities of pewter legal, one called fine pewter, which consisted of tin with the addition of as much brass as the tin " of its own nature will take." Of this kind of pewter was made almost everything that was made in pewter, i.e. esquelles (écuelles or porringers), saltcellars, platters, chargers, salvers, pitchers, cruets, chrismatories and any other articles that were made square, ribbed or fluted.

The other quality of pewter was tin and lead in the ratio of 112 : 26.

An early restriction in favour of keeping up the quality of pewter provided that no pewter should be brought into the city of London for sale without being assayed. The city of Rouen up to 1660 had the right of assaying all imported tin that came to Rouen, or was going to Paris by boat up the Seine.

The Pewterers' Company up to the time of the Reformation was a religious as well as a commercial or craft guild, as is shown by the mention in an inventory (1465), quoted by Mr. Welch, i. 33, of a gift to " the bretherhed of our lady thasumpcion of pewtrers crafte," i.e. the brotherhood of Our Lady of the Assumption of pewterers' craft.

Again, in an inventory (1489-90) of the goods of " the Crafte of pewterars within the Cyte of London " (Welch, i. 68), there is mention of " the Corporacōn of the same brethirhode and crafte under the Kynges Seal, and the Common seal of the same . . . with the ymage of thassumpcōn of our blessid lady gravyn theryn of sylver."

The fact that the Virgin Mary was regarded as the patroness accounts for the adoption of the " lely pottys," or lily-pots, which occur in the illuminated border of the grant of arms shown in facsimile by Mr. Welch (i. 127).

At the same time the freemen or the yeomanry had a guild of their own dedicated to the Archangel St. Michael. They had their own organization, but were in dependence upon the craft or mystery, i.e. the senior guild.

This fostering of the real spirit and wish to do genuine

work was the outcome of the feeling of fellowship, and it was this wish for good honest work which banded the pewterers against foreigners, a comprehensive term that included "aliens," as well as natives who wished to interfere with the trade. That this feeling of good work was strong is proved by the severe punishment that was sometimes inflicted on dishonest and on obstinate offenders, viz. expulsion from the trade.

From this religious side of the guild or mystery there developed originally the very strong bonds of union between the members of the fellowship. The same religious feeling urged the members to attend the funerals of deceased craftsmen, and led them to dine together after the funeral: to relieve distress among those of their own circles, as well as among those who on the face of it had no better claim than their own want for the time being.

Under the guild system, loyally maintained both by masters and by men, the "lock-out" or the "strike" was not a possible event. The relation between the employer and the employé was too close; and that between the master and the apprentice was almost parental in character.

The general good quality of English-made pewter was the immediate reason why so many systematic evasions of all rules regarding it were made by those of a fraudulent turn of mind. As long as pewter-ware was sold in the town where it was produced, it was easy to have some check on the quality of the ware; but as soon as it got into the hands of hawkers and tinkers, the perfect control was at an end, and the door was opened for the introduction of foreign wares.

In the reign of Richard II (1377–1399) the pewterers complained bitterly that their business was being injured by pedlars and tinkers going round the country and recasting the worn-out or damaged articles of their customers. The pewterers complained that these pedlars ruined the alloy with lead so that it was "not worth the fourth part sold for."

This adulterating with lead seems to have been a source of secret profit to these pedlars, as they charged very little for their recasting.

It seems probable that they recast principally the articles in everyday use, as plates and dishes of small size: they could hardly have carried on their backs a considerable stock of moulds, as moulds were heavy and very costly. It would be interesting to know how these roughly cast wares were finished. It is probable that they were either hammered, or scraped and burnished.

At the time of the granting of the charter to the Pewterers' Company the trade was of an importance which it is now difficult to realize, for wares in that metal were then becoming every day of more general use.

To assist in keeping up the quality, and detecting those who cheated by selling articles of light weight, a definite weight was fixed for the various articles usually made by the pewterers in 1430.

These weights were as follows:—

		Weight per doz. in lb.
Chargers	(the largest)	84
,,	next size	60
,,	middle	39
,,	small hollow	33
Platters	largest size	30
,,	next size	27
,,	middle	24
,,	small middle	22
Dishes	largest size	18
,,	middle size	14
,,	king's	16
,,	small	12
,,	hollow	11
,,	small hollow	10
Saucers	largest size	9
,,	middle	7
,,	next the middle	6
,,	small	4
Galley dishes and galley saucers (greatest size)		12
Also xiiij dishes and xiiij saucers weighing of the next galley mold.		
Small dishes of galley and galley saucers		12
Cardinal's hatte and saucers		15
Florentine dishes and saucers (greatest size)		13
Next Florentine dishes and saucers		12
Small bolles (bowls)		13

In 1444 the Warden of the Company acquired the right to pre-empt a fourth part of all tin brought into the city, whether by land or sea, at the current price. At the same time the Company obtained the right of assaying all the tin because of the complaints of "the multitude of tin which was untrue and deceyvable brought to the City, the defaults not being perceptible until it comes to the melting."

In 1473 Edward IV gave the Company its first charter in which the right of assay was confirmed, and also the right of searching pewterers' premises.

As soon as this charter was made known in the country many country pewterers joined the ranks of the London Company.

The right of search, when carried out in counties so remote as Yorkshire, Derbyshire and Somerset, was costly and troublesome, but it helped the Company to maintain the high standard of English pewter.

This regulation was similar to that under which the Nuremberg and other foreign pewterers worked.

Men were known by the particular branch of the craft in which they worked. Sadware men worked at heavy articles, such as plates, dishes, chargers and trenchers. The hollow-ware men, as the name implies, worked at large pots, measures, pint pots, quart pots, tankards and flagons of all names and sizes. Triflers worked in trifle metal and plate metal on lighter wares—spoons and, later on, forks, buckles, toys, buttons; but by 1612, from the list given by Mr. Welch, they had taken to make much hollow-ware.

The hammermen, coppersmiths and brasiers were all included among the pewterers, and had full privileges. They formed, however, a separate and smaller organization.

The lay-men worked in lay or ley, i.e. tin alloyed with lead. Hollow-ware was sometimes made of plate metal and sometimes of lay.

Metal confiscated on the ground of being bad in quality was generally stamped with a *broad arrow*. Mention is made of this mark towards the end of the fifteenth century, but, as Mr. Welch aptly remarks, " As it was doubtless the fate of all vessels marked with the broad arrow to be forfeited and melted down without delay, it is not probable that any example so marked is now procurable as a treasured specimen by the collector of old pewter" (i. 47).

Mr. Welch's book teems with references to seizures at fairs in all parts of the country, and with the records of the brass and pewter thus confiscated.

It is not more than a century since pewter was advertised to be sold at various fairs in the country. Dugdale's "Traveller" (quoted in the "Reliquary" of 1892, p. 150) mentions that at Nantwich fairs were held thrice yearly for "cattle, horses, clothes, flannels, hardware, pewter and bedding"; at Billesden the fair was held for "pewter, brass and toys"; at Hallaton, for "horses, horned cattle, pewter and clothes"; at Brigstock, "for sheep, brass and pewter"; at Rockingham, "for horses, cows, sheep, hogs, pewter, blackhats and clothes"; so too at Weldon, four times a year. In Yorkshire, Askrigg, Bedall, Coxwold, Grinton, Hedon, Kirkham, Malton, Reeth, Keighley and Stamford Bridge were all places where fairs were held, and at each of them pewter and pewter-wares could be bought.

The marking of pewter by the maker was first made compulsory by Act of Parliament in 1503 (19 Hen. VII c. 6), and the same act prohibited the sale of pewter and brass anywhere but on the premises of a pewterer, except in an open fair and market. This Act also provided that the makers of pewter-wares should mark the same with several marks of their own, to the intent that the makers of such wares shall avow the same wares by them to be wrought.

The use of false scales and weights was forbidden by this same Act.

Complaint was made in the Act, 4 Henry VIII, c. 7,[1] "that many simple and evil disposed persons ... using

[1] These extracts are taken from a book in which the Pewterers' Company caused to be reprinted (in 1741) the various "Statutes established in divers parliaments for the Mystery of the Pewterers of London; and concerning the search of Pewter Brass and untrue Beams and Weights and for deceivable Hawkers ... with the renewing and confirming of the same Statutes."

PLATE VII

TWO INKSTANDS

1. With pin-hinges and cup-feet.
2. With drawer.

PLATE VII.

the said crafts [i.e. of pewterers and brasiers] daily go about ... from village to village, from town to town, and from house to house, as well in woods and forests as other places, to buy pewter and brass. And that knowing thieves and other pickers that steal as well pewter and brass ... bring such stolen vessels to them in such places to sell, and sell it for little or nought, ... and bring it to privy places or into corners of cities or towns and there sell much part of it to strangers which carry it over the sea by stealth.... Also the said persons so going about, and divers others using the said crafts use to make new vessels, and to mix good metal and bad together and make it wrought, and sell it for good stuff where indeed ... it is not worth the fourth part of that it is sold for to the great hurt, deceit and loss of your subjects. Also divers persons, using the said crafts have deceivable and false beams and scales that one of them will stand even with 12 lb. weight at the one end against a quarter of a lb. at the other to the singular advantage of themselves and to the great deceit and loss of your subjects, buyers and sellers with them."

To remedy this it was enacted that the selling of pewter and brass, new or old, was to be restricted to open fairs and markets, or in the craftsmen's own dwelling-houses, unless they were desired by the buyers of such wares. The penalty for this was to be £10 and forfeiture of the metal.

At the same time the quality of any pewter wherever made was to be " as good fine metal as is the Pewter and Brass, cast and wrought after the perfect goodness of the same within the City of London." Here the penalty was forfeiture and sale, half the proceeds to go to the King, half to the finders.

No hollow-ware of pewter, i.e. salts and pots of ley metal, was to be made unless of the size, i.e. assize or standard, of pewter ley metal wrought within the City of London. More than this, " the makers of such wares shall mark with several marks of their own, to the intent that the makers of such wares shall avow the same wares by them to be wrought."

All wares not sufficiently made and wrought and marked, found in the possession of the maker or seller, to be forfeited. If it had been sold the fine paid as well as the ware was to be forfeited.

As might be expected, the compulsory marking of pewter-ware led to abuses, the chief of which was the counterfeiting of well-known pewterers' marks by other workmen, notably so by country makers.

As for the "deceivable hawkers," they were to lose their beam and be fined 20s., with the alternative of the stocks till the next market day and the pillory all market time.

This Act, which was in the main a renewal of 19 Henry VII, c. 6, was sought by the Company to be made perpetual instead of lasting to the end of the then Parliament.

These statutes, duly put in execution, caused the said craft to increase and multiply, to the great profit and utility of a great number of the "Kings subjects." It had the disadvantage, however, of causing " divers evil disposed persons, being the Kings subjects born, which have been apprentices and brought up in the exercise of the said craft of Pewterers," to repair, " of late, for their singular lucre, into strange regions and countries, and there exercise the said craft, teaching strangers not only the cunning of mixing and forging of all manner of Pewter vessil," but " all things belonging to the said craft of Pewterers."

The craft felt their trade might quite go from them if foreign pewter made by Englishmen could be freely imported, so they sought that such pewter should be forfeited.

Some amplifications of the Act were made in 25 Henry VIII, chiefly in the regulations as to the method of searching, which was to be lawful " for the Master and Wardens of the said craft of Pewterers as well within the City of London, as within every other City, borough and town, where such Wardens be, or to persons most expert in knowledge," appointed by the head officers or governors of the various places.

It was also to be enacted that no strangers born out of this realm were to be retained as apprentices or journeymen. Here the penalty was £10, and the ware made, " in whose hands soever it may be taken or found," was to be forfeited.

Englishmen working beyond sea, "in any strange country or region,"[1] were to have three months' notice to return, and "continually from henceforth dwell and inhabit," or else "shall be taken and reputed as no Englishman, but shall stand and be from henceforth out of the Kings protection."

The enactments as to hawkers did not seem to have much effect, as the Company complained of their misuse of royal letters patent and placards, and their continual use of "deceivable weights and beams," and sale of pewter and brass which is not "good, nor truly nor lawfully mixt and wrought." The Company sought to have the Act, previously temporary, made perpetual.

To check unlawful dealing with the metal it was agreed in 1555 that any one buying metal by night, or of tylers, labourers, boys or women, should be dismissed from the Company if the metal were found to be stolen property, and brought up before the Lord Mayor and the Aldermen for punishment.

On one occasion in 1591 the Company, for 5s., bought out a hawker, one John Backhouse, on the ground of his forestalling the Company and deceiving the Queen's subjects. He found a surety to swear that he would never hawk again. The 5s. was for him to buy pewterers' tools, with a view to becoming a pewterer (Welch, ii. 8).

The "deceivable hawkers" still gave trouble, and in March, 1621, the Company were again demanding further measures for their own protection, and "it was decided to introduce a Bill into Parliament for suppressing hawkers and the practice of buying of tynn and old pewter by brokers and others not pewterers, selling of old pewter, and transporting and uttering it."

Towards the end of the reign of Elizabeth, the Company in 1598 obtained letters patent confirming their privilege of charging a royalty on the smelting and casting of tin. Hazlitt assigns the reason to the pressure of foreign competition, which seriously affected the export of bar-tin.

[1] The "strange regions" were France, Flanders and Germany.

There was always a strong feeling that trade secrets were not to be divulged either by word of mouth or by working in public. It was this feeling that inspired the prohibition against Englishmen working in foreign parts and the exportation of English moulds. A species of *esprit de corps*, too, led the London pewterers to keep certain methods of procedure from their country brothers in the trade.

1601–2 (August 13), " by the generall consent of the whole Company it was ordered uppon the abuse of dyvers of the Company who worketh openly in the shopes with ther great wheles which is ane occasion that pewterers of the country and others shall come to great lyght of farther knowleg, to the great hindraunce of the Company as well at this present as hereafter, now there is comaundement that presently before bartelmew day [August 24th] they do reforme it, and if in case any of ther shopes be unreformed at bartelmewtyd they shall pay 13s. 4d., and at the next fawlt they shall pay 20s., and after they shalbe banyshed, and that no brother of the Company shall buy and sell with them " (Welch, ii. 34).

By the beginning of the seventeenth century the domestic use of pewter had grown far more common, and from the lists of " trifles " given by Mr. Welch (ii, 68–69) in the year 1614, there is much more variety of the ware to be had, in addition to the older patterns. We read of " deep vessells, basons, bowles, pastie plates, new fashion basons, danske pottes, pye coffins, limbecks, thurndell [new fashion of various sizes], and other pottes, hooped quarts, cefters and lavers, still heads."

At the time that the prices of these articles were fixed, the amount of rebate allowed to chapmen was also fixed, usually 1d. less in the lb. The price to be paid for giving old pewter to the pewterers in exchange for new was also arranged.

Most of the articles above mentioned were to be sold at a price per lb., tin at £4 7s. the cwt. being taken as the basis of the calculation. A small profit was fixed as a rule, 2d. per lb., or 1d. if the ware was sold to chapmen, except in the case of wares which were of recent introduction or which were sold singly.

But it was in the early years of the seventeenth century

that the Company began to lose their control over the trade; they no longer admitted country pewterers to the freedom, and thus provoked a flowing tide of irregular competition which it vainly endeavoured to check. The chief concern of the Company under the Stuarts, and indeed up to the middle of the eighteenth century, was to secure from Parliament a higher degree of protection to the trade. They objected to the royal practice of farming the Cornish tin-mines to influential syndicates, which raised the price of the metal. The Company feared, and not without reason, that England would lose the valuable export trade in pewter to the Dutch, who brought tin more cheaply from the East Indies and were in the habit of manufacturing a debased pewter threepence in the pound below the English standard. But the tin-miners were too powerful in Parliament, where Cornwall, with its many rotten boroughs, was of course much over-represented, and the Pewterers' Company expended much money in approaching various members of Parliament without result.

Self-advertisement was always sternly repressed by the Pewterers' Company, as they seem to have held that a man's reputation in the trade, and in the world at large, must depend upon the quality of his wares. The adding of *London* or an address was at one time specially forbidden, but the prohibition was repealed later, when it was found that the country makers, for the sake of a slightly larger profit, stamped *London* on their wares.

For many years the touches were quite plain, and some of them, it may be noted, were especially fine specimens of the die-sinker's art. Towards the end of the eighteenth century the labels will be found to contain statements as to the quality of the metal employed.

In 1727 it is clear from his own punch that Samuel Smith described his pewter as "*Good mettle made in London*," and in 1736 a pewterer named John Jupe was not afraid to mark his wares "*Superfine French metal*"; while Edward Box, in 1745, has on one of his punches "*No better in London*." This may have meant that his was the best, but the boast shows how the pewterers were beginning to do as to them seemed best.

Puffing of wares was as much deprecated as puffing of self, and it was mentioned as a thing to be avoided in an early regulation.

Taudin's nephew (Jonas Durand) was forbidden to add to his touch "Nephew of Taudin," and even the addition of an address, common enough later, was thought in the case of one maker, who merely added "Newgate Street," to savour too much of advertisement.

It was the right of search which originally gave the Company such an enormous hold over all the pewterers both in town and country. This hold was maintained as long as the search was effective and regularly carried out. During the Civil War, as might be expected, the actual searching became partial and less frequent; this fact, coupled with the discontinuing of the ready admission of country pewterers to the freedom of the Company, led eventually to the total loss of real control over the trade. The search had caused much opposition in the fifteenth century, was tolerated in the sixteenth, partially dropped in the middle of the seventeenth, and its attempted revival caused a renewal of the opposition. It may have been that the feeling of personal liberty was opposed to it altogether. In 1729 it was reported to the Company that much bad pewter was made at Bristol. But the Company were already beginning to feel somewhat uncertain of their position, and they hesitated to make a search at Bristol, not feeling sure whether their jurisdiction extended to places so remote from London. With the dropping of the right of search, the usefulness of the Company practically ceased. As soon as every man did what was right in his own eyes, the quality of the pewter began to deteriorate.

As to the definite position of foreign workmen in England there is very little direct evidence. There seems to have been much more jealousy among the exclusive pewterers than among the goldsmiths. The latter were, as their records show, much more willing to receive a stranger into their ranks. Entries occur, quoted by Herbert, to show that German, Dutch and Swiss goldsmiths were admitted, with due precautions and restrictions, to serve as workmen, and as masters. From Mr. Welch (i. 51) it is clear that a pewterer who was a Fleming was settled in Tower Hill as early as 1477, in which year a " pottle " (price 6d.) was bought of him to be tested for quality. Undoubtedly there must have been others.

From the provision of the Acts of Parliament passed in the reigns of Henry VII and Henry VIII, it would seem the jealousy and the exclusiveness had reached an acute stage, the enactment as to forfeiture of ware being very stringent.

Some few foreigners seem to have made ware approximating the English standard of goodness, but the fact that a man was a foreigner was certainly against him. Taudin's case is certainly a case in point (cf. Welch, ii. 122). Eventually he became a freeman, but was ordered to employ English freemen.

When English pewter was prohibited abroad, as at Bordeaux in 1658, the English workers did not like it, as it seemed to be an interference with their trade. Their policy was that of the open door, but it was only to open for English wares to go abroad. The Dutch on one occasion prohibited the sale of English pewter, but not the importation of it, which seems rather a curious regulation.

Another instance of a Frenchman wishing to work over in England was that of Mark Henry Chabroles. He was told in August, 1688, that he must not keep any " shopp, by reason he is a stranger and an alien." In 1690 the Court, learning that he was a Protestant refugee, gave him leave to work for " some time longer." This is vague, for he was in England and at work for two years longer. He was then advised, June, 1692 (Welch, ii. 165), to leave the trade of a pewterer, as " the Laws of this kingdome are against his exercising it " ; but he was allowed to continue till the 24th of August—a very significant date to a Protestant refugee.

In 1700 W. Sandys wished to have as his apprentice a " ffrench youth naturalised " ; this was opposed by the craft.

In 1709 the question arose as to the extent to which foreign pewter was adulterated, and the Pewterers' Company caused experiments to be made with various alloys,

PLATE VIII

THUMB-PIECES AND LIDS OF STUART TANKARDS

THUMB-PIECES AND LIDS OF VARIOUS TANKARDS
Early Georgian or Queen Anne. Late Georgian.
Scotch. Stuart. Early Georgian. Stuart.

(DR. YOUNG.)

PLATE VIII.

and they found (Welch, ii. 177) that 4 oz. tin with ½ oz. lead was 6¼ gr. worse than the tin bar they took as their then standard.

    4 oz. to 1 oz. lead was 13 gr. worse
    3 oz. to 1 oz.   ,,   18 gr. ,,
    2 oz. to 1 oz.   ,,   25 gr. ,,

Some foreign ware tested was found to be from 14½ to 29 grains worse than fine, French and Spanish being the worst. Some English pewter, selected at hazard from a shop, was 1½ grain less than the test piece at Pewterers' Hall.

Pewter-making in England was apparently limited to a few centres, such as London, York, Newcastle, with later, Exeter, Bideford, Barnstaple, Birmingham, Bewdley, Beverley, Bristol. In Scotland, Edinburgh and Glasgow were the chief centres; in Ireland, Dublin and Cork.

Bewdley was perhaps the most important centre of the pewter industry in the Midlands. It is not many years since the moulds used in the trade there were sold and passed into the hands of Mr. Yates of Birmingham.

In France the manufacture was more universal. Besides Paris there was early work done at Lyons, Limoges, Poitiers, Laon, Tournay, Besançon, Troyes, Tours, Amiens, Rouen, Reims, Dijon; also at Chartres, Saumur; in the south, at Nîmes, Montpellier, Angoulême, Chinon, Bordeaux, Angers, Toulouse.

In the Netherlands and Flanders the chief centre was undoubtedly Bruges and then Ghent, Mons, Namur and Liège. Much, too, was made at Brussels and Antwerp; also at Amsterdam, Breda and elsewhere.

Tin was largely used at an early date by the goldsmiths in Greece and Italy, the supply being forwarded to them *via* Venice, always an important centre.

In Germany, Nuremberg and Augsburg were the two chief centres, and mention of pewter-work can be traced back there quite as far as in France or elsewhere, one of the earliest records being an enactment made in 1324 at Augsburg, providing for visits of inspection made to the workshops by the sworn masters. These masters were empowered to test or assay the metal from the point of view of purity, and to inflict a fine upon those whose work was so bad that it had to be rejected and destroyed. Nuremberg records, too, show that pewterers worked there at an early date. Karel or Carel, a well-known maker, flourished there in 1324, with, later on in the same century, Sebaldus Ruprecht.

In Spain, Barcelona seems to have been the headquarters of the tin and pewter trade, and the place is well suited, by its natural position, for a distributing and manufacturing centre. No trace, however, of any corporation or guild has been found prior to the fifteenth century. The statutes resemble those of the workers in more northern nations.

The Italians used large quantities of tin, pewter having been made at Bologna and in other towns, possibly for tinning other metals. Much of the trade was in the hands of itinerant workmen—*stagnarini*—who travelled from place to place, very much after the manner of our tinkers, a set of men who were at one time indispensable to the housewife.

English pewter seems to have always enjoyed a good reputation both here and in foreign countries. This was mainly due to the naturally good quality of the English tin from Cornwall (it being practically one of the purest varieties of tin that is obtainable as an article of commerce), and also to the restrictions imposed upon the workers, whether masters or journeymen, as to the quality of the metal they used. Mr. Welch (ii. 137) mentions an instance of a master who broke up twenty dozen plates because they were not quite up to the standard required by the Company.

As to the reputation and skill of the English pewterers Harrison says: " In some places beyond the sea a garnish of good flat English pewter [of an ordinarie making] (I saie that, because dishes and platters in my time begin to be made deepe like basons, and are indeed more convenient both for sawce [broth] and keeping the meat warme) is esteemed almost so pretious, as the like number of vessels that are made of fine silver, and in manner no lesse desired among the great estates, whose workmen are nothing so skilful in that trade as ours, neither their mettall so good, nor plentie so great, as we have here in England."

One branch of the many into which the foreign pewterers' trade was subdivided was that of the nail-maker. These pewter nails were used for many purposes where we should now use safety-pins, and sometimes, possibly locally, for decorative purposes, being used as studs in leather.

Pewterers who did not make their wares up to the proper standard were, after being warned and fined, ordered to bring in their touches, which were then confiscated. They were then ordered to use a new touch, either bearing a knot or a double f (cf. Welch, i. 254). This enforced use of a punch, in itself bearing the visible sign of disgrace, was tantamount to compelling the offending pewterer, if a master, to shut up his shop and become a journeyman again.

In the lists of the yeomanry there are several entries of women's names, but their names do not appear in the lists of the livery.[1] As the original guild or mystery was a religious organization as well as a craft guild, there is nothing surprising in this, and mention is made of both brethren and sustren. The latter could employ apprentices, but were not allowed to work themselves.

Among the touches of the Pewterers' Company there are those of Ellen Morse and Mary ——. " Elizabeth Royd " occurs on some Church plate at Sutton, Rutland. The name, however, on another specimen seems to be Royden.

There were women pewterers in York, as is shown by a list of the Company made in 1684, in which the names of Jane Loftas and Kath. Hutchinson appear ("Reliquary," vol. vii., N.S., p. 205). In 1683 there was another, Emmatt Smith; in 1684, one Jane Waid, and her name comes in again in 1691. No doubt there were others whose names are unrecorded.

---

[1] Welch, ii, 92, mentions that Katharine Wetwood was sworn and made free of the Company; and, on p. 179, Mary and Elizabeth Witter were admitted to the freedom; and again, p. 191, Mary and Elizabeth Cleeve were also made free of the Company.

Of women pewterers in France[1] there is mention in Bapst's list of the workers of the fourteenth century of a certain Isabel de Moncel (1395). There is no statement made as to her being a widow, so she may have been either the widow or the daughter of Oudin du Moncel, whose date is given as 1383.

In 1462 mention is made of the Veuve Domey (*miraclier*), but the town is not specified. By the rules of 1613 they were allowed to keep a workshop as long as they remained widows.

Hawkers and chapmen gave trouble to the craftsmen from time to time; so, too, did the Crooked Lane men. These men seem to have been workers in tinware of a kind which they either made themselves or caused to be made for them, or else which they, somehow or other, in spite of sundry Acts of Parliament, imported from abroad. They had been apparently tolerated for some time, and in 1634 (Welch, ii. 94, 96) measures were ordered to be taken for "suppressing of the excesse and abusive making of Crooked Lane ware, whereby the so doing and counterfeiting of the reall commodity of Tynn is to the greate deceipt or wrong of his Ma[ties] subjects." What measures were taken does not appear, but as they cost £50, they were presumably of a legal description. In 1669 the Crooked Lane men tried to get a charter of incorporation, but nothing is known as to their request. As nothing is said of it they probably failed, especially as the Girdlers' Company joined with the Pewterers in paying for a counsel to plead against them.

[1] In 1300 there was in Paris "une batteresse d'étain."

CHAPTER VII

THE STANDARDS OF PEWTER

THE standards of the fineness of pewter at various times are not known with absolute certainty, and the statutes regulating the trade do not enlighten us upon this most important point. Hazlitt states that from some proceedings at Guildhall in 1350, the alloy then used and recognized by the craft appears to have been composed of 112 lb. of tin and 16 lb. of lead. 19 hen. VII cap. 6 (1503-4) dealing with pewterers and braziers, enacts that all pewter and brass worked or cast within the realm shall " bee as good fine mettal as is the pewter and brasse cast and wrought after the perfyt goodness of ye same within the city of London, and by the statutes of the same ought to bee." It further enacts that no one shall make any " hollow wares of pewter, that is to say, salts and potts that are made of pewter called lay mettal, but that it may bee after the assise of pewter lay metall, wrought within the Citie of London." From this it appears that at least two legal qualities or standards of pewter were then in use, but unfortunately the fineness of either is not specified. 25 Hen. VIII, cap. 9 (1533-34) makes mention of pewter " which is not good nor truely nor lawefully mixt." The ordinances of the York company of Pewterers (" Reliquary," v. 2, 1891) ordain that "none of the said Crafte shall hearafter cast anye vessell but of good and fine metell, and shall not put any sowder or leade therein, or amongst the same." The name " vessel " comprised such articles as were then made to hold any liquid, and appears to have been cast in brass moulds ; further on the ordinances proceed to speak of the quality of the pewter to be used for " hollow wares " which, as we see from the Act above recited, were chiefly salts and pots; and were perhaps wrought throughout and not cast; hollow ware metal it ordains " shalbe of one saye (assay) or assize, viz. of the assize of pewther laye mettle wrought in London."

In the eighteenth century the legal standards for pewter are said to have been as follows :—

1. Fine or Plate Metal the one containing the highest proportion of tin, of which plates and dishes were made. It was composed of 112 lb. of tin and usually of 6 to 7 lb. of regulus of antimony.
2. Trifling Metal or Trifle, the next standard, was composed of pewter of the highest standard lowered one halfpenny in value by the addition of lead. This standard was used for ale-house pots.
3. Ley or Lay Metal, the lowest standard, was compounded of the highest standard and a further addition of lead, reducing its value two pence in the pound. Of this winepots were made.

The above proportions and ingredients must not, however, be taken to be fixed and invariable, for from the articles following on the Assay of Pewter it will be seen that the standards were fixed not by the fineness or proportion of tin in the pewter but with reference to the specific weight of the alloy as compared with that of tin. The ingredients used by the pewterers were variable and every pewterer had his particular mixture which he kept secret. Antimony, bismuth or tin-glass, copper and lead were commonly used and it is said sometimes silver. It is probable that traces of iron, zinc and even of silver (with the lead) found their way into the alloy.

THE ASSAY OF PEWTER

The assay of the purity of tin and of the quality or standard of fineness of its alloy, pewter, was as early as the sixteenth century conducted as follows :—

A mould, such as is now used for casting lead bullets, was taken, and a ball of the particular standard of pewter in question was cast therein; then in the same mould another ball was cast of the pewter the quality of which it was desired to ascertain. The two balls were then weighed. If the latter ball was equal in weight to or lighter than the first or standard essay it was of the requisite quality; for the lighter the tin or pewter the purer it is. If it weighed more it was rejected as being of inferior quality.

From the little book published by the authority of the Pewterers' Company in 1772 it appears that the mould then used was of such a size that a ball of fine tin, absolutely free from any admixture, cast therein, weighed 182 grains; a ball of Plate Metal not more than $183\frac{1}{2}$ grains or $1\frac{1}{2}$ grains heavier; a ball of Trifling Metal not more than $185\frac{1}{2}$ grains or $3\frac{1}{2}$ grains heavier; and a ball of Ley Metal not more than $198\frac{1}{2}$ grains or $16\frac{1}{2}$ grains heavier.

Another method, but less exact, was sometimes used for the assay of Pewter. It was as follows:—

A half-round cavity was scooped out of a piece of what was known as thunderstone and from this cavity a narrow and shallow channel was cut in the surface of the stone about 2 in. in length, the melted pewter was allowed to run along this channel into the scooped-out hole until the latter was full. The quality of the pewter was judged when cold by the appearance and colour of this sample. This method required a practised eye. Another method, and one commonly practised by the pewterers, was to touch the pewter to be assayed with a hot soldering bit; the quality was estimated by the appearance of the streak left by the hot bit.

A collector of pewter will have to learn betimes the difference between pewter and Britannia metal, or he will be paying pewter prices for its rival and substitute. It will be best for him to boldly ask for a piece of Britannia metal, take it home and after cleaning it properly test it by rubbing it on clean white paper, not once but several times, and note the resulting marks or smears comparing them with the marks made by a piece of genuine pewter either genuine antique or genuine new. Both can be got with a little trouble and the tests will teach the collector a lot of useful knowledge.

Next he may try the so-called knife test. To do this it is

PLATE IX

Various Spoons

(Left to right of page)

(a) Hexagonal stem, *temp.* Henry VIII. Maker's mark N. E., with cardinal's hat.
(b) Elizabethan spoon, found in crypt of Gloucester Cathedral.
(c) Slip-top spoon, found in the Thames. Date 1679.
(d) Pied-de-biche, rat-tail. W. L., 1668.
(e) Pied-de-biche, rat-tail. I. N., with fleur-de-lys and date 1678.
(f) Rat-tailed spoon.
(g) Rat-tailed spoon. Maker's mark T. P. in small beaded shield. Found in Chester.
(h) Rat-tailed spoon, with quality mark. Maker's mark B. T. G. with a crown, a fleur-de-lys, rose below.
(i) *Temp.* William IV

PLATE IX.

THE STANDARDS OF PEWTER

just as well to get a strip of ordinary commercial sheet lead, a piece of sheet pewter of known quality, and a piece of Britannia metal. Then with the knife—a broken blade is quite useful for this—draw it slowly and steadily along the metals in order, lead 1, pewter 2, Britannia metal 3.

It will be noticed that in the lead the knife sinks deepest and with the least trouble. Less so in the pewter and still less so in the Britannia metal. If the furrow that is made in each case be examined with a lens the difference in each will be easily apparent and a similar furrow recognized on the occasion of any future tests.

Anyone skilled in metallurgy will be thirsting to assay his and his friend's pewter, but this is expert's work and should be paid for according to results.

It is no use for a tyro to begin a series of tests with strange alloys of which he knows nothing.

Another test which is often applied to pewter is to bend it backwards and forwards holding it close to the ear, listening the while for the characteristic noise made by the metal—the French call it *cri de l'étain*—while being bent. It is not an infallible test because the addition of a very small percentage of zinc to the alloy will stifle the *cry* for ever.

Another thing to be remembered is that it is not good for pewter to be bent backwards and forwards indefinitely. It is bound to break at the bend eventually.

In repairing pewter it is advisable to examine the piece, and see whether it has come unsoldered or whether it is broken. Many pots and tankards, especially those with bulbous lower halves, are made in two pieces, and a careful examination will show the line of juncture. If this line has received a hard blow there will in all probability be a cracked joint, and this—after scraping the edges clean—may be resoldered.

If a handle—from rough usage—has come away from the body of the pot or tankard it must be cleaned, bent back and resoldered.

If a portion of a vessel be absent, or has been destroyed by crass negligence or carelessness the missing portion may be restored either by casting a piece of the required size in a plaster of Paris mould and soldering it when fitted to its place, or by fusing pewter, without solder at all, in the place where the gap is, bit by bit, till the gap is rather more than filled. The surplus metal may then be removed by filing and scraping.

When no solder is used there is no trace of any join whatever.

When a mercurial solder is used the line is faintly visible and the solder will tarnish slightly more quickly than the adjoining pure metal.

Common lead solder will also show up as darker in colour and tarnishes very quickly.

CHAPTER VIII

THE ORNAMENTATION AND DECORATION OF PEWTER

THE nature of the metal is not such as greatly to encourage the worker in repoussé or the engraver. Easy as it is to cut and to work, it wears out quickly, and any elaborate design soon becomes illegible. Deep-cut lines help to weaken the work, and in view of this, linework proper has generally been kept very thin and delicate. Broken or wavy linework has frequently been done by holding a flat tool, such as a flat scorper, at an angle of 50° or so, and by forcing it forwards in the direction required by the design with a regular rocking motion. It is easier to do than to describe, as any one interested may see by experimenting on a piece of sheet lead with a carving chisel, say one-eighth of an inch wide. The quality of the " wriggled " or " joggled " line thus made will vary with the speed and the regularity of the rocking, and with the width of the tool selected. Borders have been produced by the combination of different lines similarly worked.

Sometimes a running pattern is carried all over the object, and at first sight seems to be composed of dots, but on closer inspection the traces of the connecting lines will be seen, but less plainly than the deeper-cut dots.

Frequently the border of a plain dish or plate, which for strength is made considerably thicker than the body of the article, is decorated with a kind of bead ornament, produced presumably by milling or by a stamp. Occasionally the ornament of the rim consists of a faint moulding.

In many plates and dishes the simple lines of the circle or oval are broken, and the dish takes a cinquefoil shape, often with an elaborate edge.

Much of the linework on pewter is done with a graver,

some of the metal being removed at each cut of the tool. Much, too, is done with a chasing-tool called a tracer. The difference in the lines thus produced will soon be perceived, as in some specimens the two methods are both used, if not side by side, at any rate on the same article. A peculiar effect can be got by the use of a wedge-shaped punch.

The graver removes a portion of the metal at each cut, driving it forward in front of the tool. Of course the shape of the piece removed depends upon the size of the graver, the way it is ground, and the intention of the workman who is using the tool. In the case of the chasing-tool no metal is removed, as the tool, which is held vertically, is struck with a hammer and displaces the metal, into which it is forced, very much in the way in which a furrow is formed. The tool is moved along in the required direction, and, tapped regularly with the hammer or light mallet, produces a long furrow. If the furrow be examined with a lens the hammer-blows will be clearly seen.

Curved lines, if intricate, are done by means of a curved tracer; but the straight tracer, when not too large, is capable of doing most of the work, if the user of it knows its capabilities.

Many objects in pewter, in addition to the line ornament, are decorated with patterns impressed by means of punches. The plates—judging from the backs—have been held on an anvil while the blows were given to the punches, and the resulting inequalities on the backs removed by scraping or by filing. The effect of the combination of the two styles of ornamentation is not always good. Handwork and machine-work, by such close juxtaposition, are too prominently pitted one against the other, and neither is so effective when combined.

As samples of engraved and chased work applied to pewter, the screen of twenty-four pewter plates and dishes in the President's Court at South Kensington may be cited. They are small in size, the engraving (some of it is of unpleasant subjects) is overdone, and overcrowding is the result.

Mouldings in the best pewter-work are very much kept down, and where they are added for strengthening the rim of a dish or other article are usually underneath the rim. In the Briot and Enderlein type of salver the mouldings are very massive, but not out of proportion to the size and weight of the articles to which they are applied.

Pewter as a rule looks best when quite simple and unadorned, and it is only in rare cases that it has been successfully combined with other metals or materials. A small tankard in the Rijks Museum at Amsterdam has its more prominent mouldings and features in brass. The latter is not allowed to predominate at all, but is carefully subdued, and thereby the pewter vessel, which is in itself delicate in form and workmanship, is enriched. Had the brass been overdone or allowed to overpower the rest, the effect in so small a vessel would have been crude and disastrous. Copper similarly handled would have looked well. There is another similar specimen in the Victoria and Albert Museum, but the effect is lost, as the brass has become quite black.

Pewter pierced work applied to wooden vessels never looks quite right. There is no strength in it, and when the wood swells or starts, the pewter cracks, and the days of the vessel are as a rule numbered. Specimens of such work exist, called *Pechkrüge*.[1]

Perhaps the height of absurdity is reached in a small tankard in the Victoria and Albert Museum, the body of which is made of serpentine rudely wrought, and mounted in pewter far too slender in section for the weight it had to support and the consequent strain.

Another form of ornamentation which was easily applied to pewter-ware, and which soon wore out, was " pricked " work. Fine work when carefully done (the tool being forced vertically into the metal) outlasts the carelessly done work which was done with a tool or picker held at an angle of about 45°. This pricked work is either finished by an incised line on either side or left by itself. Sometimes the pricked work is done more boldly, with a larger picker or possibly a drill point, and the lines so obtained look well if the design is kept to simple S curves.

[1] They derived their name from the coating of pitch applied to the inside to render them water-tight.

Pointillé ornament looks well when restrained in amount. As a border in the flat part of a plate, just finished and accentuated with a kind of feather edge, it has quite a rich appearance, but its richness depends chiefly on the lines which bound it.

Some pewter is ornamented with stamps either straight or slightly curved, with a plain edge on one side and a serrated edge on the other.

Sometimes the metal is worked on the surface with a chasing-tool for the bolder lines, and the finer lines are added with a graver. The two processes may be seen in the set of engraved plates in the South Kensington Museum.

Another method of producing ornament is to combine two methods, viz. the point work with either stamped work or the raised blobs, circular or oval in shape.

Pewter is frequently engraved, but it is very rarely that the decoration suits the object to which it is applied.

A common pewter tankard with shallow scooped cuts in it has a very plebeian look about it; but the cuts soon wear out.

Good pewter will stand good engraving, not the *pointillé* work, nor the joggled ornament, but regular burin work. There are some excellent examples in the Rijks Museum, Amsterdam, of ordinary plates, with armorial bearings well engraved on the rim.

Nothing, too, looks more decorative than the simple direct lettering on some of the Corporation *hanaps*, whether on the body of the vessel or on a shield on the lid.

Italics do not look so well as the upright capitals, but it is mainly a question of the way in which the engraver does his work, as good simple lettering well done is always decorative. As instances of this the Corporation cups in the Cluny Museum may be compared with the tankards in the Museum at South Kensington. Script well done is unusual on pewter, but the " Elizabeth Dering " on the back of the Charles II dish at South Kensington is excellent.

The miserable style of engraving on beer-tankards was probably brought into use by the engraving being required to be on the inside of the rim at the bottom, where there was not enough room for the proper use of the graver. When the style was set it was used indiscriminately, even on surfaces where the graver could be used in the ordinary way. This style of engraving consists in detached curves, no attempt being made to complete the curves in the loops of any letters.

A shield or a coat of arms held up by a figure on the lid is often added to the lid of a large flagon, and gives a clue to the original owner of the pot, and in this way to its date.

In salvers a boss is usually the centre of the ornamentation, as in the Briot and Enderlein specimens, and in the works copied from them. Occasionally the boss is of Dutch or gilding metal enriched with a plaque or enamel, with a happy effect.

In a large rose-water dish with a raised boss $2\frac{1}{4}$ in. in diameter, bearing the arms of C. R. (Charles I) on a brass plaque, enamelled in colours, the chief ornaments are a circle of lenticular *perles* round the rim, and another similar circle about midway between the boss and the rim. These were raised above the flat surface by being struck from the back by means of punches.

Occasionally silver was applied to the ornamental pewter-work used as coffer and furniture decoration, and to the ornaments which when painted and lacquered were fixed on beams and rafters.

At one time this use of gilding was restricted to church plate, chiefly chalices; but in the reign of Louis XIV this restriction was relaxed in favour of pewter in ordinary domestic use.

Another absurdity sometimes committed was the painting and lacquering of domestic pewter. There is a cruet-stand at South Kensington enamelled or painted white and picked out with gold. The effect, combined with that of the gilt incised work on the cruets, is not happy. In the Museum at Nuremberg is a crucifix made of wood overlaid with pewter. The latter has been mercurially gilt.

Silvering has also been applied to pewter in modern times, though manufacturers do not recommend the practice. A flagon at Higham Ferrers, which has been

PLATE X

Two Large Dishes

1. Reeded rim. 20¼ diam. Made by Pettit, 1685.
2. Flat-beaded rim. Arms dated 1677.

PLATE X.

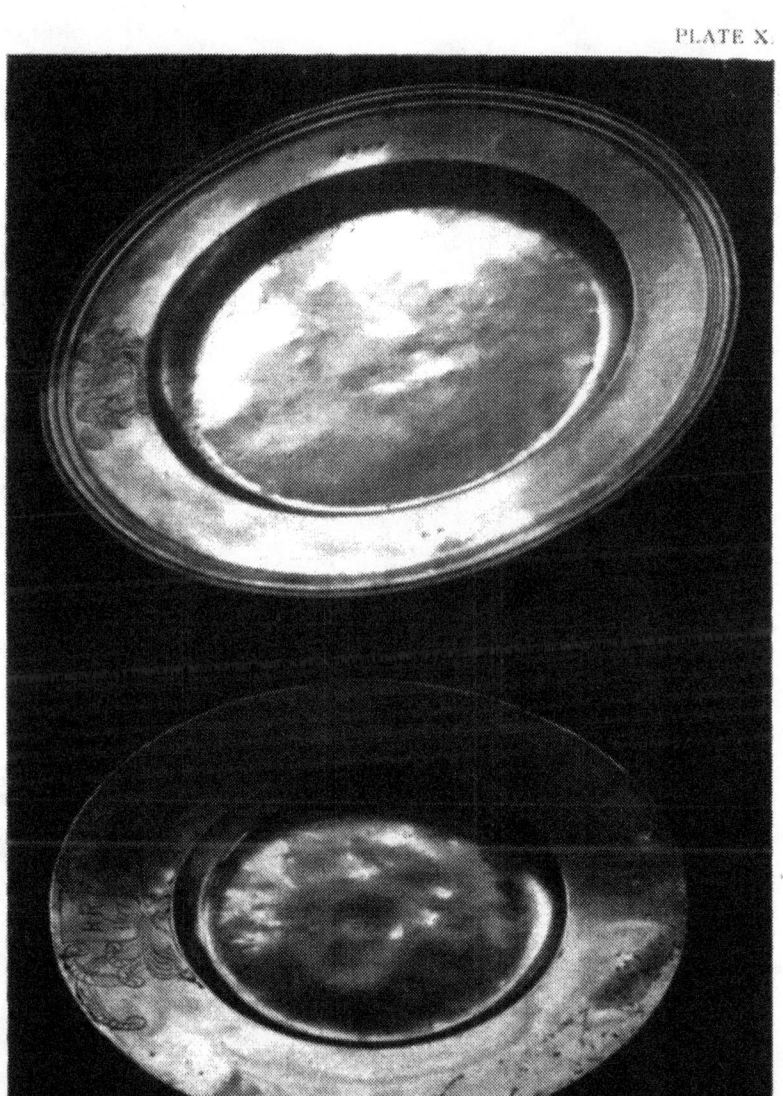

restored, is thickly plated with silver. Some of the existing alms-dishes of pewter have also been treated in the same way.

The painting and gilding of tin or pewter was in England always very stringently forbidden. Mr. Welch (ii. 80) mentions "some smallest paynted beakers and salts" which were confiscated at a search made in 1622.

It had been allowed, however (in 1564), to decorate in this manner objects if made for presents, provided that the objects were small, and that it could be proved that they had been given away. Mr. Welch (i. 248) mentions formal warning given to Richard Harrison and Robert Somers for this offence. When Louis XIV confiscated the plate of his subjects, the latter had to choose between pewter and faïence. If the choice fell upon pewter the users of it were allowed to paint and gild it, a concession which hitherto had been reserved to pewter for church use. This decorated pewter did not become very common, and few genuine specimens have come down to us. Henry de Béthune, Archbishop of Bordeaux in 1680, had various vases lacquered black and ornamented with gold. Fifty years later, in the inventory of goods at the Château of Rochefoucauld, mention is made of "a goblet of pewter, gilt."

Pewter was used to inlay furniture and domestic woodwork as early as the fifteenth century, in the same way that buhl-work was used at a later date, and that tin, nearly pure, was used to inlay papier-mâché work.

In the Musée Plantin at Antwerp is a magnificent cabinet in mahogany, all inlaid with pewter of good quality. The dark tone of the wood and the silvery colour of the metal make a fine contrast, and give a far finer effect than the black cabinet inlaid with brass in an adjoining room. There is another specimen in the Cluny Museum in Paris.

In recent years pewter has been used in the same way, but in a very tentative and not always successful manner. The colour of the metal—provided it did not tarnish—would be effective enough; but it shows very little in a light-coloured or stained wood. If protected from oxidation by lacquer, it is apt to look hard and uninteresting, and is very different in appearance from pewter regularly and carefully handled. It looks best if inlaid in a wood of light or medium tone, and left unlacquered.

It would be better in pewter-inlay work to keep to a metal of the same composition as that used for the same purpose in the papier-mâché ware of the last century.

Professor Herkomer commissioned for his house at Bushey some doors in which pewter and copper were cleverly combined, the copper being inlaid in the pewter.

Pewter *appliqué* work was sometimes used to decorate small caskets and coffers. In the "Catalogue raisonné" of Monsieur Darcel, one of these coffers is described as follows: "Les côtés sont formés de trois frises; l'une de griffons, d'aigles éployées, de basilics, de lions passants, etc., dans des disques circulaires reliés par des barres horizontales, bordées de fleurons symétriques dessus et dessous, comprise entre deux frises de rinceaux, à feuilles d'érable. Une bande de cuivre rouge doré, à saillie, forme soubassement."

Very often the shape of a vessel has been altered and ornamented after manufacture. There are tankards and coffee-pots extant which have circular bases and lids, but with octagonal or sometimes fluted bodies.

The vertical is not so common as the diagonal fluting, but it is used with good effect, especially in cases where the fluting is only done to a portion, say one-third of the body.

There is not much to be said of the ornamentation applied to church plate of pewter. It was, when applied at all, kept particularly simple and restrained. The commonest devices used were the sacred monogram (frequently on the rim), the emblem of the Trinity, the Instruments of the Passion, or a Sacred Heart.

St. Margaret Pattens, to mention one of our City churches, has plain dishes, with, for ornament, an eight-pointed star radiant with flames, containing in the centre I H S and a cross above it, with the three nails.

At St. Katharine Cree are some fine alms-dishes 18 in. in diameter, considered by Mr. Philip Norman to be some of the finest pewter dishes in existence. He dates them 1628–31, the date of the rebuilding of the church, and of the silver plate also in the church, and says: "There are three pewter alms-dishes of remarkably fine workmanship, and no doubt all of the same date; they have bosses in their centres; on one are the royal arms and the initials C.R.; on another, a sword in saltire, crowned with a rose (this and the harp crowned), and the initials C.R.; on a third, the Prince of Wales' feathers and the initials C.P. All these embellishments are beautifully worked in enamel. There is a fourth pewter dish, identical in design, with a double rose in the centre, also enamelled, but this has been electro-plated."

Of engraved work the most delicately done is French, as the two specimens shown by Herr Demiani in "Edelzinn."

Of inlaid work, perhaps the finest existing specimen is the flagon which was once in the possession of Mr. Gurney, and which now belongs to Lord Swaythling. It was for some time a loan exhibit at South Kensington Museum.

Some Chinese and some Russian pewter is found with very clever inlaid work.

The various decorative panels of figure-subjects in salvers of the Briot and Enderlein type were, like other cast pewter-work, sometimes cast separately with a view to their use as decoration, either alone, or as insets in combination with furniture. Sometimes, as is clear from the plates in Herr Demiani's book, the panels of a salver were utilized in the various sections of a tall flagon. A dish in the Louvre is built up of cast sections, some of them repeated, interspersed with plain pieces.

A small finely moulded tankard, which is in the Victoria and Albert Museum, South Kensington, is composed of three separate panels, the line of juncture being quite clearly visible.

Arabesques, properly worked and well designed, are most effective decorations on pewter. Nothing can be more dignified and attractive than the work of the Nuremberg master, Nikolaus Horchheimer, perhaps the father of German pewter arabesques. There is no necessity for high relief; in fact the lower the relief, the better the effect. Some very fine specimens are illustrated by Herr Demiani in his "Edelzinn"—mostly from his own collection. One good specimen is in the British Museum. It is the design that tells, for when once the mould was finished there was little need of further workmanship.

Another method of ornamenting pewter which is rarely met with is that of lacquering with semi-transparent lacquers. The effect is sombre in the extreme. A painted or enamelled and gilt cruet-stand in South Kensington Museum, with gilded glass bottles, is now almost grotesque, though it was probably highly prized by its original owner.

CHAPTER IX

PEWTER IN THE HOME

PEWTER nowadays is not found in use in any ordinary household. It can be kept in a condition rivalling silver, but it is rarely so found. Occasionally a pewter tundish or funnel is found in use in a farm in the country; and in some country and even town kitchens there will be found the Britannia metal teapots that delighted our forebears of three generations ago—pots which still enjoy a mythical reputation—quite undeserved—for making such excellent tea.

Pewter was, in the end of the thirteenth and the beginning of the fourteenth century, of sufficient importance to be specially mentioned in official documents.

In a pipe-roll of Edward I we read that leaden (more probably pewter) vessels were used for cooking the boiled meats for the feast given to celebrate the King's coronation. By 1290 this king had over three hundred pieces of pewter plate in his possession, the pieces consisting of dishes, platters and salts. Clement of Hungary in 1328 possessed nearly a gross of porringers.

In the fourteenth century pewter was used more in the houses of families of rank than those of lesser degree, and it was usual even in large houses to hire pewter services for special occasions, such as Christmas festivities.

In 1380 Michelet le Breton supplied to Charles VI 6 dozen dishes and 12 dozen porringers, weighing $474\frac{1}{2}$ marks.

In 1390 the households of high dignitaries, such as the Archbishops of Rheims and Rouen, were thoroughly equipped with pewter.

It seems from Jean de Jeaudun that the French pewter had more style about it than that made in England. Mention of everything that could be made in pewter is found in inventories of the time, viz. porringers, flagons, cans, cups and tankards (with or without covers), plates, dishes and alms-dishes, cruets, decanters and candlesticks.

Isabelle of Bavaria in 1401 bought from Jehan de Montrousti for her kitchen 9 dozen dishes and 23 dozen porringers, weighing 782 marks.

Charles VII in 1422 bought from Jehan Goupil of Tours 64 dishes and 158 porringers.

The various City Companies[1] had services of pewter, and it was in general use, in the Inns of Court, in the fifteenth and sixteenth centuries, and, according to Hazlitt, up to a recent date.

At the Universities of Oxford and Cambridge the colleges had their garnishes of pewter, but with few exceptions there is little now remaining. Queen's College, Oxford, has perhaps the best specimens.[2]

Pewter-ware began to come into more general use by the gentry in the fifteenth century, but it was in price at first beyond the reach of the humbler classes. Gradually, however, it began to supersede the domestic utensils of wood. Harrison, in his "Description of England," wrote: "The third thing they tell of is the exchange of vessels, as of treene [i.e. wood] platters into pewter, and wooden spoons into silver or tin. For so common were all sorts of treene stuffe in olde time, that a man should hardly find foure pieces of pewter (of which one was peradventure a salt) in a good farmer's house." "Old time" is sufficiently vague an expression, but as Harrison wrote shortly before 1587 it is easy to understand what he meant.

In the Reading Museum there are some wooden dishes

---

[1] Cp. the records of the Goldsmiths' Company, 1470: "For a garnish of 2 dozen pewter vessels to serve the company, £1 17s. 6d." (Herbert.)

[2] Queen's College, Oxford, has seventy-two specimens, mostly made by and bearing the marks of Samuel Ellis. Some of it bears the additional marks of other makers, such as A. Cleeve, Rd. Norfolk, Thos. Chamberlain.

(one square, two round) exhibited side by side with the pewter by which they were superseded.[1]

One of the rules at Clifford's Inn was to the effect that each member was to pay thirteen pence for vessels of pewter, and was bound to have in the kitchen "two plates and dishes of pewter each day for his own use." Some of the Staple Inn pewter is now in the Guildhall Museum.

The following four instances of the mention of pewter are of interest :

In the will of John Ely (1427), vicar in Ripon Minster, mention is made of " di. dus. garnes de vessell de pewdre cum ij chargiours," or the half of a garnish, i.e. of a set of twelve of each.

In the inventory of John Danby of Alveston (1444) mention is made of " ix pece led and pewd[er] vessall ij.s. iiij^d."

By the will of Elizabeth, Lady Uvedale (1487), a bequest is made of " a hoole garnish of peautre vessel, two round basin of peautre."

There were in the inventory of the College of Auckland (1498) " xx pewder platters, xij pewder dishes, viii salters, ii payre of potclyppes, j garnishe of vessell, j shaving basyn."

At the time of the Dissolution of the Monasteries very little pewter was confiscated. In an inventory of the goods of the Cell of Stanlowe (1537) there is mention of " iij counterfettes otherwise called podingers of pewter, whearof on[e] olde "; and in the kitchen were " vij pewther dyshes " (" Reliquary," vii., 1893, p. 30). At Whalley Abbey there were " iiij garnisste of pewter vessell."

Harrison, who has been quoted before, wrote at the end of the sixteenth century (1577-87) that " Such furniture of household of this mettall, as we commonly call by the name of vessell, is sold usually by the garnish which doth conteine 12 platters, 12 dishes, 12 saucers, and those are either of silver fashion or else with brode or narrow brims, and bought by the pound, which is now valued at sevenpence, or peradventure at eightpence."

[1] In one country house the writer has seen the pewter used by three successive generations, and also the Chinese ware by which it was superseded, all religiously preserved.

PLATE XI

1. Various measures and a teapot.

    (Colonel Balfour.)

2. Two measures, showing different ways of fixing handles to the body.

PLATE XI.

When more was required than the limited garnish, additional plate could be hired, called "feast-vessels," and the letting out of such was a source of much profit to the lenders. The pewterers clubbed together and shared the profits if more was required than was in one man's available stock.

The hiring out of new pewter-ware was forbidden, though no doubt the rule was, like the other regulations of the Pewterers' Company, often broken.

From the Northumberland Household Book we learn that the price of hiring was fourpence for each dozen articles per annum. For buying pewter the same book contains: "Item, to be payd . . . for the bying of vj dossen nugh pewter vessels for servying of my house for oone hole yere after vj shillings the dossen."

In the same book (1500) is a note that pewter vessels were too costly to be common.

From the "Ménagier de Paris," the requisite service of pewter for a dinner of state was 6 dozen écuelles, i.e. porringers, the same of small plates, 2½ dozen large dishes, 8 quart and 12 pint tankards, and 2 dishes for the scraps for the poor.

In the reign of Henry VIII the following was one of the regulations of the royal household (Cap. 20):

"Officers of the squillery[1] to see that all the vessels, as well silver as pewter, be kept and saved from stealing."

This shows that pewter held an honourable position in the furniture of a house, and bears out the note quoted above, that pewter was too valuable to be common.

Harrison (1577–87) wrote: "Likewise in the houses of knights, gentlemen, merchantmen and some other wealthy citizens, it is not geson[2] to behold generallie their great provision of tapestrie, Turkie work, pewter, brass, and fine linen and thereto costlie cupboards of plate, worth five or six hundred or a thousand pounds to be deemed by estimation."

In the later sixteenth and early seventeenth century

---

[1] i.e. scullery, from the O.F. *escuelles*, i.e. *écuelles*.
[2] Uncommon.

pewter may be said to have begun to be commonly used by the people as well as in many households of quality, as the inventories clearly show.

To this period of display pewter must be attributed the appearance of the highly decorated work, beginning with that of Briot (1550) and followed by that of Enderlein, and later by the florid work of the Nuremberg workers (1600-1660). The wares of the ewer and basin type may have been designed for use on ceremonial occasions, but the smaller elaborate plates, such as the Kaiserteller and the plates with religious subjects, though sometimes called and possibly used as patens, were no doubt intended to be used as decorative adjuncts to the house.

In the sixteenth century in France, according to the "Ménagier de Paris," the *bourgeois* class made brave displays of pewter-ware on their sideboards and dressers in imitation of the similar displays of gold and silver made by the upper classes. The *bourgeois* consoled themselves by calling their pewter "à façon d'argent," a consolation for which, no doubt, they had to pay the pewterers.

At that time, just as now, there was a craze for *nouveuatés de Paris*, and it led people to pay fancy prices for their pewter. In the "Journal d'un Voyage à Paris" (1657) it is stated that "L'après disnée nous fusmes nous promener à pied, et, en passant devant la maison de cet homme qui a trouvé le secret de raffiner si bien l'estain qu'il puisse resister au feu autant de temps que l'argent et les autres métaux les plus difficiles à fondre nous y entrasmes et treuvasmes que c'est une merveille de voir que dans un plat de son estain il en fait fondre un d'argent. Voilà un beau secret découvert, et qui faict desjà que les personnes de condition se servant de sa vaisselle, qui couste moins et faict le mesme effet que celle d'argent, estant aussi belle, aussi legère, et d'autant d'esclat. Il les vend cent sols le livre, quand ce sont des pièces où il y a peu de façon : celles qui en ont beaucoup, il les vend plus cher."

Matthew Parker, Archbishop of Canterbury in 1575, had 370 lb. of pewter in the kitchen in jugs, basins, porringers, sauce-boats, pots and candlesticks; also pewter measure in the wine-cellars, together with salt-cellars. He had more, too, in his house at Addiscombe.

Lord Northampton's kitchen alone had about 3 cwt, of pewter vessels, and his house may be taken as a typical example of the larger establishments of that time. In households of this size there were yeomen of the ewerie whose business it was to look after the pewter.

In the inventory of Sir Wm. Fairfax's house at Gilling in 1594 (given in " Archæologia," vol. xlviii.), there were in the " wine-seller one quart pewter pott : in the pantrye 2 basins and ewers of pewter valued at xiij^s iiij^d and ij pewter voyders trays—valued at x^s. In the kytchine xij sawcers, xij dishes, xij great dishes, xij great platters, xij lesser platters, iiij chargers, sawcers xij, dishes xij." Of new vessels there were " xij sawcers, xij sallite dishes, ij dozin great dishes, xviij great platters, xviij lesser platters, and i charger of the greatest sorte. Valued altogether xiiij^{li}. vi^s. viii^d."

In an inventory of Sir Thomas Hoskyns, Kt., of Oxted, in 1615, there were in the kitchen " 8 dozen of pewter dishes of all sortes, five dozen of sawcers, thirteene candlestickes of pewter, fower pewter flagons."

From a " trew inventory taken in 1618 of the goods and chattles of Sir Richard Poullett, late of Herryott in the C^o of Southampton, Knight, deceased," were : " in the pantry and seller 9 pewter candlesticks : in the wine seller a still of pewter with a brasen bottome : in the kytchin and the kytchin entry—one pewter flaggon pott, nyne pewter candlesticks, 14 small sallet pewter dishes." Then follows a list of " Boylemeat dishes, deep platters, large platters, washing bason, pye plates, small d^o, small saucers and 7 old counterfett dishes, 14 old sawcers, and 18 pieces of severall sortes of old pewter."

At Walton the inventory (dated 1624) runs : " There should be of nyne severall sizes of pewther dishes which came from Newcastle, and have not your name on them, 6 dishes of each size, which in all is 54 dishes "—but of these it states 9 are missing.

" There came with the dishes above 2 long dishes for Rabbittes which are both in place . . . likewise 12 saucers whereof . . . now wanting 8, also 2 chargers, 2 long pyplaites and a voyder which are all in place. All the above . . . are of the silver dishes fashion.

"Other silver fashioned dishes changed at Beverley at severall tymes by Ralph Hickes whereof now in place which are marked with your own and my Lady's name." Of these there ought to have been 12 and a rabbit dish, but 6 were missing. Of "other vessell in the kitchin chest which are now in place," of various sizes, "27 dishes, 1 charger, 4 pye plaites, one Cullender and one baking pan."

One more inventory[1] of pewter and other ware is that taken at Chastleton House near Moreton-in-the-Marsh in 1632. It is interesting as showing the pewter equipment of a country mansion at that time.

"In the Gallery.

"Item, Pewter platters of divirse sortes, 8 doz and 10 platters, one large boiler, five basons, two spout potts, seaven pie plates, three great flaggons, two quart potts, one pott costerne, one cullinder, one baie pott, one puddinge coffin, ix candlesticks, nine chamber potts weighinge 443 li."

This was valued then at £22 3s., or just one shilling per pound.

The main portion of the Chastleton pewter is now on a dresser in the kitchen, extending the whole length of one wall. Much of the pewter is of a date subsequent to the making of the above inventory, as the names and stamps of Samuel Ellis (1748), Robert Nicholson (1725), A. Nicholson (?), Townend and Compton (1809), John Home (1771), W. Brayne (1705), clearly prove.

A smaller dresser with plates in better condition is in one of the passages upstairs, and some chargers are displayed in the embrasure of a window on the main staircase.

The pewter is not used, and that in the kitchen has assumed a venerable appearance, in keeping with the kitchen, which has never been rewhitewashed since the house was built by Henry Jones in 1611.

There is one curiously shaped dish in the kitchen

---

[1] From "Three Centuries in N. Oxfordshire."

equipment—perfectly straight on one side and oval on the other—like the tinned iron receptacles that are used when meat is roasted on a jack in front of the fire.

Pewter played an important part in the first colonial households in America, as it was the only available ware in many cases. But it had to give place, as in England, to the introduction of china.

In France, at the same time, in the inventory of Marie Cressé mention is made that " Dans la salle servant de cuisine, il a esté trouvé, en pots, plats, escuelles et autres ustensiles d'étain, cent-vingt-deux livres d'étain sonnant, prisé la livre douze sols " (Paris, 1633).

Boston was the chief seat both of its manufacture and also of the distribution of English pewter. The use of whale oil necessitated the introduction of lamps of a form peculiar to the country.

In the century from 1680 to 1780 the use of pewter at first was steadily continued, but later, owing to the introduction of domestic pottery from abroad and from our own Staffordshire works, began to decline.

A similar state of things prevailed in France, in spite of Louis XIV's appointment of a Royal Pewterer. The King could compel his nobles to give up to him most of their silver plate, but he could not compel them to go back to the use of pewter, even with the grant of special permission (previously restricted to church plate) to adorn it with lacquer and gold. With the middle classes it continued to be used.

Pewter, however, managed to keep its place in the kitchens of the houses of the gentry, and in many houses of the middle class. In some of the larger domestic establishments it continued to be used regularly till within the last thirty years, and there are even now two or three houses where it is still used in the servants' hall.

Any inventories taken now of a middle-class house would, probably, contain no mention of pewter at all. It would occur in some old family houses which have not changed hands, and in which the pewter has been reverently laid aside, in some cases with the chinaware by which it was immediately superseded.

Plates and dishes with salvers and chargers of all sizes (and there were many, as may be seen from the list of the moulds of the London and the York pewterers) were made by the men known as sadware-men. The term is of doubtful origin and meaning, but it is still in use among pewterers where they exist.

Sadware was cast in moulds and finished by the hammer on an anvil or swage. These moulds left the metal in a somewhat rough condition and the hand-finishing was essential. In quality the sadware was good, and to finish it the proper method was by striping and burnishing. Sadware-men do not seem to have received very high wages, nor to have been held in very high estimation, and, like the humble spoon-makers, tried to do their work as easily as possible, e.g. by turning it on a lathe. This was forbidden in 1681 in very definite terms (Welch, ii. 155).

Sadware from its quality has survived ordinary wear and tear very well, almost down to our time.

Pewter lingered on longest in the taverns and inns, and in the London chop-houses till the latter were assailed by the introduction of coffee-palaces and tea-rooms.

Pewter platters were in use thirty years ago at the Bay Tree Tavern in St. Swithin's Lane. These were veritable platters, absolutely flat, with a moulding round the edge for strengthening the platter. They were about nine or perhaps ten inches in diameter, and had been well used in their time, as the knife-marks on the upper surface clearly showed. With the rebuilding of the tavern and its conversion into a restaurant these platters would seem to have disappeared.

About the same date some of the many chop-houses in Eastcheap had displays of pewter plate, but they were not then in common use.

Salvers with feet are not unknown. A clumsy specimen with three long feet is preserved in the church of Erchfont-with-Stert (Wilts). Salvers of this kind have survived in the form of hot-water well-dishes, which are still made but often with china plates inserted.

In these days, when portability and lightness are regarded as so essential, it requires an effort to think of pewter plates having ever been chosen for an officer's camp equipment. However, they were so used, and there are many specimens in existence which are said to have been used by Lord Marcus Hill through the Peninsular campaigns.

Small bowls or porringers, sometimes called counterfettes, are very common objects in museums and collections. As a rule they are simple in section, strongly made, with ears or handles of shaped and perforated work, and usually a large cinquefoil or Tudor rose ill-stamped on the bottom.

They are very often of Dutch make, but such bowls in various sizes were in common use in England. In the Museum at South Kensington there is a pair of large size, quite plainly finished, but one has graduations engraved in the inside showing that it was a barber-surgeon's bleeding-dish.

These porringers date back from very early times. From the Old French name of *escuelles* our word scullery is derived.

Harrison, quoted before, writes: "Of porringers, pots, and other like I speake not, albeit that in the making of all these things there is such exquisite diligence used, I meane for the mixture of the mettall and true making of this commoditie (by reason of sharpe laws provided in that behalfe) as the like is not to be found in any other trade."

The eared cups or porringers have often lost their ears or handles owing to defective construction. A projecting handle of such thin metal was bound to get bent, and by being bent back into position was bound to crack. They survived best when cast thick, or in some cases when strengthened with a circular ring, soldered on to the body of the cup and on to the handle.

Blood porringers, cupping dishes, or bleeding dishes are still made in pewter, and the ear or handle is more or less traditional in pattern, being from one of Townend and Compton's old moulds. It has, however, been found necessary to strengthen the ear by thickening it, and to give a little solid metal at the point of juncture with the bowl.

Some of the Scotch "quaighs" are similar to these

PLATE XII

Two old measures, with photograph of the lid stamped rather unusually in five places.

PLATE XII.

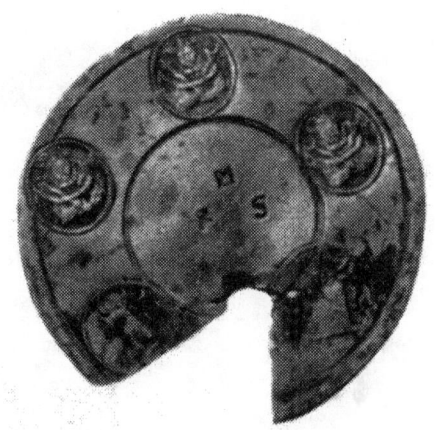

bowls, but in many cases the ears or handles are shaped, not pierced with any pattern.

Some eighteenth-century vegetable dishes with similar handles seem to be the latest development of these very convenient vessels.

It is to be noted that the number of spoons which have come down to the present time in good condition is comparatively small. This is partly due to the fact that the early spoons had been made, or at any rate finished, by hammering. The metal was soon bent by the pressure put upon it during use and the number of breakages must have been enormous.

Spoons were, from the necessity of living, invented earlier than forks, which are comparatively late comers.

Wooden spoons were no doubt the first to be made and were contemporary almost with those made of horn. Neither material is ideal. Wood retains a suspicion of the viands or fluids for which it has been used, and horn when heated unduly, either in use or when being cleaned—cracks easily, loses its shape and so deteriorates very quickly. Horn was replaced by *laiton* (a variety of brass) or latten, as it is usually spelled in English, and the forms of the latten spoons were at an early date copied by the spoonmakers. These latten spoons were introduced by traders from abroad and very early specimens are extremely rare.

By the end of the fourteenth century the various types of spoons were beginning to come into use, and in the fifteenth century we find spoons with knops shaped to represent acorns, diamond points, or lozenge points, images of the Blessed Virgin Mary called Maidenheads, heads of women wearing horned head-dresses, heads representing the Apostles, hexagonal knops, lions, writhen balls, baluster-tops, seal-tops and strawberry-tops.

All these were elaborate and were sometimes gilded or lacquered.

In the next century a cheaper and simpler spoon came into use. There was no ornamental knop or top, but the stem was sliced off at an acute angle. From this kind of cutting or slipping (gardeners use the same word to-day) the spoons are known as slipped tops, or slipped in the stalk. The stalk was irregularly hexagonal as a rule and later tended to become a square and sometimes an oblong in section.

The next development gives us the Puritan spoon. In these the ornamental hexagonal, being considered frivolous, gives way to an uncompromising square.

The next stage was the flattening out of the square end so as to balance the bowl, and in so doing the chance splitting of the hammered end fixed the pattern and the name given to it was the split end or *pied de biche* or deersfoot.

With this type of spoon the strengthening band, or tongue, or rat's-tail has its genesis, and it prevailed up to 1720 or thereabouts.

The *pied de biche* end was followed by the shield end or wavy end spoons, and the wavy end finally gave way to the simple round end.

In the museums at Haarlem and elsewhere the japanned racks with supports for three rows of four spoons in each are to be seen.

It was not a sign of cleverness if a workman had to be kept at spoon-making, though this branch of the trade was sometimes left open for a man whose eyesight had failed. Mr. Welch notes cases of men finishing their spoons improperly, i.e. by grating them and burnishing instead of beating them. This was a saving of time, no doubt, but it left the spoons softer than they should have been. In 1686 a maker, Burton by name, was found fault with for using an " engine," presumably a press of some kind, for making spoons. Fortunately for him his spoons were well finished, and he undertook not to sell them in the country under six shillings, and in town for four shillings, a gross, so that no injury might be done to the other spoon-makers.

Punch ladles have survived in fairly good condition—they are later in date than the ordinary spoon, and are fairly hard metal. Frequently, where oval in shape and deep in the cup, they are stronger than the circular type. The handles are usually slender specimens of turned wood.

Perforated spoons, or sugar-sifters, are rarely quite perfect. The ornamentation is frequently produced by punching the open work of the pattern out with a punch, and the bowl suffers in consequence.

Pewter toys date back to Roman times, and have been dug up at various places in England and on the Continent. They may have been the actual toys which gladdened the hearts of their actual possessors during life, but from the way they are made they seem, like the chalices buried with deceased ecclesiastics, to have been intentionally counterfeit representations of the real toys used by the youthful deceased during life.

Though hardly toys, it may be as well to mention here the buttons, brooches and spinning-whorls, unmistakably Roman, that have also been found.

Tin soldiers would seem to have been used for children's playthings quite as early as Queen Elizabeth's time, for one Anthony Taylor was heavily fined for making " manekins " " 10 grains worse than fine."

In the seventeenth century tin and pewter toys were quite common in Germany and the Netherlands, and specimens are to be seen in the Nuremberg Museum and in the Nuremberg dolls' house at South Kensington. This dolls' house is well worth careful study. In France the *bimbelotier*, or toymaker, was a recognized worker in tin or pewter, and his trade was large.

A pewterer in 1668, Francis Lea, was fined ten shillings for " his Toy Pestell and Morter, and other toyes at 5 grains," i.e. not quite up to the high standard of quality required by the Pewterers' Company. As a rule the toys seem to have been diminutive copies of the full-sized articles in everyday use in the household. Dolls'-house furniture constituted a distinct branch in the trade.

In our own time a common toy for boys was, and perhaps still is, a pewter squirt ; another, perhaps not quite so generally known, was a circular disc with a serrated edge strung on a string that passed through two points in a diameter and had its ends tied. By means of the two loops it was rotated quickly backwards and forwards, to the accompaniment of a siren-like noise which varied according to the speed of the rotation, and the size and method of setting of the teeth.

Bird-cages, fenders for dolls' houses, tiny mirror-frames, *étagères*, plate-baskets were objects to please the smaller hearts of the gentler sex, but their attractions paled before those of a tea-set complete on its tray.

Candlesticks and candelabra for dolls, both based on earlier patterns and pleasing in themselves, were also commonly made. But most, if not all, the dolls' pewter lacks the grace of the old pewter toys for this reason, that the old toys were diminutive copies of the articles in everyday use. Modern toys are for the most part "creations" of the artist.

Tea-cups and saucers, or tea-things, as they are more often called, have long since ceased to be made in pewter, but the traditional shape on a much smaller scale has lingered on in the tiny sets still sold for dolls'-house use or ornament. These diminutive sets are cleverly made, and are rarely worked upon after leaving the mould, for the low price precludes any such outlay of labour.

In style they are far superior to nearly all the silver and other metal teapots produced commercially at the present time.

Drinking vessels fall into two main classes—those without and those with handles—and the variety of shape in either class is almost endless.

It was no doubt recognized at an early date that the branch of the trade which dealt with drinking vessels was important, and worth while fostering.

In 1423 a regulation was made by Robert Chichely, Mayor, "that retailers of ale should sell the same in their houses in pots of 'peutre' sealed and open, and that whoever carried ale to the buyer should hold the pot in one hand and a cup in the other; and that all who had pots unsealed should be fined."[1]

This extract is interesting from the use of the word "sealed," which would seem to point to the stamping of a mark, about eighty years before the Act of Parliament

---

[1] Herbert, "History of the Livery Companies."

made such stamping necessary, and about 120 years before the first recorded use of official touches.

Drinking cups of the beaker form were probably derived originally from the earlier cups of horn, which were used contemporaneously with those of wood and pewter. The outward curves of the lip and of the foot were common-sense as well as decorative additions, as the curves gave an additional element of strength where it was most required.

Pewter pots from a very early date seem to have formed part of the equipment of a cabaret in France, or a tavern in England. They must have been regarded as an improvement upon vessels made of copper, wood, or rough earthenware. That they were found convenient as weapons of offence or defence appears from a case quoted by Bapst, where one Jean Lebeuf in 1396 was charged with hitting his boon companion with a pewter wine measure. The practice has undoubtedly been continued since that time.

Our English taverns had their pewter pots and tankards from a very early date, and the manufacture was certainly profitable—in fact, so profitable that when, at the end of the seventeenth century, glass and earthenware began to be used to some extent the Pewterers' Company were anxious (at the request of the Potmakers) to procure an Act of Parliament to make it obligatory to sell beer, wine and spirits on draught in pewter measures, sealed. It was suggested, not altogether from disinterested motives, that the earthenware and other drinking vessels were not good measure. This argument was very ingenious, but it was not successful. It savoured too much of the monopoly system.

Harrison, in his "Description of England," wrote: "As for drinke, it is usuallie filled in pots, gobblets, jugs, bols of silver in noblemens houses, also in fine Venice glasses of all formes, and for want of these, elsewhere, in pots of earth of sundrie colours and moulds, whereof manie are garnished with silver, or at the leastwise in pewter."

The "fine Venice glasses of all formes" do not here concern us, nor do the "bols of silver," but the "pots, gobblets, jugs and bols" were made in Harrison's time of pewter. What Harrison quaintly terms "pots of earth of sundrie colours and moulds, whereof manie are garnished with silver, or at the leastwise in pewter," formed in the fourteenth and subsequent centuries a large and important branch of the pewterers' trade.

The pot-lids formed a branch of the London pewterers' craft, and they worked under very special regulations. In 1552 " yt was agreed that all those that lyd stone pottes should set their own marck on the in syde of the lyd, and to bring in all such stone potts in to the hall wherby they may be vewed yf they be workmanly wrought, and so be markyd[1] w^t the marck of the hall on the owt syde of the Lyd. Also every one that makyth each stone pottes shall make a new marck, such one as the M^r and Wardens shalbe pleased w^{t}all whereby they maye be known from this daye forward. Theise potts to be brought in wekly upon the Satterdaye and if the Satterdaye be holly daye then to bring them in upon the ffrydaye. And loke who doth the contrary shall forfayte for every stone pott so duely proved iiij^d in mony over and besydes the forfayte of all such pottes as be not brought in according to this artycle " (Welch, i. 174).

In 1548 they were ordered to be stamped with a fleur-de-lys (Welch, i. 157).

Four years later the Company appointed one Harry Tompson to have the " vewe and marking of all stone pottes and he should mark none but those that be substancyally wrought " (Welch, i. 190). He was removed from his office in 1559.

The cost of making the lids was fixed in 1581 at two shillings a dozen, unless the customer were a brother of the Company (Welch, i. 289).

Another version of this in the Jury Book says the mark was to be on the outside. This may be so, for in 1559 it was settled that if a lid were badly made the potte was to be broken as well as the lid, and " that from hensforth the makers of stone pott lyddes shall set theire marcke on the inside of the Lyddes " (Welch, i. 202).

There is as great variety in the shape of the body of

---

[1] The price of the marking was a farthing a dozen.

tankards as in their names, the fashion of the purchase or thumb-piece, the shape of the lid and the curve of the handle.

Mr. Welch (ii. 61, 62), under the date 1612-13, about twenty-five years after Harrison's time, mentions in a list of pewter wares and their specified weights: "Great beakers, wrought or plaine middle and small beakers, as well as childrens beakers, also wrought or plaine, greate and smale beere bowles, with large wrought cuppes. There were also middle and smale French Cupps, with high wyne cupps, wrought and plaine and the cutt shorte, plaine and wrought." As to jugs and pots for holding the beer there were (p. 62) "'spowt potts' containing a potte, quart, pint and half pint of fluid. Ewres were known as Hawkesbills and Ravensbills, both greate and small, with very little difference in the weight between the sizes, with greate and smale French of the same weight. There were new fashion thurndells[1] and halfe thurnedells—new quarts, new great, smale and halfe potts, hooped thurndells, great hooped quarts, Winchester quarts and pints with or without lidds, long hooped Winchester pyntes and Jeayes danske potts." The list concludes (p. 64) "with greate middle and smale jugg potts not sized, and measures for aquavitae."

A weak point in many tankards and flagons has been the hinge of the lid. Some of the hinges are quite simple, consisting of three leaves; others have five. Friction, dust and frequent use have soon caused the hinges to work loose, and have been assisted by occasional falls, the evidence of which is generally clearly to be seen.

To remedy this weakness of the hinge, bone was tried as a substitute, as in the church flagon at Milton Lilburne. Brass pins are sometimes found.

Flagons with feet are common enough in German museums, and there are specimens in the museum at South Kensington.

In Germany, in the seventeenth century, tankards for beer were made of wood and ornamented with *appliqué*

[1] These are sometimes called thirdendales or thriddendales. Sir W. H. St. John Hope says it is a Wiltshire word, meaning a pot to hold about three pints, hence the name.

PLATE XIII

Stuart Tankards

1. Height, 5 in. ; base, 4⅝ in.
2. ,, 6 in. ,, 5 in.
3. ,, 7½ in. ,, 5¼ in.
4. ,, 6 in. ,, 4½ in.
5. ,, 5 in. ,, 4½ in.

Sizes are from top of lid to base.

Capacity of No. 3 is smaller than 2 and 4, as base is raised up.

(Dr. Young.)

The two illustrations have been made from photographs giving front and side view respectively, slightly different in scale.

PLATE XIII.

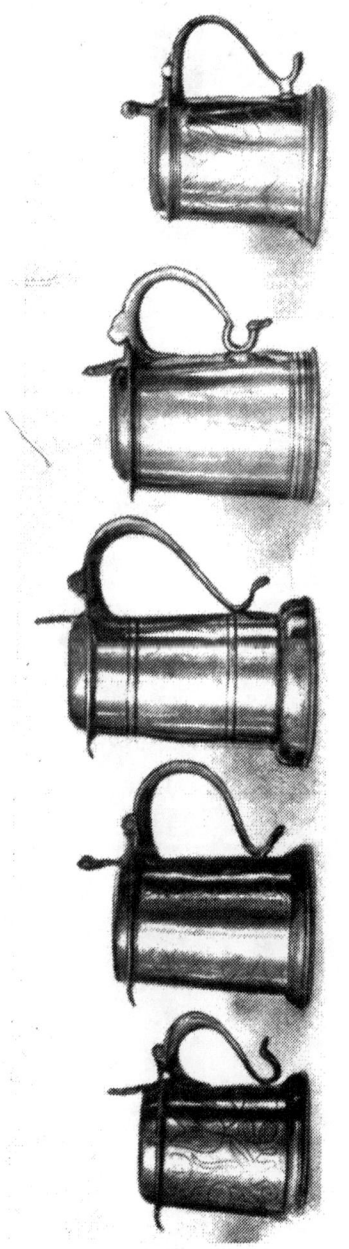

work of a simple kind, chiefly scroll-work. Sometimes these tankards were partly inlaid as well. The interior was made water-tight with pitch, and from this the tankards took the name of *Pechkrüge*.

The modern German glass beer-tankard is often fitted with a pewter lid, but the weight of the lid is generally carried on an upright pewter pillar, which is clamped on the upper side of a C-shaped handle. The metal employed is rather bright-looking and garish, and is frequently overelaborately worked, and with the glass vessel the colour effect is not satisfactory. The metal has the appearance of type metal rather than of ordinary pewter, and the nature of the composition may be influenced by the supposed necessity to have the ornament very sharply cut and clear in every detail.

In most western European countries pewter was largely used for measures either for dry goods or for liquids, and for use in scales where small goods were to be sold by weight, such as salt. Oil, wine, beer, were the fluids most commonly measured in the pewter measures, and the metal, from its capacity of withstanding rough usage, was found to be especially convenient. The ware was in common use for these purposes in the whole of France.

"Tappit-hens"[1] is the name given to Scotch jugs, usually found in sets of three, and used for beer. The form is quaint, but quite suitable for the metal from which the "hens" are made. In South Kensington Museum there is an early measure of English make which suggests the tappit-hen. The Jersey measures resemble the "hens" in shape.

Previous to the Union with England in 1707 the Scottish standard measures were :—

    4 gills   1 mutchkin
    2 mutchkins 1 chopin (i.e. $1\frac{1}{2}$ pints, English)
    2 chopins   1 pint (i.e. 3 ,,   ,,)

The Scottish pint, when made in a particular shape with a crested lid, was commonly called a tappit-hen.

[1] Tappit, i.e. with a top. Possibly they took their name from a breed of domestic hens which had crested heads.

The type without a crest is certainly earlier in date. The range of sizes was greater and probably included a ¼ gill (a thimble full) and ½ gill.

At a loan exhibition in Glasgow in 1909 there were on view :—

1. ¾ gill
2. 1 gill
3. 1½ gill
4. 2 gill
5. Small mutchkin (3 gills)
6. Mutchkin (4 gills)
7. Chopin
8. Tappit-hen.

and 9 (a very rare size) holding 3 chopins or 4½ pints (English).

In these early " hens " the bottom end of the handle is soldered directly on to the body.

Some of the larger " hens " were made with a cup fitting inside the top, with a slight rim.

The Scotch " quaighs " were also used as drinking vessels.

Cups and tankards are often scored at intervals with lines all the way down the inside circumference. It is difficult to see the object of this, and the effect is not decorative. Pegs in a peg-tankard are justifiable, and so are the lines in a graduated bleeding-dish.

Many tankards have an ornament such as a rose in the inside at the bottom. In some cases the ornament is cast, and then soldered upon the metal.

A large Tudor rose is often found in the bottom of the porringers or eared dishes.

A medallion is often found soldered on to the bottom (inside) in German drinking vessels. A rose is a common device; so too a lily, or a scroll, or a cross with the Virgin Mary and St. John—the last-named in the case of conventual pewter plate.

CHAPTER X

CHURCH PEWTER

EARLY chalices are known to have been made of horn, marble, glass, copper and lead. Horn was forbidden by Adrian II in 867, but it was used in France in the twelfth century; marble, earthenware and glass were found to be rather fragile; bronze and copper, unless tinted or gilded, and lead vessels were found to have an injurious effect upon the wine that was poured into them.

The three permissible metals, then, at first, were gold, silver and pewter, but the last was not supposed to be used unless for economic reasons. In later times pewter vessels seem to have been used as a general rule, and the more elaborate plate kept for festival use.

For the celebrant the usual type was the chalice with or without handles; for the use of the congregation, up to the end of the thirteenth century, large chalices with handles were used. From these the wine was sometimes taken by means of a tube permanently fixed on the side of the cup, or else taken in the usual way.

At the Council of Westminster held under the presidency of Richard, Archbishop of Canterbury, in 1175, it was ordered that "the Eucharist shall not be consecrated in any other than a chalice of gold or silver, and from this time forward we forbid any bishop to consecrate a pewter chalice."

Necessity, however, knows no law, and in spite of the Canon Law the English ecclesiastics had to put up with pewter communion plate after the bulk of the church plate had been collected and disposed of to make up the 100,000 marks required to ransom Richard Cœur de Lion in 1194.

In France pewter church plate was expressly permitted to be used by poor parishes by the Council of Nîmes in 1252, and by the Council of Albi held in 1254. As it was used in some dioceses in cases not necessarily on account of poverty, it must be assumed that the rule had its occasional local exceptions.

Sepulchral chalices, said to be made of pewter, though in many cases more probably of lead, have been dug up in many places during the progress of structural alterations, and restorations. These articles for sepulchral use are not well finished as a rule, but are rather rough. Abbots and bishops were as a rule buried with a crosier, sometimes of gold; priests with a chalice. St. Birin, Bishop of Dorchester, who died in the seventh century, was buried with a crosier and a chalice of pewter, as was proved when the tomb was opened in 1224. Chalices have been found in graves at Chichester, Cheam in Surrey, in Gloucester Cathedral and in other places, quite frequently enough to show that the custom was common. They have been found too, at Troyes in tombs dating between 1188 and 1395, at Jumièges, at Geneva, date 1423, with paten and crosier. It is rare that these chalices are found much later than the middle of the fifteenth century.

When the church at Nassington was under restoration in 1885 a grave was opened in the north aisle, near the third pillar. In this were found a pewter paten and chalice, both much damaged, and three palmers' shells or scallops, each of them pierced with two holes for affixing to the wearer's dress. The vessels were early in date, probably the middle of the thirteenth century. The paten was 4 in. in diameter, and had a single circular depression, the edge being rather broad. The chalice was 4 in. in diameter at the lip, and $4\frac{1}{2}$ in. high, with a shallow bell-shaped bowl, a slender cylindrical stem with a knop and a circular foot.

At Mont Saint-Michel in Normandy, when the tombs of Robert de Torigny and Martin Furmendeius were discovered and opened in 1885 by M. E. Corroyer, crosiers were found, and in each grave a round disc of pewter with inscriptions, showing the rank and names of the former occupiers of the graves. Robert de Torigny was abbot from 1154 to 1186, and Martin, his immediate successor, died in 1191.

These plaques are preserved in the muniment room at Mont Saint-Michel. They may have been pectoral plaques, similar to the roughly made pectoral crosses, usually of the shape known as Maltese, which have been found in graves of the same date, i.e. the twelfth century. These seem to have been inscribed with a prayer of absolution (scratched on the metal with a stylus) and placed under the crossed hands of the deceased before burial.

The heart case of Richard Cœur de Lion was found at Rouen in 1838, and that of Charles V was found in 1862, and one has been found at Holbrook in Suffolk. All these seem to have been made of pewter.

Large pewter vessels, called in Latin "amphorae," for conveying the sacramental wine in bulk from cellar to sacristy, and for water for the ceremonial washing of the celebrant, as well as of the sacred vessels after use, were common from the thirteenth century, at any rate on the Continent.

Where pewter was not in use tinned copper vessels were probably used.

In the fourteenth century the use of burettes, or small pewter bottles for the sacramental wine and the water, is first mentioned. These are called *cruets* later on in English; and in France by many synonyms, such as pochon, pitalpha, vinateria, canette, chaînette, choppineaux, chaupineaux—the last-named suggesting our old word chapnet or chapnut, which was in use in English in 1612–13, as it was specified in the official list of the Pewterers' Company[1] as a vessel of which six were to weigh 1½ lb., and in a smaller size six were to weigh 1 lb.

Pewter candlesticks were used in churches about the same time that the burettes came in fashion, but were apparently of small or moderate size. The larger kind and the hanging candelabra seem to have been of iron tinned or of copper. An early mention of an English chandelier is in the inventory of Whalley Abbey in 1537.

Portable bénitiers were often made of pewter. In shape

---

[1] Welch, ii. p. 61.

they resembled small pails, a convenient form for carriage round the church. Mention is made of one in 1328 in the private chapel of Clemence of Hungary; in the inventory of Jean de Halomesnil, 1380, a canon of the Sainte-Chapelle in Paris; in 1430 at Mons, in the chapel of the Hospital of St. Jaques; in 1438 in the inventory of Pierre Cardonnel, canon of Notre Dame at Paris.

It is difficult to say exactly at what time hanging stoups or wall-bénitiers of pewter came into use. Those in the Cluny Museum are much later than the fourteenth century; in fact those that have come down to our own time are as a rule seventeenth-century work or a little later. From the size they were undoubtedly meant for private domestic use, and in some cases they were richly painted and gilt. There is a plain one in good preservation in the museum at Ghent.

These bénitiers varied considerably, but they generally took one of two main forms, viz., the kind that was intended to stand upon a ledge, table or shelf, and the kind that was designed primarily to be hung upon a nail, but which as often as not had a container with a base, upon which it could safely be placed on a shelf if required. The shape of the container gave most scope for the designer's fancy. An inverted truncated cone was a very common shape.

The pentagon too was, from its solidity, a not uncommon shape. Many of the Flemish stoups have very elaborate crosses, with figures far inferior in execution to the rest of the work. Their containers are of a domestic rather than an ecclesiastical type, and in spite of the lids, or remains of lids, much resemble shaving-brush bowls. Some of the containers seem as though they were the halves of bowls of an ordinary type.

It is the exception to find one of these bénitiers in perfect condition. They have usually broken at the point where the cross is joined to the bowl, the reason being that the cross, when of any height, is disproportionate in weight, and has had a tendency to lean forward, and so in time has been broken.

Font ewers and font basins have been made of pewter, but actual fonts of pewter are rare. Professor Church found a pewter at Cirencester of thirteenth-century design. It seems to be an open question whether it was intentionally or accidentally made of pewter, as there are many lead fonts in existence in this country. A lead font, of course, will last perfectly well if properly designed and made thick enough to stand usage. Thin lead or pewter that could be bent backwards and forwards would last but a very short time. A baptismal ewer made of pewter, and gilded, was scheduled by Mr. R. C. Hope at Ashwell, Rutland.

In 1643 many fonts were either utterly destroyed or summarily removed from our churches; substitutes were introduced in the form of pewter basins or bowls, and large ewers for the water before use. There is a pewter font basin at Wellington Church, Sussex.

The church of St. Giles-in-the-Fields was provided with a pewter font in 1644, and it was cut square on one side.

Altar crucifixes were sometimes made of tin, and the example in the museum at Nürnberg is a very fine specimen. Recognizing the soft nature of the metal, its maker mounted it on wood to protect it from injury. The cross was richly ornamented by gilding.

Other church vessels were the dishes or trays upon which the cruets or burettes were kept; ampullae of various forms for the storing of incense; ewers and basins; small boxes or chrismatories for the consecrated oil required for use in extreme unction.

Monstrances and pyxes were undoubtedly made in pewter in the sixteenth century. There is in the museum at Stonyhurst College a chalice, in the foot of which there is a pyx.

At the dissolution of the monasteries in 1537 very little pewter seems to have been confiscated, and what little there was seems to have been domestic rather than ecclesiastical in character.

At Whalley Abbey there were in the abbot's kitchen " iiij garnisste of pewter vessell, ij dosen of vessell," and in the convent kitchen " xxxi dishes, xxij doblers, and xxviij sawsers." These are not said to be pewter in so many words, but it is more than probable that they were. The same was the case at Stanlow and elsewhere.

PLATE XIV

1. Chalice. Dated Assoc. Congreg. Edin., 1794.
2. Flagon. Scotch. Relief Kirk, Musselburgh, 1786.
3. Early chalice. No marks.
4. Early chalice (No. 22 in Touch Plates) (C. S. and rose).
5. Flagon or laver. Scotch. No marks. Note double bands, usually single, as above (Musselburgh one).

(Dr. Young.)

Two flagons and paten from Somersetshire.

PLATE XIV.

1   2

3   4   5

After the Reformation, when Communion in both kinds became the rule, a change in the size of the cups was necessary, as well as in the size of the flagons.

The 20th Canon of 1603-4 enacts as follows: " Wine we require to be brought to the Communion table in a clean and sweet standing pot or stoup of pewter—if not of purer metal." Previous to this date and this enactment, flagons were extremely scarce in churches, and it is probable that none were in use for the Communion before the last ten years or so of the sixteenth century.

The earliest tall straight-bodied flagons, made in *silver*, were made in 1602. Some of these are still extant. There are two at New College, Oxford (1602). Brasenose has a pair dated six years later, and Salisbury Cathedral has a pair made in 1610.

These silver flagons, as was usually the case, set the fashion, and the shape was copied in pewter. At Strood, near Rochester, an inventory notes " the purchase from Robert Ewer in 1607 (for 9/6) two pewter pots to serve the wine at the Communion."

Invaluable work has been done by the compilers of the various county histories of church plate, and to them inquirers as to existing church plate in pewter must be referred.

Northamptonshire is especially rich in the variety of its pewter church plate, both flagons and dishes. The earliest dated example (1609) of a flagon is at Werrington. It is a tall flagon, 14 in. high, $6\frac{1}{2}$ in. at the base, and $4\frac{3}{4}$ in. in diameter at the top, but it is without makers' marks of any kind. Many flagons were but 11 or $11\frac{1}{2}$ in. in height. That at Earl's Barton was especially noted in an inventory of 1647 as " a great flaggon pewter," and is 13 in. high.

There are in Northamptonshire many specimens of pewter basins or bowls, probably used as *lavabos* for the celebrants to wash their hands at Holy Communion just before the consecration, a custom which was still common in the seventeenth century.

In Dorsetshire the pewter church plate has in nearly all cases disappeared, and in the few places where it has survived it has almost invariably ceased to be used. In

Nightingale's "Church Plate of Dorset" the earliest specimens mentioned are two flagons at Puddlelow, inscribed: "Ex dono Henrici Arnoldi, Ilsingtoniensis. 1641." At Iwerne Minster there is a dish dated 1691; at Allington a flagon of 1694; and at Winterborne St. Martin a flagon of 1698.

Of eighteenth-century pewter there are plates at Bradford Peverel, 1707 and 1713, at Wyke Regis, 1717; and of flagons a specimen inscribed "Shaston St Peters 1770."

Mr. Nightingale mentions that at Cerne Abbas in 1630 "item p^d for a new pewter pott for wine for the Com' [Communion] x^s." This is a high price for that date.

At Sturminster Marshall mention is made in the churchwardens' accounts: "1780. p^d for A Bason to care [carry] to the vant [font] £0 1s. 2d."

Much of the church pewter has been improved away from the churches, sometimes being converted to other uses, as the entry for Gatesbury shows: "In 1854 the old chalice and paten, with a very large flagon and an alms dish, all of pewter, were melted up and cast into a large ewer for Baptism." The same thing was done at Lalton in the same county.

In many cases it is to be feared that the parish clerks, or other so-called responsible persons, have parted with them for a consideration.

A complete set of late seventeenth-century church plate in pewter, originally at Midhurst in Sussex, is now in the Museum at South Kensington.

No one looking at the seventeenth-century pewter which has fortunately survived in some of our churches will fail to admire the stately grandeur of the average flagons, and the simplicity of the plates and dishes.

In some few cases the lids have, through wear and tear, cracked at the juncture of the lid and the hinge, and have been repaired by some over-zealous workman, who thought it his duty to add a meaningless and useless knob to the centre of the lid.

The flagons are of various types, and they might be classified either from the shape of the body of the flagons or from that of the handles,

There is the type represented by the flagon at Lockington (Leicestershire), dated 1612. It is an upright flagon, tapering upwards with a graceful curve from the foot, and capped with a simple moulded lid.

Another type is represented by the Lubenham flagon, also in Leicestershire, and dated 1635. In shape it is somewhat like the copper coffee-pots that were once so common.

Communion plate made of pewter is still in use in some places, either by itself, or as an adjunct to plate of either silver or silver-gilt. Express mention of such use is to be found in most of the histories of county ecclesiastical plate; but the more usual remark is to the effect that the pewter vessels are not now in use. Sometimes the note added is that, though disused, it is carefully preserved. This is as it should be, for the early seventeenth-century flagons and cups had a dignity of form that is quite lacking in those of later date.

The use of such plate was more common in poorly cultivated and sparsely populated districts, e.g. Friesland on the Continent, and the extreme northern parts of Britain. Much existed in the diocese of Carlisle and much more in Scotland. It is perhaps in Scotland that pewter lingers on still more than elsewhere in the service of the Church.

In one Scotch church (North Leith), besides the silver church plate, six pewter flagons are still used at the Communion Service. Of these four are small, and are inscribed: "North Kirk of Leith 1788." These were made by Gardner, Edinburgh, and bear his mark. Two others, rather larger, were made by R. W. (Robert Whyte), and are stamped with a thistle. A pewter paten was in use up to 1881. It was of Edinburgh make, dated 1762, maker W. H. The four small marks on it are a thistle, a rose, W. H. and a skull.

Mr. Ferguson, in his book on the church plate of the Carlisle diocese, quotes the Bishop of Carlisle as having said, "There is much of historic interest attaching to these pewter vessels, and they deserve a place in the treasury of the church to which they belong."

From this standpoint alone they are worthy of preservation, but more so from the artistic point of view. Most of them are superior in beauty of form to the productions of later times by which they have unfortunately been superseded.

It is sad to read in the inventories of church plate that the simple old pewter alms-dishes have given place to so-called art-brass trays mechanically engraved, with no feeling in them, and frequently overloaded with sham jewels made of plain or coloured glass.

In Scotland Communion tokens, made under the superintendence of church members in a stamp or mould designed for that special purpose, were adopted, after the model of the lead tokens used as early as 1560 by the French Calvinists. Sometimes they were of lead, sometimes of brass, or tin, or pewter. Some were square, not more than an inch in width, sometimes round or hexagonal with a rim. They were quite plain, and were marked as a rule with the initial letter or letters of the parish.

In the seventeenth century they were made larger, the date and a monogram being added, and the custom grew up of recasting them in new patterns whenever there was a new minister. By the eighteenth century the minister's initials were regarded as more important than those of the parish.

The tokens were officially issued a day or two before the Communion Service was to take place, and were officially collected before the service. Whenever a new set was required the old ones were collected and sent to the pewterer, who, from the accounts, seems to have charged very little for the recasting and very little for the new metal. It is a curious fact that tickets of paper, or cards, were first used, and that modern feeling has now reverted to this description of token.

Communion plate is still made in Britannia metal, and a very early specimen made by Messrs. Dixon and Sons, dated 1751, is preserved in the Museum at York.

It is a pity that the seventeenth-century type of flagon was superseded by that of the nineteenth, for the modern flagon is painfully like a coffee-pot, both in the elaborate handle and in the knob on the lid, the purchase, or thumb-piece, at the side near the hinge having apparently been discontinued.

The spout too and the foot have been broadened, over-developed with heavy mouldings, and in this way the balance of the whole thing has been marred.

In the chalices the lower half is as a rule plain, but the bowl portion is too heavy, and not graceful in its curves.

The patens resemble the older plain plates, but are mounted on feet which are rather too high.

MISCELLANEOUS ARTICLES IN PEWTER

In the Middle Ages we know that badges, or tokens, of pewter, or sometimes of lead, were in great demand by pilgrims as souvenirs of their visit, and as proofs of their having made the actual pilgrimage. There are specimens extant of palmers' shells that have been buried with deceased pilgrims. A common device is a scallop-shell or a cockle-shell, in commemoration of S. James of Compostella, or in the latter case S. Michael.

Tokens commemorating Thomas à Becket, the martyr of Canterbury, bore the inscription CAPUT THOMAE. These were generally worn by pilgrims in the twelfth century, who, as Chaucer wrote,

> Set their signys upon their hedes
> And some oppon theyr capp.

In the Guildhall Museum there are many of them of various sizes and shapes. In the same museum is a badge representing Edward Confessor, which was found at Westminster. There are also a reliquary in the form of Canterbury Cathedral; a badge to commemorate St. Hubert; and an effigy of Erasmus, who suffered martyrdom under Diocletian in 303 A.D. In the same museum is a stone mould for a twelfth-century religious badge, with the legend SIGNUM SANCTE CRUCIS DE WALTHAM. It is figured in vol. xxix. of the "Journal of the B. A. Association," page 421.

A mould for casting badges of a religious character

(seventeenth century) is to be seen in the Cluny Museum. It is well carved in what looks like lithographic stone. The device consists of a heart-shaped frame of floral design, containing the initials I.H.S. and at the top a floriated cross.

Another specimen of these moulds for casting badges for pilgrims, or other signs, is to be seen in the National Museum of the Society of Antiquaries at Edinburgh.

This custom of wearing badges prevailed, if it did not originate, in France. In the north S. Denis was the favourite saint until he was replaced by S. Michel, while the southern part of the country favoured S. Nicholas. There were, however, many local patron saints, pewter reproductions of whom were in great demand, e.g. S. Jean at Amiens.

Mont Saint-Michel was a most important centre for these badges, and the cockle-shells found on the sands there are supposed to have been the original type of the palmers' shells. This may or may not have been so, but a large trade was done in pewter or leaden shells. Besides these there were more or less rude representations of S. Michel routing and slaying the dragon.

Rings and models of horns were also made and sold.

The trade in these articles was considerable, and in the fourteenth century a tax of "12 deniers par livre" was imposed on the sale. Naturally the pewterers and dealers protested and made out a very strong case, showing that with the tax pressing on them they could not live, that the pilgrimage was falling into disrepute, and that the personal devotion of the pilgrims was on the wane. Upon this the King, in a lucid interval, gave the people of Mont Saint-Michel exemption for ever from the objectionable tax.

Among the articles specially mentioned in the document[1] are "enseignes de Monseigneur Saint Michiel, coquilles et cornez qui sont nommez et appellez quiencailleries, avecques autre euvre de plon et estaing, getté en moule."

This document distinctly shows that the articles were at

---

[1] "Ordonnances des Rois de France" (Secousse), vii. pp. 590, 591.

that time made on the spot, and it states that they were cast in moulds.

Monsieur Corroyer in his book on Mont Saint-Michel gives illustrations of these and of the mould in which some of them had been cast. The badges were obviously intended to be sewn upon the garments, loops in the metal being left for the purpose, or affixed by tangs left upon the back of the badge.

The adjacent island of Tombelaine had a shrine to Notre Dame de Tombelaine, and badges with her image are—in fragments—extant.

Some of these badges would seem to have been made to wear as large brooches or buckles, or, in some cases, as pendants upon the chest. After the pilgrimage was over they were often fixed up in a prominent place in the home of the pilgrim with other cherished possessions.

Monsieur Corroyer gives a restoration of a pewter horn which, from the figure upon it, must have been designed for use by the Mont Saint-Michel pilgrims. Like the *ampullae*, it bore the fleurs-de-lys of France, and a rough representation of S. Michel transfixing the dragon.

Another pewter badge which was much in demand was that representing the so-called *chemise* of the Virgin Mary at Chartres. It is figured in the " Grande Encyclopédie " (*sub voce* " Chemise "), and from the illustration it can easily be seen how the badge was to be attached to the pilgrim's dress.

Rings, too, were made in pewter; one is shown in M. Corroyer's book on Mont Saint-Michel.

Beggars' and porters' badges were sometimes made in pewter, though more generally in brass, and in later times of zinc.

At South Kensington Museum is a porter's badge of pewter, by no means a common object. There are also some few specimens in the Guildhall Museum.

Beggars in Spain, as early as 1393, had to wear badges or lead. In Edward VI's reign, by Act of Parliament, beggars were to " weare openly . . . some notable badge of token."

In the Musée Royale at Brussels there is a beggar's

PLATE XV

Two Scottish Episcopal Church flagons and a christening bowl.

PLATE XV.

badge, such as was in use up to the end of the eighteenth century by the *Arme Camer* or *Chambre des pauvres*. It consists of an A and a C, with a lion rampant between, holding the A between his front paws and the C in a fold of his tail. The badge is fitted with three loops for attaching to the wearer's cloak or coat.

An *ampulla*, Fr. *ampoule*, was a small vessel for containing incense, for consecrated oil for the sacrament of extreme unction, or oil for the lamps which were kept burning in such sacred places as the tombs of saints. In form they varied, but were often circular, with two handles rather more than half-way up the side. Similar shaped bottles are still made in glass, covered with fine basket- or straw-work, and are used as travelling flasks.

The *ampullae* were used for many purposes, mainly private and devotional. Pilgrims to the Holy Land treasured in them a little dust or sand from Calvary, or some from the site of the Holy Sepulchre, or, again, from the Garden of Olives. Pilgrims to Rome collected dust from the Catacombs. Pilgrims to Mont Saint-Michel brought away some few grains from the treacherous and ever shifting sands. Originally the pilgrims had chipped off pieces of the tomb of S. Aubert, very much in the fashion of some modern tourists, but such vandalism being officially stopped, recourse was had to pewter and leaden keepsakes.

These *ampullae* had wide mouths, sometimes carried up somewhat in the shape of a funnel. They were closed merely by pressure, and were worn suspended to the person of the pilgrim by a cord.

The decoration of the *ampullae* varied according to the place at which the relics were collected; but the French ones almost invariably had the three fleurs-de-lys on one side. On the other side there was scope for the pewterer. M. Forgeais ("Plombs historiés de la Seine") describes a noted *ampulla* called "*la larme de Vendôme*." In this case the three fleurs-de-lys gave way to what was considered more pictorial material. On one side was an altar, and upon it a large ciborium. A saint on the left holds up a large tear over the ciborium; the saint on the right carries a lighted taper. To the left of the altar is a cross *pattée*, with its foot *flèchée*, and over it the legend : LACR | IMA DEI. On the reverse, a knight in full armour, on a horse, clothed. In the field there are leaves and small fleurs-de-lys, and above is the legend : S^r. GEO | RGIUS.

A variety of pewter, as a metal for coinage, was used in the East[1]—it was probably a very hard and pure alloy—and in England, from the time of Elizabeth up to the reign of Charles II, for tradesmen's tokens.

In the time of the Commonwealth (1653) there were pewter farthings made. They had stamped upon them "¼ of an ounce of fine pewter," and were looked upon as quite safe, being intrinsically worth their money value.

James II, in his last campaign in Ireland, was driven by lack of money to coin crowns and half-crowns in pewter. He obtained the metal cheaply by appropriating what he found in the houses of the Protestants, and the coins bore the legend : MELIORIS TESSERA FATI. When such coinage as this was current, one can hardly be surprised to hear that "people absconded for fear of being paid their debts."

In the time of James II, and of William and Mary, there were other issues of pewter coins. These had a small piece of copper, usually square, though sometimes round like a rivet, inserted in a hole in the centre, and clenched by the press when the pewter disc was struck. Some of the William and Mary coins were made entirely of pewter.

For presentation purposes the *cymaise*, *cimaise*, or *cymarre* was often in request. It was the custom when a king or prince approached a city to which he was about to pay a visit, for a deputation from the city to wait upon the king and offer him wine in a *cimaise*—very much in the way that bouquets of flowers are presented at public functions by small children. The king's attendants had the custom of appropriating as perquisites the wine-vessels so offered; hence, in a practical age, pewter became quite the usual metal for the manufacture of these vessels. They are found fairly generally from the fourteenth to the sixteenth

[1] The Siamese coins from the district near Tenasserim were flat and round, four inches in diameter, with rudely drawn birds or dragons

century, and specimens are to be met with in most of the museums in the north-east of France and in Belgium.

Cimaises are mentioned as early as 1370, in the inventory of Henri de Poitiers, Bishop of Troyes.

The *cimaise* was often fitted with two handles: one fixed at one side for holding the vessel when the contents were being poured out; and the other a swing handle, its pivot-points being near the top edge. These swing handles were elaborately wrought and often enriched with cleverly turned work, and were used for carrying the vessels.

Vessels of a similar type were offered as prizes to be competed for at shooting-matches, and both the victors and the vanquished seem to have been rewarded with pewter cups.[1] These prizes bore the arms of the town, and a device of a gun, or a bow and arrow.

These *cimaises* are chiefly interesting from the fact that they are the principal representatives of the pewter of their epoch which have come down to the present time.

Inkstands of varying form date back to an early period, though they were not in common use amongst the lower middle and lower classes. The form of the early metal inkstands is a matter of conjecture, but as the earliest of all were in horn (hence their French title of *cornet*) it is probable that the form was round.

Bapst, quoting from some early document, mentions that 17 sols. 6 deniers were paid to " Goupil, pintier, pour un aincrier d'estaing double d'estaing tout rond, à mettre aincre, plumes, gettouères [jetons] et deux bobéches dedans."

The fact of its being double seems to imply that it had an outer casing to keep safely the miscellaneous items mentioned above, though it may mean that the ink-well was also of pewter.[2]

They were often made of lead, as the specimens in South Kensington Museum, the Cluny and other museums clearly

---

[1] Pint pots and tankards, nominally of pewter, but really of Britannia metal, are still rowed for in college races at Oxford and Cambridge, and elsewhere.

[2] Rymer's " Foedera," iii. Part 3, under date 1382, mentions an inkstand of pewter, " unum calamare de stanno."

prove, and highly ornamental. Havard gives an illustration of one of the fourteenth century in lead.

The Nuremberg Chronicle represents S. Luke seated with a round pewter inkstand in his left hand.

The later form was a flat tray or dish, with two or three receptacles for the ink and the sand, or the pens and the wax.

The varieties were: oval standish; large, middle, small chests; large, middle and small Dutch with drawers; cabinet with drawers; and then the type that still survives, large, middle and small loggerheads. The last-mentioned are now, to suit a depraved public taste, made in an alloy very little better than black-metal.

In a picture gallery it is easy to study the various types, and there is no better collection for the purpose than the set of Corporation pictures by Rembrandt in the gallery at the Rijks Museum, Amsterdam.

Our present-day pewter inkstands, called "loggerheads," consist of a circular base and a circular receptacle with lid, with a chinaware well for the ink, and holes to hold the pens, are an old type and will be familiar to many. In some of the early ones there was no ornament at all, or occasionally a few lines on the flat base or on the walls of the receptacle. Occasionally they are met with made of very good pewter. The ink-well was sometimes pewter, in shape something like a tall hat, but the metal was not good for the colour of the ink.

A weak point in these inkstands was the hinge of the lid, and even in most specimens not of modern make the lid is missing. The reason is not far to seek, for the lid was often placed in such a way that it could not remain open. The same force that was required to give the lid the absolutely necessary angle caused a crack near the hinge, and as force was required to make the lid shut, the perpetual see-saw was fatal. The lids were usually far too heavily weighted in their moulded edge.

This type of pewter inkstand, as we know it, is not beautiful, but its redeeming points were that it would not upset, and that it had a lid to keep out the dust. In the latest pattern, which is made for export, the makers omit the flat base so as to make the "loggerheads" cheap.

CHAPTER XI

PEWTER MARKS

IN France—we have no record of anything of the sort in England—the Paris pewterers were under the wing of the goldsmiths and their ordinances were codified by the Provost as early as 1268, and revised in some respects in 1304. Again in 1382 the pewterers of Paris were forbidden by their ordinances to sell any wares of hammered work made in Paris or in the suburbs without first stamping them with their mark according to the usual custom. As the rules of the trade were practically the same in all countries it is more than probable that the same regulation was in force in England.

No doubt the necessity for marking arose from the insistence on a definite standard, and a maker would make his own private mark on his ware so that he would know it again. Self-preservation in fact, when the right of search was a living reality, became the chief object for the pewterer—then later, what was probably done fairly generally became compulsory.

The practice may too have originated in the pewterer's desire to do the same as the goldsmiths and the silversmiths were obliged to do by their craft rules.

By 19 Hen. VII, cap. 6 (1503-4), the makers of hollow-wares such as salts and pots which were made of the pewter called " lay metal " were required " to marke the same wares with severall markes of their owne, to the entent that the makers of such wares shal auow the same wares by them as is above said to be wrought." Here would probably be, as before mentioned, a stamp with a device and the initials or the full name of the maker, which is the earliest mention we have found in England of the maker's mark. It is curious that no mention is made in the Act of marks to be put upon other wares made of pewter of high standard. It is probable that it had been customary to mark all other wares, but that wares of inferior pewter had not been so marked. Consequently the alloy used had become further debased, for as it was not marked the maker of such debased wares escaped detection and the usual fines. We next meet with a notice of pewterers' marks in the York ordinances of the year 1540 which prescribes a maker's mark to be placed on pewter of the higher quality, as to which the above Act is silent, confirming the opinion that this had all along been required by the laws made by the pewterers themselves; it ordains " that euery of the sayd Pewderers shall sett hys marke of all suche vessell as they shall cast hereafter and to have a counterpayne thereof to remayne in the said common chambre upon payne of euery of them that lackes such a marke, and doyth not mark ther vessell therwyth before that they putt them to sayle, to forfet therefore iij s. for euery pece to be payd as is before sayd. And euery of the sayd occupacion to have a proper mark before the feast of the nativity of our Lord (September 7th) next to come, uppon payne of xl. s. to be payd as ys aforesayd."

The " Counterpayne " was a sheet of metal, which was kept at the Pewterers' Hall, upon which was stamped an impression of each maker's private punch with which he stamped his wares before offering them for sale.

In the year 1599 the pewterers' ordinances of the same city were reformed and enlarged. Makers of hollow wares it says " shall mark the same with severall markes of their owne, to the intent, that they shall avowe the same accordinge to the Statute in that behalfe," the statute being the 19 Hen. VII, cap. 6, above cited. Later on is a very important clause where we first meet with a precise statement as to the description of mark to be used by the maker. It is worth while to print it in full: " Item, that every Master of the sayd Craft, nowe beinge or which hereafter shalbe, shall have a proper marke, and two Letters for his name, to marke his vessell and waire withall and shall therwith marke all suche vessell and Waires, as he shall hereafter cast and make, so sone as he shall have made up the same waires fit for saile, upon payne of everye one wanting suche a marke and Letters to forfait for every moneth that he shall want the same 1s., to be payde and devided as aforesayd. And further to forefait for every pece unmarked iij s. iiij d. to be payd and divided as aforesayd."

Paris, just as London to the English, was the headquarters to which the workers all over the country looked for a lead, and the regulations of many towns mention that pewter is to be *a l'usage et façon de Paris*, just in the same way as the York Pewterers specify that their regulations are the same as those of the citizens of London.

As late as the end of the seventeenth century we find an Irish statute of William III (passed in 1697) enacting pewter vessels were to be of the same quality as those cast in London

From a memorandum in the old Book of Inventories belonging to the Company, and quoted by Mr. Welch (i. 165), it appears that "a table of pewter, with every man's mark therein," was in existence as early as 1540. This may have been one of the earliest touch-plates that were ordered to be made, as Mr. Welch thinks that the practice of requiring the pewterers to register their marks formally originated in 1503-4, when an Act, 19 Henry VII c. 6, made it compulsory (Welch, i. 94). This touch-plate unfortunately has been lost. Such touches were preserved at the Hall of the Pewterers' Company as early as 1540. But some system of marking[1] wares must have existed at a still earlier date, for in the days when work was liable to confiscation if it fell a few grains below a certain specified standard, self-protection would suggest some private mark or means of identification.

These touch-plates[2] have been exhibited privately at various times and places, and the Pewterers' Company have had them reproduced in collotype in Mr. Welch's book.

[1] In 1492 the Company had four new "markyng irons for Holoweware men" (Welch, i. 78). This entry shows that marking had been done before this date. The reference (on p. 97) to "pots, *sealed*," must also point to the practice of marking.

[2] By special permission of the Company verbal descriptions of the touches are given in Appendix A.

PLATE XVI

German flagon (right).

Flemish measure (left).

PLATE XVI.

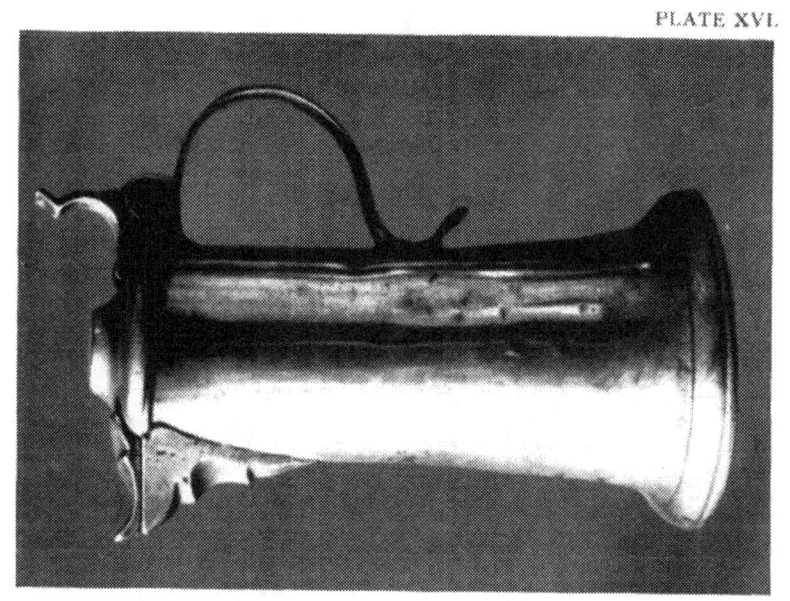

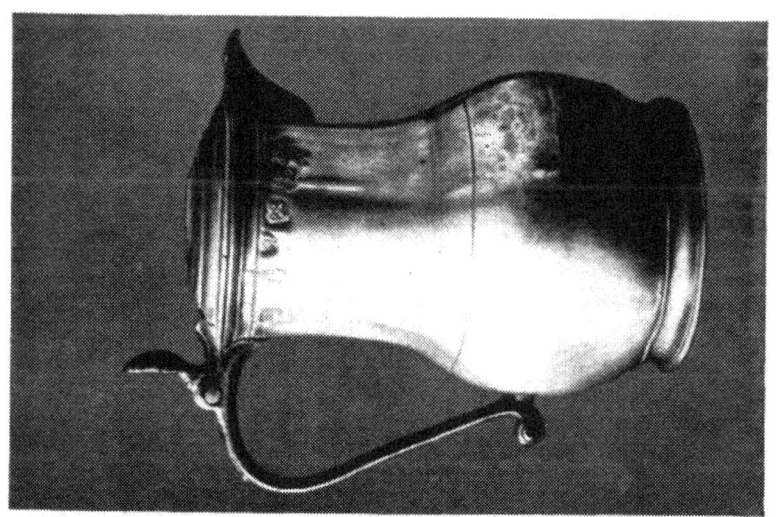

The register that seems to have been kept of the members who struck their touches on the touch-plate has unfortunately been lost. If it had had entries no more irregular than those of the touches, it would have still been valuable as a means of throwing light on many touches which are now and will long remain riddles. Mr. Welch unfortunately found that no such register was in existence, and for that reason, no doubt, passed over the subject of the marks.

The touches are not in chronological[1] order. They seem to have been punched more or less where the owner wished to put them, and the blank spaces have been filled up subsequently with other touches and of other years.

Many of the earlier touches are officially dated, and may be said to cover, with a few intervals, the time from 1673 to 1824. It seems that the usual object of ordering a touch to be dated was that it might be known who were the offenders, the majority of touches being undated. Occasionally, however, new touches were ordered to be used by everybody, and this would account satisfactorily for the fact that quite different touches are found on the existing touch-plates for the same pewterer. The touches vary in size according to the articles on which they were stamped: the smallest punches were used on spoons, and those of larger size on dishes and chargers. The touch-marks usually were the initials of the maker of the pewter, and various other devices such as the Company's quality mark, i.e. the rose or stryk, generally, though not always, with a crown above it, and the maker's mark, as a sun in glory, a hand, a heart, a Catharine wheel, a dolphin, a dog, a caduceus, an angel on a globe, and many other devices. Many marks have been punched upside down, or carelessly, on the top of other marks, making both difficult to decipher. Two instances are known of one mark being surcharged with the name or initials of another. Guy Earle of Warwick is surcharged with T.W., the initials of Thomas Wigley, and Carpenter and Hamberger is found surcharged with the name of Stiff, to whom the business had been transferred.

[1] The earliest on the first touch-plate is 1644.

Sometimes the full name of the pewterer is given, sometimes the initials only. This, however, was a matter on which the regulations varied at different times.

The marks were not required by any of the regulations of the Pewterers' Company, and seem to have been impressed on pewter from Elizabethan times merely to look like silver marks.

No one need refuse a good dish or a plate because of the absence of these small marks, nor need he acquire an inferior dish merely because it has the four small marks.

In the earlier dishes these small marks are larger and bolder than in the later dishes.

The same marks, i.e. the large touches and the smaller or hall marks, are found on plates of every size that was made for sale.

Foreign pewterers, especially those in the Netherlands, copied the quality mark and the four small marks without any valid reason.

In marking their larger tankards the German pewterers were in the habit of stamping the touch thrice over. The plan has its advantages, for it is not so easy a thing as it sounds to impress a large touch on the thin bottom of a deep tankard. By doing it thrice over there was a certainty that from the three impressions—even if all were imperfect—it would be possible to arrive at the town of origin and the name of the maker.

It is the rule in foreign pewter generally that the touch gives the arms of the town of origin, and in this way it is easy to discover whether the piece comes from Nürnberg, Augsburg, or is of Swiss or Netherlandish manufacture.

Up to 1635 many of the pewterers marked their wares with very colourable imitations of the genuine hall-marks of the Goldsmiths' Company. These marks, no doubt, were intended to deceive the public, and must have done so to some extent; for the Goldsmiths' Company remonstrated very strongly, and appealed to the Privy Council, with the result that the Court of the London Aldermen in the same year made an order that the pewterers should stamp their pewter with one stamp " as anciently hath been accustomed, unless the buyer shall desire his own arms or stamp of his sign to be strucken thereupon " (Welch).

This excellent regulation was not observed, and probably not enforced, for there is plenty of pewter extant with the silver marks, or the colourable imitations thereof, that was made many years subsequently to 1635.

A misconception as to marks on pewter needs some explanation. The Pewterers' Company required the maker, under a penalty, to mark all the pewter he made with his own registered[1] mark, and, if the pewter were of a certain quality, with the mark so well known of an X with a crown above it. This X is sometimes found repeated, and occasionally without the crown.

The London Goldsmiths' Company required all plate exposed for sale to be brought to that Company's Hall to be stamped there with the stamp or hall-mark.

Though the Company did not object to the silver marks, they interfered when these were the only marks on the ware; e.g. in 1681 " John Blackwell was charged with selling trencher plates without any other mark than the silver mark and was fined 20s." (Welch, ii. 155).

Yet in 1754 two members were allowed to sell " 12 dozen scalloped raised brim plates and dishes in proportion without any other touch than their Silver Touch " (Welch, ii. 194).

In 1688 complaint was made by Mr. Stone that the 17th Ordinance was frequently broken, i.e. that pewterers struck touches upon their ware other than those they had struck on the Company's plate of touches.

In November, 1690, complaint was made to the Court against Samuel Hancock for striking his name at length upon his trencher plates, and at each end thereof is struck his own touch and the rose and crown, and for striking the letter X upon ordinary ware, which is a mark generally used by the Mystery to distinguish extraordinary ware.

This touch of the crowned rose could only be used by express permission of the Company.[2] In 1671 it had been

[1] Enforced by the Act 19 Henry VII, 1504.
[2] Certain objects of domestic use (specified in Welch, i. 288) had to be brought (in 1580-1) to the Hall to be stamped with the mark of the Hall by the beadle, after he had found the weight of each article to be 5 lb. the piece.

agreed (Welch, ii. 144) that from henceforth no person whatsoever shall presume to strike the rose and crown with any additional flourish or the letters of his own or another's name, whereby the mark which is only to be used for good exported may in time become as other touches and not distinguished.

After consideration the Court, in December, ordered that "no member of the Mystery shall strike any other mark upon his ware than his touch or mark struck upon the plate at the Hall, and the Rose and Crown stamp, and also the Letter X upon extraordinary ware" (Welch, ii. 164). At the same time, though, it was left open to any member to add the word London to the rose and crown stamp, or in his touch, and the proposed striking of the name in full upon hard metal or extraordinary ware was negatived.

In October, 1692-3, "such as have not their names within the compass of their touches" were allowed to put them "at length within the same."

Six months later "this Committee, debating the matter of persons striking their names at length upon their ware within or besides their touches or marks struck on the Hall plate," held that "the practice of striking the worker's or maker's name at length within or besides their touches registered or struck at the Hall is against the general good of the Company; and that all such persons as have set their names at length within their touches now in use shall alter their several marks or touches by leaving out their name, and register and strike at the Hall their respective new or altered marks or touches without any person's name therein" (Welch, ii. 166).

This, however, was not taken as final, and on August 11th, 1697-8, it was ordered that none should strike any other mark upon ware than "his own proper touch and the rose and crown stamp"; that any member may strike his name at length between his touch and the rose and crown, also the word London, but that none may strike the letter X except upon extraordinary ware, commonly called "hard metal" ware.

A rose and crown is found also on Scotch, Flemish, Dutch, French and German pewter. It is said by Bapst that it was the distinguishing mark of pewter of the second quality made at Mons.

In spite of Acts of Parliament and other stringent regulations, there seems always to have been a considerable amount of copying, if not counterfeiting, the marks of other pewterers. This will be seen by any one who peruses the lists of pewter plate in the various accounts of church plate that have been published.

As late as 1702 (in the reign of Queen Anne) the Pewterers' Company obtained a charter giving them power to make regulations as to counterfeit. Each member was obliged to deliver to the Master for the time being " one peculiar and selected mark or touch solely and properly of itselfe and for yourselfe only, without adding thereunto any other man's mark in part or in whole, to be struck and impressed on the plate kept in the Hall of the said Company for that purpose; which said mark and none other he shall strike and sette upon his ware of whatsoever sort that he shall make and sell, without diminution or addition, and shall upon striking of such his mark or touch, pay to the renter-warden 6s. 8d. and 2s. 6d. to the clerk for entering the same, and 6d. to the beadle."

Then followed a regulation, or rather repetition of previous regulations, as to untruly mixed wrought or unmarked pewter, which was to be fined one penny a lb.; and another as to pewterers boasting of their own wares, and disparaging that of others, or improperly enticing away another man's customers. For these offences the fine was forty shillings.

One of the chief causes which militate against the making of a complete and correct list is that, apart from the occasional public change of the touches by order of the Court of the Pewterers' Company, private changes were sometimes made. Touches, too, were borrowed or lent in early times by permission of the Company, and for approved reasons.

The following instances from Mr. Welch's book clearly show this.

In 1622-3 Walter Picroft was ordered to change his mark of " three ears of corn " to one ear and his initials.

Thomas Hall had leave to use Mr. Sheppard's touch. Three weeks later it was granted to John Netherwood.

In 1654–5 William Pettiver, apprentice to Oliver Roberts, is not to be made free till next Court, but hath leave to strike Mr. Barnard's touch in the mean time.

[Ralph] Cox was ordered to use as a touch a rose and crown with a knot about it and 1656.

R. Goudge was ordered to make his touch R. G. with a knot about it and 1656.

Thos. Porter in 1683 was ordered to strike as his touch "the Angell and glister serreng" (Welch, ii. 156). This seems to have been a mark of disgrace.

Sands (1689) altered his rose and crown stamp by taking out the place of his abode.

John Blenman in 1725–6 had leave to strike the same touch as Abraham Ford, who had retired from his trade and consented to Blenman's request.

Charles Puckle Maxey (1749) to have pelican and globe instead of James King's touch.

Richard Warde claimed the right of using as his mark a hammer and crown. He based his claim on the fact that his wife had been the widow of Wm. Hartwell, who used it before.

Occasionally a device of what seems to be a portcullis is found on pewter, and this is sometimes the only surviving mark. This portcullis[1] is in reality the English form of the pewterers' sign—so common in France—a trellis of pewter. It was usually circular in form, and the *raison d'être* of the trellis was the ease with which tin in that form could be cut up and used as required, tin in the form of the large bars called *saumons* being far less easy to handle. In the "History of the Pewterers' Company" there are entries at different times of hammers and chisels for making the assay of tin, whether it was the proceeds of sale or of confiscation.

In 1747 a committee made a report on touches, and the following by-law, based on their recommendations, was passed on June 25th: "That all . . . wares capable of a large touch shall be touched with a large touch with the Christian name and Surname either of the maker or the

---

[1] It is sometimes found crowned.

vendor at full length in plain Roman letters. And . . . small wares shall be touched with the small touch—with a penalty of one penny per pound for default" (Welch, ii. 193).

This points to the fact that the old rule of one man one touch had been found impracticable.

It must be remembered that the large touch is the most important of any impressed on any pewter. The smaller (so called) "hall-marks" may often, however, help to give a clue, especially where they give the initials. On the other hand the initials in the small marks may differ from those of the name in the large touch, when the ware was made by a manufacturer for sale by a dealer in London or elsewhere. Much of the pewter at Queen's College, Oxford, was made by Samuel Ellis, but some of it bears the additional marks of Thomas Chamberlain; some again bears the name of Alexander Cleeve, and some the name of Richard Norfolk.

PEWTER HALL-MARKS

The pewter hall-marks, for want of a better name, seem to have been made small designedly, after the manner of the silver marks; the shields containing them have often been copies of the silver hall-mark then in use; and the number of the pewter marks has been kept the same as the silver marks, the pewter stamp being repeated in some cases in four shields side by side, or in others two stamps have been repeated alternately to make up a set of four in all.

These marks being then colourable imitations of silver hall-marks often bore facsimiles of parts of the latter. In this way only is it possible to account for the presence of the leopard's head, the lion passant, a figure of Britannia—and it may be noted that the cross surmounted by a crown, a very common stamp on pewter, is in itself a silver mark that was formerly placed on silver-ware that came from Exeter.

The presence of single letters as date-marks is not *per se* objectionable, but the practice was copied from that of the

Goldsmiths' Company, and probably with intent to deceive.

On many articles of pewter there are found large plain letters punched in the ware, or sometimes smaller letters in shaped punches. These latter are occasionally found crowned. From the fact that the letters A. R., G. R. or W. R. are so found crowned, it has been assumed that they give a clue to the date by accentuating the name of the reigning sovereign. On officially stamped standard measures this is no doubt the meaning of the crown, but V. R. with both letters crowned is found long before 1837, and seems to point to the indiscriminate use of crowned letters. On an alms-dish of 1745 the writer has seen on the rim W. T., W. W., A. P., E. P., A. B., 1745, each letter being crowned.

In the cases where letters such as G. R. with a rose or other device crowned occur in one punch, the letter may be assumed to be a Government stamp. They are found so on pewter measures, frequently with the initials of a maker and a date in another stamp. The makers no doubt kept sets of punches with which to stamp any required initials upon the rims of the plates or other articles.

Long inscriptions done with punches invariably spoil the appearance of the articles so ornamented, especially where the rest of the article is properly engraved.

When letters are given on the rim of a plate in a triad they are usually taken to be the initials of the couple to whom the plates once belonged.

One of these triads was vouched for by the then owner as follows:—

    C   C was the initial of the surname, and
  J B   J was for John, and the B for Barbara,

the Christian names of the couple who possessed the pewter.

CHAPTER XII

LIST OF THE NAMES OF PEWTERERS, ENGLISH, SCOTTISH AND IRISH, COLLECTED FROM VARIOUS SOURCES OFFICIAL AND UNOFFICIAL

TO compress the list within a reasonable number of pages it has been necessary to abbreviate considerably.

Figures in brackets (1), (2), (3) are used when there have been found to be two or more of the same name. In some cases the two references may belong to the same pewterer, as frequently many years elapsed between the time of joining the yeomanry and that of taking up the freedom.

A ? means that up to the present the name of the pewterer is known, but that the date of his floruit is not certain.

Edinburgh means that the name is in the list of Edinburgh Pewterers as given by Mr. L. Ingleby Wood.

A † added to Edinburgh means that the touch of that pewterer is to be seen on the touch-plates preserved at Edinburgh.

The names printed in italics are the names of those pewterers whose touches are impressed on the five touch-plates which are still preserved at Pewterers' Hall, London.

Portions of names or whole names in brackets are conjectural only, but in some obvious cases are intended to show variant spellings.

The dates are given from the list of the Yeomanry and of the livery which have been preserved at Pewterers' Hall. Where two dates are given they are the earliest and the latest known from existing records.

It will be noticed that many names are dated 1670. These were derived from a special list (at Pewterers' Hall) made to verify the number of men who were enrolled

among the yeomen, but whose admittance, for som
reason or another, had not been officially recorded. It is
most useful list.

The Irish names are inserted by very kind permission o
Mr. Howard B. Cottrell and Mr. M. S. Dudley Westropp
from the list in their work mentioned in the preface.

The value of the list, which represents over forty years
work, lies in the chance that it gives a collector to dat
approximately work done by men whose names are no
on the touch-plates.

Abbott, John	1693
Abbott, Thomas (1)	1712
Abbott, Thomas (2)	1792, 1811
Abernethie, John	1678 (Edinburgh †)
Abernethie, James	1660 (,,)
Abernethie, William	1649 (,,)
Abram, Henry	1561, 1571
Ackerman, N.	1640
Ackland, Thomas	1728, 1743
Acton, Samuel Etheridge	1755
Adam, W.	16—
Adam, J. T.	?
Adams, Henry	1692, 1724
Adams, Nathaniel	1692
Adams, Robert	1667, 1683
Adams, Thomas	1670
Adams, William	1662, 1671
Adenbrook, William	1756
Adkinson, W.	c. 1670
Adswick, Giles	17—
Afferton, John	1495, 1506
Ainsworth, Jeremiah	1702
Alcock, C. B.	1808 (Dublin)
Alder, Thomas	1667
Alderson, George (1)	1728
Alderson, George (2)	1817, 1823
Alderson, John	1711, 1782
Alderson, Thomas	?
Alderwick, Richard (1)	1748
Alderwick, Richard (2)	1776
Alef, William (? Ayliffe)	1668
Alexander, Paul	1516

LIST OF THE NAMES OF PEWTERERS

Alger, Robert	1670
Alexaunder, Thomas	1488
Almond, Wm.	1670
Allanson, Edward	1702
Allen, George	1790
Allen, Henry	1670
Allen, James	1740, 1766
Allen, John	1679, 1697
Allen, Joshua	1689
Allen, Richard	1668
Allen, Robert	1670
Allen, Thomas	1553, 1584
Allen, William	1736
Allom, Peter	1709
Alyssandre v. Alexaunder.	
Alyxander, Paul	1516
Ambrose, William	1763
Amerson, Michael	1774
Aniss, Josiah	1727
Anderson, John	1798–1829 (Dublin)
Anderson, John	1693 (Edinburgh †)
Anderson, Robert	1697 (,, †)
Anderton, James	c. 1700
Andrews, Randall	c. 1679
Andrews, Robert	1703
Anderson, Thurston	1575 (Dublin)
Andouit, James	1682 (,,)
Angel, John	?
Angell, Philemon	1691
Annison, William Glover	1742
Ansell, John	1714
Appleton, Henry	1751
Appleton, John (1)	1779
Appleton, John (2)	1803
Apps, Philip	1751
Apps, John	1785
Archer, William	1646, 1653
Arden, Joseph	1821
Arlicheseye, John	1346
Armiston, Henry	1753 (Cork)
Arnott, George	1735
Arnott, Thomas	1702
Arthur, John	1803
Arthur, William	1668
Ash and Hutton	c. 1750 (London)

Ashenhurst, Peter	1759 (Cork)
Ashley, James	1824
Ashley, Thos. J. Thurston	1824
Ashlyn, Lawrence (Astlyn)	1599
Astlyn, John	1514
Astlyn, Lawrence W.	1487, 1522
Astlyn, Stephen	1670
Astlyn, Walter	1518, 1534
Asplin, William	1614
Asserton, John	1495, 1506
Asshe, William	d. 1541
Atkinson, Christopher (?Adkinson)	d. 1600
Atkinson, Joseph	1763
Atkinson, William	1718
Atlee, William	1696
Attersley, Robert	1788
Atterton, Robert	1693
Attley, Samuel	1667
Attwood, William	1718, 1736
Augustone, John (?Augustine)	1692
Aunsell, Stephen	1451
Austen, Robert	1651, 1659
Austen, Thomas	1639
Austen, Johns	1800–1, 1852 (Cork)
Austen & Son	1820 (Cork)
Austen, Joseph	1795 (,,), 1817
Austen, Robert	1812 (,,)
Austin, John	1719
Austin, J. Ralph	1806
Austin, James	1764
Austin, Samuel	1693
Austin, William	1667
Ayers, Wm.	1670
Aylif(f)e William (? Alef)	1667
Aymes, John	1670
Babb, Bernard	1700
Baby, Jesse	1805
Bache, Richard	1779
Bacon, Benjamin	1749
Bacon, George	1746, 1762
Bacon, Thomas	1717
Badcock (s), John	1764

LIST OF THE NAMES OF PEWTERERS

Badcock (e), Thomas (1)	1688
Badcock (e), Thomas (2)	1787
Bagford, Thomas	c. 1610
Bagshaw, George	1810
Bagshaw, Richard	1809
Bagshaw, Thomas	1810
Bailey, John	1750, 1789
Bailey, Zachary	1626
Bainton, Jeremiah	1718
Bainton, Ralph	1670
Baker, Charles	1783
Baker, Humphrey	1598
Baker, Samuel	1678
Baker, William (1)	1450
Baker, William (2)	1553, 1558
Baldwin, R.	(? Chester)
Ballantyne, John	1755 (Edinburgh †)
Ballantyne, William (1)	1742 (,,)
Ballantyne, William (2)	1749 (,,)
Ballard, William	1741
Ball, Thomas	1726
Ball, William	?
Bampton, Thomas	1775
Bampton, William	1742, 1785
Banckes, Nicholas	1648 (Dublin)
Banck(e)s, Andrew	1624–1647 (Dublin)
Banfield, John	1732 (Dublin)
Bangham, William	1805
Banks, John	1620
Banckes, Ralph	1610 (Dublin)
Banckes, Roger	1627 (,,)
Banckes, Peter	1713 (,,)
Banckes, William	1583 (,,)
Banckes, William	1687 (Kilkenny)
Banckes, Francis	1620–1637 (Galway)
Bannister, Thomas	1701
Barber, Joseph	1777, 1797
Barber, Nathaniel	1782
Barber, Samuel	1786
Barclay, Robert	1756
Baring, John	167–
Barker, John	1577, 1585
Barlow, John	1698
Barnard, —	1654
Barnes, John	1717

Barnes, Thomas	1738
Barnes, William	1770
Barnet, ——	1641
Barnett, Robert	1783, 1815
Barrett, Lancelot	1763
Barrington, William	1824 (Dublin)
Barron, Robert	1786
Barrow, Richard	1667
Bartlett, Walter	(Northampton)
Bartlett, William	?
Barton, Daniel (1)	1678, 1699
Barton, Daniel (2)	1700
Barton, Joseph	1718
Barton, Richard	1718
Barton, William	1693
Baskerville, John	1695
Baskerville, Thomas	1731
Basnett, James	1821
Basnett, John	1821
Basnet, Nathaniel	1767, 1777
Bassett, Isaac	1722
Batchelor, John	1762
Bate, John	1746–1780 (Dublin)
Bateman, Aaron (1)	1721
Bateman, Aaron (2)	1734
Bateman, Aaron (3)	1744
Bateman, John	1663, 1670
Bateman, Francis	1708
Bateman, Benjamin	1719
Bateman, Moses	1700
Bateman, Thomas (1)	1733
Bateman, Thomas (2)	1742
Bateman, Thomas (3)	1774
Bathurst, John	1715
Bathus, William	1797
Batteson, Abraham	1675–1707 (York)
Batteson, John	1684 (York)
Batteson, John	1707–26 (York)
Battisford, (? John)	? (London)
Baxter, John	1513, 1531
Beale, John	1670
Beaumont, William	1706
Beard, Sampson	1691
Beard, Thomas	1688
Bearsley, Allison	1711

Bearsley, Edward	1735, 1749
Bearsley, Job (1)	1678
Bearsley, Job (2)	1711
Beck, William	1725
Beckett, Thomas	1702, 1730
Beddon, Nathaniel	1730
Bee, John	c. 1693
Beecraft, Richard	1736
Beehoe, Josias	1720
Beeslee, Francis	1693
Beeston, George	1743, 1765
Beeston, James	1756
Bell, John	1724
Bell, Robert (1)	1670
Bell, Robert (2)	1748
Bell, Thomas	c. 1660
Bell, William	1703
Belson, John	1734
Belson, Richard	1724
Belville, R.	c. 1705
Bennett and Chapman	c. 1760
Bennett, Edward	d. 1773 (Bandon)
Bennett, John	1653, 1679
Bennett, Philip	1542
Bennett, Thomas (1)	1670
Bennett, Thomas (2)	1700
Bennett, Thomas (3)	1807
Bennett, William	1662
Bennett, William	1758
Benson, John	1740
Benton, Ralph	1681
Benton, William	c. 1708
Bernard, Onesiphorus	1722
Berners, Thomas	1699
Besouth, Joseph	1759
Bessant, Nathaniel	1702
Betchett, Thomas	c. 1702
Betts, Thomas	c. 1680
Bidmead, Jonathan	1728
Billing, Samuel	c. 1700 (London and Coventry)
Bills, William	1701
Binfield, John	1710
Birch & Villiers	1755–1805 (Birmingham and London)

Birkenhead, John	1670
Bishop, James	1724
Biship, Piers	1452, 1479
Blackman, John	1703
Blackwell, Benjamin	?
Blackwell, Daniel	c. 1679
Blackwell, John	1681
Blackwell, Thomas (1)	1547
Blackwell, Thomas (2)	1706
Blackwell, Timothy	1670
Blagrave, William	1664
Blake, John (1)	1699
Blake, John (2)	1793, 1832
Bland, Henry	1732
Bland, John	1730
Bland, William (1)	1703
Bland, William (2)	1726
Blaydes, Ralph	1535–1546 (York)
Blenman, John	1726
Blewett, John	1707
Blewett, Robert	1738
Blewett, Thomas	1736
Bliss, John	1708
Bliss, Robert	1735
Blissett, William	1697
Bloxham, Edward	1719 (Dublin)
Blundell, Peter	c. 1588
Blunt, John	1681
Blunt, Thomas	1746
Bly, F.	?
Boardman, Robert	1730
Boardman, Thomas (1)	1728, 1756
Boardman, Thomas (2)	1763
Boase, Samuel	1695, 1715
Bode, Philip	1761
Bond, John	1775
Bonkin, Jonathan (1)	1699
Bonkin, Jonathan (2)	1720
Bonvile, John	c. 1688
Bogg, John	1642 (York)
Boost, Isaac	1744
Boost, James	1744, 1767
Boost, Samuel	1695
Booth, John S.	1755
Borman, Robert	1700

LIST OF THE NAMES OF PEWTERERS

Borthwick, Andrew	1620 (Edinburgh †)
Borthwick, William	d. 1664 (,,)
Boss, Samuel	1695
Boston, Ebenezer	1670
Bosworth, Thomas	1699
Boteler, John	1748
Boulton, Richard	1614
Boulton, Thomas	?
Boultinge, John	1575
Bowal, Robert	1621 (Edinburgh †)
Bowcher, Richard	1727
Bowden, John	1701
Bowden, Joseph	1687
Bower, Richard	?
Bowes, James	?
Bowler, Henry (? Bowles)	1757
Bowler, Richard	1755
Bowler, Samuel Salter	1779
Bowyer, John	c. 1590
Bowyer, Nicholas	1607
Bowyer, Richard	1670
Bowyer, William	1642
Bowring, Charles	1820
Box, Edward	c. 1745
Boyden, Benjamin	1693
Boyden, Thomas (1)	1706
Boyden, Thomas (2)	1735
Boylson, Edward	1610
Boys, Nicholas	1728
Bradford, Richard	1705
Bradley, John	1657 (York)
Bradley, Henry	1678
Bradshaw, William	1670
Bradstreet, Edward	1720
Bradstreet, Richard	1727
Brailsford, Peter	1667
Braine, John	?
Brand, Henry	1672
Brant, John	1818
Brasted, H.	1692
Bravell, William	1692
Bravell, Mary	1712
Bray, Charles	?
Bray, Thomas	c. 1730
Brayne, William	1705

Brereton, George	. .	1749 (Dublin)
Brett, Thomas H.	. .	1773
Brettell, James	. .	1688
Bridger, Joseph	. .	1723
Bridges, Stephen	. .	1692
Bright, Allen	. .	c. 1750
Brigstock, Joseph	. .	1733
Bristow, Nicholas	. .	c. 1684
Britton, H.	. .	1670
Broad, John	. .	1704
Bro(a)dhurst, Jonathan	.	1731
Bro(a)dhurst, John	.	1719
Bro(a)dhurst, Saul	.	1748
Bromley, —	. .	1603
Brocklesby, Peter (1)	.	1629
Brocklesby, Peter (2)	.	1636
Brocklesby, Peter (3)	.	1667
Brocks, David	. .	1702
Brodshoe, Robert	.	1589 (Dublin)
Bromfield, John	. .	1745
Bromfield, William	.	1777
Bromley, William	.	d. 1589
Brooke, Peter	. .	1764
Brooke, Richard	. .	?
Brooke, William	. .	1603
Brooks, John (1)	. .	1637
Brooks, John (2)	. .	1699
Brooks, Rice	. .	1667
Brooks, Richard	. .	?
Brooks, William	. .	d. 1603
Brown, Alexander	.	1717 (Edinburgh †)
Brown, Coney John	.	1786
Brown, George	. .	1711–15 (Edinburgh)
Brown, Ignatius	. .	1671 (Dublin)
Brown, John	. .	1757
Brown, John (1)	. .	1712
Brown, John (2)	. .	1756
Brown, John	. .	1744 (Dublin)
Brown, John	. .	1761 (Edinburgh †)
Brown, Joseph	. .	c. 1750
Brown, Philip	. .	1757
Brown, Richard (1)	.	1729
Brown, Richard (2)	.	1784
Brown, Robert	. .	1614
Brown, Thomas	. .	? (Edinburgh)

LIST OF THE NAMES OF PEWTERERS

Brown, William	1741 (Edinburgh †)
Browne and Swanson	1753–1770
Browne, Benjamin	1726
Browne, John	1777
Browne, Martin	1690
Browne, Ralph	1670
Browne, Robert	d. 1745 (Edinburgh †)
Browne, William	1705
Broxup, Henry	1757
Broxup, Richard	1793
Bryan, Egerton	1674
Bryant, John	1749
Bryce, David	1660 (Edinburgh †)
Bryden, Alexander	1717 (,,)
Bryers, John	1715
Buckby, Thomas	1716
Buckby, T. and ?	1716
Buckley, William	1689
Buclennand, James	1643 (Edinburgh †)
Buckmaster, Thomas	c. 1630
Budden, David (1)	1670
Budden, David (2)	1702
Budding, Henry	1739
Bugby, Thomas	1694
Bull, John	1678
Bul(l)mer, Richard	(Leeds)
Bullevant, James	1667
Bullock, H.	1670
Bullock, James	1752. Struck off 1754
Bullock, James	1763, 1770
Bullock, John	1688 (Cornish)
Bunkell, Edward	1729–1756 (Edinburgh †)
Bunnerbell, Robert	1633 (,,)
Bunting, Daniel	1783
Bunting, Robert	1691
Burch, Edward	1720
Burch, Samuel	1715
Burford and Green	1746
Burford, Thomas	1750, 1779
Burges, Robert	1670
Burges(s), Thomas	1701
Burgum and Catcott	1768–1773
Burnett, Edward	1727
Burns, Robert	1694 (Edinburgh †)
Burren, Edward	?

Burroughs, Edmond	1747–1778 (Dublin)
Burroughs, William	1768–1771 (,,)
Burges, Edward	1636
Burt, Andrew	1802, 1813
Burt, Thomas	1630
Burton, John (1)	1514
Burton, John (2)	1689
Burton, Mungo	1709 (Edinburgh †)
Burton, Robert	1619
Burton, Thomas	1569
Burton, William	1675, 1685
Busfield, John	1656–67 (York)
Busfield, Thomas	1653–65 (,,)
Bush, R. & Co.	1780 cir. (London)
Bush, Robert	
Bush and Perkins	(London)
Bush, Robert & Co.	(Bristol)
Bush, William	1709
Bushell, John	1728
Butcher, Gabriel	1627, 1635
Butcher, Robert	1625, 1639
Butcher, James	(Bridgwater)
Butcher, John	169–
Butcher, Thomas	1645, 1652
Butler, James	1720 (Irish)
Butler, John	1770
Butler, Joseph	1739
Butterton, Jonathan	1663–1683 (Dublin)
Buttery, James	1765
Buttery, Thomas (1)	1692
Buttery, Thomas (2)	1730
Byrd, John	1648, 1654
Byrne, Gerald	1791 (Dublin)
Cable, Joseph	1699
Cable, Peter	1717
Cable, Thomas	1706
Calcott, John	1699
Callie, William	1510
Cambridge, John	c. 1687
Campbell & Co., Belfast	c. 1850 (Belfast)
Campion, John	1662, 1681
Canby, George (? Candy)	1694
Caney, Joseph	1748
Cardwell, Joseph (1)	1707

LIST OF THE NAMES OF PEWTERERS

Cardwell, Joseph (2)	1730
Cardynall, John	1473, 1480
Carloss, Edward	1718
Carloss, Henry	1708
Carman, John	1803
Carnadyne, Alex.	1595
Carpenter, Henry (1)	1708
Carpenter, Henry (2)	1740
Carpenter, Henry (3)	1757, 1816
Carpenter, John (1)	1701
Carpenter, John (2)	1711
Carpenter, Thomas	1713
Carpenter & Hamberger	c. 1790
Carr, John (1)	1696
Carr, John (2)	1722
Carr, John (3)	1744
Carr, John (4)	1760
Carr, Richard	1737
Carr, Robert	1736
Carron, David	1722
Carter, A.	? (London)
Carter, James	c. 1685
Carter, John	1688
Carter, Joseph	1784, 1812
Carter, Peter	1699
Carter, Richard	1725
Carter, Samuel	1771, 1794
Carter, Thomas	1644, 1648
Carton, Joseph	1659 (Dublin)
Cartwright, Thomas	1719, 1743
Cary, John	1543, 1552
Cary, Thomas	1675
Casimir, Benjamin	1704
Casse, Francis	1674
Castle, F.	c. 1690
Castle, George	1670
Castle, John	1703
Castle, Woodnutt	1732
Catcher, Edward	1544, 1561
Catcher, John	1577, 1585
Catcher, Thomas	1584
Cator, John (1)	1725
Catlin, John	1693
Cator, John (2)	1752
Cavanagh, John	1761–1772 (Dublin)

Cave, Thomas	c. 1664
Cave, William	1728
Cayford, Francis	1707
Caesar, William	1712
Certain, John	1743
Chalk(e), William	1482
Chamberlain, Johnson	*c.* 1705
Chamberlain, Thomas (1)	1500, 1536
Chamberlain, Thomas (2)	1732, 1765
Chamberleyn, Robert	1450, 1466
Chambers, Richard (1)	1684 (York)
Chambers, Richard (2)	1691–1731 (York)
Champion, Edward	1688 (Cork)
Chandler, Benjamin	1721
Chapman, Catesby	1721
Chapman, George	1772
Chapman, Oxton (1)	1729
Chapman, Oxton (2)	1760
Charlesley, J. T.	1730
Charlesley, William	1738, 1764
Charleton, George	1758
Charleton, Nicholas	1759
Chase, Richard	1670
Chassey, Joseph	1650
Chaulkley, Arthur	1722
Chawner, Robert	1568, 1580
Chawner, William	1757, 1761
Checkett } Joseph Chegnett }	1670
Cherry, George	1729
Chesslin, Richard	1662, 1682
Chester, George	1615, 1634
Chetwood, James	1736
Child, John (1) (Chyld)	1534
Child(e), John (2)	1621, 1643
Child, John (3)	1700
Child, Lawrence (1)	1702, 1723
Child, Lawrence (2)	1727
Child, Richard	1758
Child, Stephen, jun.	1758
Chitwell, Samuel	1691
Christie, William	1652 (Edinburgh †)
Churcher, Adam	16— (London)
Clack, Richard	1735, 1754
Claridge, Benjamin	1672

LIST OF THE NAMES OF PEWTERERS

Claridge, Charles	1758
Claridge, Joseph	1724, 1739
Claridge, Thomas	1716
Clark, Charles	1791
Clark, Henry	1541, 1555
Clark, James	1784
Clark, John (1)	1667
Clark, John (2)	1773, 1788
Clark, Josiah	1690
Clark, Mark	1699
Clark, Samuel	1720
Clark(e), William (1)	1695
Clark, William (2)	1721
Clark, William H.	1819
Clark and Greening	c. 1760
Clarke, Charles	1790–1801 (Waterford)
Clarke, George	1647 (York)
Clarke, James	1735
Clarke, James	1722 (Edinburgh †)
Clarke, James	1745
Clarke, John (1)	1756
Clarke, John (2)	1765
Clarke, John (3)	1814
Clarke, Mark	1699
Clarke, Nathaniel	1730
Clarke, Richard	1736
Clarke, Samuel	1732
Clark(e), Thomas	1543
Clarke, Thomas	1699, 1711
Clarke, William (1)	? 1695
Clarke, William (2)	1726, 1755
Clayton, Richard	1741
Clayton, Robert	1772
Cleeve, Alexander (1)	1689, 1727
Cleeve, Alexander (2)	1716, 1724
Cleeve, Boucher	1736
Cleeve, Edward	1716
Cleeve, Elizabeth	1742
Cleeve, Giles (1)	1706
Cleeve, Giles (2)	1740
Cleeve, Mary	1742
Cleeve, Richard	1743
Clements, Christopher	1697 (Cork)
Clements, John	1747, 1782
Clemmons, Thomas	1713

Clenaghan, William	1740–1773 (Dublin)
Cliffe, Francis	1687
Cliffe, John (Clyffe)	1588, 1607
Cliffe, Thomas	1630, 1639
Clift, Joseph	1696
Clothyer, William	?
Cloudesley, Nehemiah	c. 1707
Cloudesley, Timothy	?
*Coates, Alexander	1693
Cobham, Perchard	1732
Cock, Humphrey	1670
Cock, William	1688 (Cornish)
Cockey, W.	1740–1770 (Totnes)
Cockins(k)ell, Edward	1693
Cocks, Samuel	1819
Codde, Stephen	1458, 1467
Coe, Thomas	1807
Coggs, John	1712
Coke, John	1694
Coldham, John	1456, 1465
Coldwell, George	1773 (Cork)
Cole, Benjamin	1672, 1683
*Cole, Henry	c. 1687
Cole, John	c. 1712
Cole, Jeremiah	1692
Cole, Rowland	c. 1724
Coleborne, Richard	1724
Coles, Alexander	1693
Collet, George	1787 (Youghal)
Collet(t), Edward	1773
Collet(t), Thomas	1737
Collier, Nicholas	1600, 1604
Collier, Peter	1720
Collier, Richard (1)	1669
Collier, Richard (2)	1728, 1737
Collier, Richard	1706
Collings, John	1690
Collins, Charles	1734–1753 (Cork)
Collins, Daniel	1776, 1805
Collins, Daniel Thomas	1804, 1812
Collins, Henry (1)	1704
Collins, Henry (2)	1751
Collins, James	1803, 1811
Collins, Samuel	1732, 1768
Colson, Joseph (1)	**1670**

Colson, Joseph (2)	1700
Colton, Jonathan	?
Compere, John	1696
Compton, Thomas	1802, 1807
Comyn and Rowden	c. 1770
Coney, John	1755
Cooch, Joshua	1761
Cooch, William (1)	1731, 1761
Cooch, William (2)	1775
Cook, Andrew	1670
Cook, Edmund	1701
Cook, Richard	1756
Cook, Thomas	1690
Cook(e), William	1707
Cooke and Freeman	o. 1725
Cooke, Charles William	1810
Cooke, Edward	1769
Cooke, Francis	1670
Cooke, Isaac	1692
Cooke, John	1770
Cooke, Ralph	1536 (Newcastle-on-Tyne)
Cooke, Richard	1599 (York)
Cooke, Samuel	1727
Cooke, Thomas	c. 1699
Cooke, White	1720
Cooke, William (Junior)	1599
Cooper, Benjamin	1684
Cooper, Benjamin	1727
Cooper, George	1777
Cooper, George H.	1802, 1819
Cooper, John	1688
Cooper, Joseph	c. 1690
Cooper, Richard	1818
Cooper, Thomas (1)	1668
Cooper, Thomas (2)	1817
Cooper, William	1655
Cordell, John	1765
Cordell, Joseph	1729
Cordwell, William	1756
Cormell, John	c. 1684
Cornewall, John	c. 1684
Cornewall, William	1614
Cornhill, Gilbert	1670
Corse, Joseph	1694
Cortyne, John	1630 (Edinburgh †)

Cotton, Jonathan (1)	1711, 1736
Cotton, Jonathan (2)	1736, 1759
Coton, Jonathan (3)	1750
Cotton, Thomas (1)	1716
Cotton, Thomas (2)	1747, 1778
Coulter, William	1751 (Edinburgh †)
Coulthard, Alexander	1708 (,, †)
Coulton, Charles	1711
Coulton, Robert	1662–1677 (York)
Coulton, Robert	1642–1688 (,,)
Coulton, Robert (Junior)	1677–1688 (,,)
Coursey, John	1667
Coutie, William	1619 (Edinburgh †)
Coverham, William	1423
Cowderoy, Thomas	1689
Cowdwell, John	1606, 1620
Cowes, Henry	1626, 1645
Cowes, Thomas	1601, 1605
Cowley, John (1)	1724, 1730
Cowley, John (2)	1747
Cowley, William (1)	1669, 1695
Cowley, William (2)	1709, 1734
Cowling, Abraham	
Cowling, William	1737
Cowlston, —	c. 1603
Cowper, James	1704 (Edinburgh †)
Cowper, Thomas	1721
Cowper, William	1750
Cox, Charles	1724
Cox, John	1679
Cox, Ralph	1656
Cox, Richard	1712
Cox, Stephen	?
Cox, William (1)	1708
Cox, William (2)	1756
Cranley, Charles	1692
Creak, James	1738
Crellin, Horatio N.	1821
Crellin, Philip (1)	1788
Crellin, Philip (2)	1814, 1820
Crichton, George	1673 (Edinburgh †)
Crichton, John	1687 (,, †)
Crief, Richard	1639 (Dublin)
Cripps, James	1735
Cripps, Mark	1736, 1762

LIST OF THE NAMES OF PEWTERERS

Crisp, Ellis	1670
Crook, Richard	1710
Crooke, Robert	1738
Crooke, William	16—
Crook(es), William	c. 1685
Croop, William	1706
Crop, John	1683 (Dublin)
Cropp, William	1667
Cross, Abraham	c. 1674
Cross, Abraham	1695
Cross, William	1659
Cross, William	1668
Crosby, Daniel	1683 (Dublin)
Crossfield, Robert	1701
Crosswell, Robert	1570
Crostwayt, Richard (Crosthwaite)	1541, 1550
Crostwayte, Nicholas	1551, 1559
Croswell, Thomas	1670
Crowde, William	1454, 1474
Crowe, William	1512, 1528
Crowling, Abraham	? (? Cowling)
Crowson, John	1586
Cuming, Richard	c. 1690
Curd, Thomas	1729, 1756
Curns, Robert	1486, 1491
Curtis, Benjamin	1697
Curtis, Habakkuk	1599
Curtis, Henry	1670
Curtis, Peter (Curtys)	1525
Curtis, Thomas	1538, 1546
Curtis, William	1558, 1586
Cuss, John (Guss)	1455
Cuthbertson, John	1712–1730 (Edinburgh †)
Cutler, T.	c. 1276
Dackombe, Aquila (1)	1746, 1773
Dackombe, Aquila (2)	1801, 1818
Dackombe, William	1819
Dadley, Edward	1775, 1804
Dadley, Mary	1815
Dadley, William	1818
Dafforn, Joseph	
Dakin, Robert	1698
Dale, John	1670

Dale, Richard	1709
Dalmer, Symeon	1705
Daly, John	1635 (Dublin)
Damport, Edward	1569 (Coventry)
Daniel, Thomas	1723
Daniell, Alexander	1812
Daniell, George	1806
Darby, John	1694 (Dublin)
Darling, Thomas	1736, 1758
Davenport, Christopher	1602 (Coventry)
Davenport, Edmund	1550 (Coventry)
Daveson, William	1667
Davidson, Thomas	1807
Davies, David	?
Davis, John (1)	1687
Davis, John (2)	1715, 1747
Davis, Joseph	1720
Davis, Richard	1664
Davis, Thomas	1788
Davis, William	1748
Davison, George	1700–1728 (Dublin)
Davison, John	1687
Davison, William	1733 (Dublin)
Davy, Edmund	1688 (Cornish)
Daw, William	?
Dawe, Richard	1780 (Exeter)
Dawe, Robert	1690 (,,)
Dawes, Richard	1652
Dawkins, Pollisargus (Policargus)	1628
Day, John	1540, 1565
Day, Thomas	1703
Deacon, Thomas	1780
Deacon, Thomas	1780
Deacon, William	1755
Deale, George	1711
Deane, John	1775
Deane, Robert	1692
Deane, William	1731
Deeley, William	1726
de Jersey, William	1744, 1773
Denby, William	1170
de St. Croix, John	1729
Devey, John	1768
Devon, John	1777

LIST OF THE NAMES OF PEWTERERS 165

Dewell, Joseph	1734
Dickinson, Charles	1770–1817 (Cork)
Dickinson, Paul	1622
Dickinson, Robert	1762
Dickinson, Thomas	1667
*Dickson, William	1607
Digby, John	1670
Digges, William	1699
Dimocke, William	c. 1690
Dirley, John	1708
Distin, Anthony	1696
Distin, Giles	1667
Ditch, William	1669
Dixon, Henry	1790
Dixon, John (1)	1688
Dixon, John (2)	1739
Dixon, William (1)	c. 1612
Dixon, William (2)	1704
Dobney, John	1744
Dobson, Richard	1746
Dockron, William	1576 (Dublin)
Dockwra, John	1670
Dod, —	c. 1665
Dodson, Thomas	1769
Dolbeare, John (1)	1630
Dolbeare, John (2)	1740
Dolby, Francis	1697
Done, John	16—
Donne, James	1701
Donne, John	1716
Donne, Joseph	1727
Donne, William	1722
Dorman, John	1815
Dottowe, John	1460
Dove, John	1684, 1713
Downton, John	1478, 1481
Dowell, Jeremiah	1721
Downing (?) John	1670
Doyle & Co.	1798 (Dublin)
Doyle, Patrick	1771
Drabble, William	1819
Draper, James	1598
Draper, John	1638 (Dublin)
Draper, John	1712
Drayton, Symkin	1466

Drew, Edward	1728
Drew, John	1720
Drinkwater, Richard	1712
Drinkwater, Timothy	1676
Dropwell, Robert (? Crosswell)	1571
Drury, John	1655, 1673
Drury, —.	1705
Duckmanton, John	1690
Dudley, —.	c. 1600
Duffield, Peter (1)	1654, 1688
Duffield, Peter (2)	1697
Dunch, Mary Ann	1724
Duncomb(e), John	c. 1700 (Birmingham)
Duncomb(e), Samuel	c. 1750 (,,)
Dunn, John	1736
Dunne, Richard	1691, 1696
Dunning, Thomas (1)	1604, 1617
Dunning, Thomas (2)	1617
Durand, Jonas (1)	1692, 1726
Durand, Jonas (2)	1732, 1763
Durnford, Francis	c. 1674
Duxell, Richard	1616, 1629
Dyer, John	1669, 1703
Dyer, Lawrence (1)	1657, 1675
Dyer, Lawrence (2)	1694, 1728
Dyer, Richard	1699
Dyer, William	1667, 1682
Eames, Richard	1697
Eastham J.	1748
Eastland, B. R.	1748
Eastwick, Adrian	1730
Eastwick, Francis	1694
Eastwick, Henry S.	1740
Eastwick, Isaac	1736
Ebsall, John	1706
Eddon, William	1689
Eden, William	1697, 1737
Edgar & Co.	? 1850
Edgar, Preston & Son	c. 1850 (Bristol)
Edgar & Son	?
Edgar, Robert	1684 (Edinburgh †)
Edgar, Thomas	1654 (,, †)
Edgell, Simon	1709

LIST OF THE NAMES OF PEWTERERS

*Edward(s), Edward . . c. 1670
Edwards, John . . . 1718
Edwards, J. . . . 1739
Edwards, William . . 1697
Egan, Andrew . . . 1783
Eells, Levy . . . 1744
Eells, William . . . 1752
Eiddy, James . . . 1600 (Edinburgh †)
Elderton, John . . . 1696, 1731
Elderton, Savage . . 1740
Elice, Wm. (Ellis) . . 1481, 1490
Elinor, Christopher . . 1755
Elliot, Bartholomew . . 1746
Elliott, Charles . . . 1704
Elliott, Thos. (Elyot) . . 1587, 1604
Elliott, William . . . 1823
Ellis, Edward (1) . . 1700
Ellis, Edward (2) . . 1762
Ellis, John . . . 1688 (Cornwall)
Ellis, John (1) . . . 1754, 1770
Ellis, John (2) . . . 1754
Ellis, Samuel (1) . . 1721, 1748
Eliis, Samuel (2) . . 1754
Ellis, William (1) . . 1702
Ellis, William (2) . . 1726
Elphick, Thomas . . 1670
Elwick, Henry . . . 1707
Ellwood, William (1) . 1697, 1733
Ellwood, William (2) . 1723, 1749
Elwood, James . . . 1777–1790 (Dublin)
Elton, J. . . . 1725
Elyot, Thomas (1) . . 1579, 1604
Embry, William . . . 1727
Emes, John (1) . . . 1676, 1700
Emes, John (2) . . . 1700
Emmerton, Thomas . . 1715, 1736
End, J. Jacob . . . 1815
End, Richard . . . 1777
End, William . . . 1774–1805 (Limerick)
Engley, Arthur . . . c. 1700
Enos, Thomas . . . 1612 (Dublin)
Estwicke, Francis . . 1694
Evans, Charles (1) . . 1737
Evans, Charles (2) . . 1760
Evans, Ellis . . . 1690

Evans, Humphrey	(Exeter)
Evans, James	1816
Evans, J.	1720
Evans, Richard	1756
Evatt, Thomas	1797
Eve, Adam	1769
Eve, Joseph	1725
Everard, George	1696
Everett, Henry	1717
Everett, James	1711
Everett, G. (Everitt ?)	1664
Ewen, John	1700
Ewsters, Richard	1717
Ewsters, Thomas	1752
Eyre, William	1452, 1475
Exall, Christopher	1700
Excell, James	1718
Fairbrother, R. (? Farebrother)	?
Farley, John	1727
Farman, Edward	1786
Farman, J.	1764
Farmer, George	1688
Farmer, Henry William	1811
Farmer, John (1)	1687
Farmer, John (2)	1725
Farmer, Richard	1728
Farmer, Thomas	1688
Farmer, William (1)	1765
Farmer, William (2)	1795
Farshall, Richard	1692
Farthing, Roger	1573
Fasson, Benjamin	1797, 1815
Fasson, J.	1725
Fasson, John (1)	1745
Fasson, John (2)	1753, 1762
Fasson, Thomas	1783, 1803
Fasson, William	1758, 1787
Fasson & Son	177–
Fawcet, James	1749
Fawler, Daniel	1698
Febbard, Richard	1690
Febbert, William	c. 1720
Feild, Henry	1719

LIST OF THE NAMES OF PEWTERERS

Feildar, Henry (Fieldar)	1704
Fell, George John	1796
Ferguson, Alexander	1678 (Edinburgh †)
Ferner, John	1595
Festam, Thomas	1749 (Dublin)
Fethers, Francis	1815
Fevrier, William	1776
Fewtrell, Edward	1605
Fiddes, James	1754
Field, Edward Spencer (1)	1749, 1771
Field, Edward Spencer (2)	1787
Field, H.	1693
Field, Robert Spencer	1782
Fielding, Charles Israel	1778
Finch, John	1670
Findlay, Robert	1717 (Edinburgh †)
Fisher, Paul	1798
Fisher, Samuel	1744
Fisher, William	1771
Fitzpatrick, John	1768 (Dublin)
Fitzrere, Patrick	1559 (,,)
Flanagan, James	1730 (,,)
Fleming, William	1717 (Edinburgh †)
Fletcher, Hannah	1714
Fletcher, James	1775
Fletcher, Richard	1681, 1701
Flood, John	1537
Flood, Walter	1630 (Dublin)
Floyd, John	1769, 1787
Floyde, J.	1748
Fly and Thompson	c. 1735
Fly, Timothy	1713, 1739
Fly, William	1691
Fontain(e), James	1752, 1786
Ford, Abraham	1719
Ford, John	1701, 1723
Ford, Roger	1692–1752 (Dublin)
Ford, William	d. 1731 (Dublin)
Forman, Simon	1608
Fort, Roger	? (Lurgan)
Foster, Benjamin (1)	1706
Foster, Benjamin (2)	1730
Foster, Bomford	1371
Foster, Boniface	1574
Foster, Edward	1734

Foster, John	1810
Foster, Joseph	1757
Foster, J.	1789
Foster, Thomas	1742
Foster, William	1709
Fothergill, M.	(Bristol)
Fountain, Thomas	1670
Foull, Thomas	1541
Fowler, J.	1744
Fowler, Samuel	1769
Fox, Edward	1617
Fox, Thomas	1689
Fox, William	1670
Foxon, William	1723
Foy, Philip	? (Exeter)
Francis, John	1670
Franklyn, Jeremiah	1729
Franklyn, Richard	1689, 1730
Freeman, Henry	1669, 1671
Freeman, James	d. 1772 (Dublin)
Freeman, Thomas	1694
Freeman, William	c. 1727
French, Alexander	1670
French, John (1)	1687
Frith, J. M.	1760
French, John (2)	1780 (Bristol)
Frend, Nicholas	1620 (Dublin)
Frend, Robert	1625
Friend, Edward	1636 (Dublin)
Frith, John	1670
Frith, Thomas	1693
Frith, William	1700
Froome, William	1760
Frost, John	1777
Fryer, John	1696, 1715
Fryer, John	1668 (Clonmel)
Fulham, Andrew	1614
Fulham, John	1637, 1651
Fulshurst, Abraham	1689
Funge, William	1701
Galbraeth, —.	(Glasgow)
Gamble, Nicholas	1687
Game, Hugh	1436
Gardiner, John	1764 (Edinburgh †)

LIST OF THE NAMES OF PEWTERERS

Gardiner, Joseph	c. 1690
Gardner, Allen	1555, 1578
Gardner, Thomas	1783 (Dublin)
Garioch, Patrick	1735
Garle, Christopher	1714
Garmentin, William	1613 (Edinburgh †)
Garratt, Joseph	1734
Garton, Joseph	1677 (Dublin)
Gascar, Percival	1581, 1597
Gasse, James	1670
Gatcher, John (? Catcher)	c. 1588
Gauls, —.	(Exeter)
Geary, Thomas	1740 (Cork)
Gee, George	1764 (Dublin)
Geffers, —	1688 (Cork)
George, William	1670
Gery(e), John	1559, 1574
Gepp, Matthew	1715
Geohegan, John	1714 (Dublin)
Geraghty, John	1816 (Dublin)
Gerardin, Watson	c. 1825 (London)
Gibbings, J. J.	? 1850 (Cork)
Gibbons, —	1670
Gibbs, Henry	1729
Gibbs, James	1741
Gibbs, John	1756
Gibbs, Lawrence	1670
Gibbs, Matthew	1719
Gibbs, William	1804
Gibson, Edward	1719 (Edinburgh †)
Gibson, Elizabeth	1762
Gibson, Robert	1668
Gibson, Thomas	1626 (Dublin)
Giddings, Joseph	c. 1709
Giffin, Jonathan	1723
Giffin, Thomas (1)	1726, 1757
Giffin, Thomas (2)	1760
Gilbert, Edward	1654, 1662
Giles, William	1741, 1769
Gill, Robert	1437–1493
Gill, William	17—
Gillam, Everard	1702
Gillam, Jonas	1708
Gillam, William	1698
Gillate, George M.	1807

Gilligan, Roger	1709
Gillman, Henry	1734 (Cork)
Gisburne(erne), John	1691
Gisburne(erne), J.	1696
Gisburne(erne), Robert	1691
Glass, William	1754
Gledstanes, George	1610 (Edinburgh †)
Glover, Edward	1610, 1620
Glover, Henry	1620
Glover, John	1779 (Edinburgh †)
Glover, Richard	1559, 1611
Glover, Roger	1605, 1615
Glover, Thomas	1814
Glynn, Thomas	1670
Glynn, William	1691
Goater, Thomas	1729, 1758
God, J.	16—
Goddard, William	1670
Godeluk, Thomas	1468
Godfrey, John	1612
Godfrey, Joseph Henry	1807
Godfrey, Stephen	1679
Godfrey, Peter	1688 (Cornwall)
Godfrey, William	1796
Going, Richard	1696, 1766 (Bristol)
Gold, Richard	1737
Goldie, Joseph	1633 (Edinburgh †)
Gollde, Wm. (? Crowde)	1470
Good, Robert	1709
Goodale, John	1454, 1457
Goodison, Richard	1771–1788 (Dublin)
Goodluck, Robert	1771
Goodluck, William Richard	1823
Goodman, Edward	1670
Goodman, Harry	1693
Goodman, Philip	1587, 1596
Goodwin, Richard	1783
Goodwin, Thomas	1707
Goodyear (Gudeyere), Thomas	1534–88
Goose, Thomas	1770
Gorwood, Joseph	1684 (York)
Gosle(r), N. (? Gosling)	c. 1690
Gosling, Thomas	1721
Gosnell, William	1670

LIST OF THE NAMES OF PEWTERERS

Gould, William	1712
Gowet, Robert	1621 (Edinburgh)
Graham, Basil	1699
Graham, Joseph	1758
Graham, Wardrop	c. 1770 (London)
Grahame, Alexander	1654 (Edinburgh †)
Grainge, John	1799, 1816
Grainger, William	1620, 1638
*Graime, Thomas	c. 1700
Grant, Edward	1698, 1741
Grant, Joseph	1801
Grant, N.	c. 1695
Gratton, Joseph	1817, 1839
Graunt, John	1669
Graves, Alexander	1752
Graves, Francis	1621, 1629
Graves, T. O.	?
Gray, John	1757
Gray, Thomas	1782
Gray and King	c. 1710
Greatrakes (? Greatrix) James	1780 (Cork)
Greatrix, John	1783 (,,)
Greaves, Francis	1610
Greaves, John (1)	c. 1609
Greaves, John (2)	1733
Green, James	1718, 1778
Green, John Gray	1793
Green, Joseph	1803
Green, Nathaniel	1722
Green, William	1684
Green, William Sandys	1725, 1737
Greene, Jacob	1670
Greenbank, William	166–
Greener, Thomas	1700
Greenfell, George	1759
Greening, Richard	1756
Greenwood, John	1731
Greenwood, Thomas	1759
Gregge, John (Grigge)	1722
Gregg(e), Robert	1678, 1683
Gregg(e), Thomas	1654, 1677
Gregory, Edward	? c. 1720 (Bristol)
Gregory, George	1740
Grendon, Daniel	1735

Greschirche, William de	d. 1350
Grey, John	1712
Grey, Richard	1706
Gribble, William	1688 (Cornwall)
Grier, James	1694
Grier, John	1701 (Edinburgh †)
Griffith, John	(Irish)
Griffith, Richard	1712 (Cork)
Grigg, Samuel	1734
Grimshaw, James	1714
Grimsted, John	1701
Groce, Thomas	1737
Groome, Randell	1615, 1624
Groome, William	1698
Grove, Edmund	1753
Grove, William	1779
Groves, Edmund	1773
Groves, Edward	c. 1677
Grunwin, Gabriel	1693
Grunwin, Richard	1714, 1729
Griffin, Elizabeth	1749
Guld, John	1677
Gunning, James	1782 (Eyrecourt)
Gunthorp(e), Jonathan	1699
Gurnell, John	1768
Guss, John	1455
Guy, Earle of Warwick	cf. Thomas Wigley
Guy, John	1692
Guy, Samuel	1729
Gwilt, Howell	1697, 1709
Gwyn, Bacon	1709
Hadley, Isaac	1668
Hagger, Stephen Kent	1754
Hair, William	1695
Hale and Sons	? 1700
Hale, George	1675
Hale, William	1670
Halford, Simon	1726
Halifax, Charles	1670
Halifax, Christopher	1704
Halifax, Francis	1690
Halifax, Henry	1698
Hall, John (1)	1810
Hall, John (2)	1823

LIST OF THE NAMES OF PEWTERERS 175

Hall, James	1699
Hall, Robert (1)	1639
Hall, Robert (2)	1793
Hall, Thomas (1)	1620
Hall, Thomas (2)	1711
Hall, William (1)	1670
Hall, William (2)	1687
Hamberger, John	1794, 1819
Hamilton, Alexander	1721, 1745
Hamilton, William	1613 (Edinburgh †)
Hamilton, William	1760–1796 (Dublin)
Hammerton, Henry (1)	1706, 1733
Hammerton, Henry (2)	1748
Hammerton, Richard	1751
Hammon, Henry	1647–1691 (York)
Hammon, John	1647–1656 (,,)
Ham(m)ond, George	1703, 1709
Hamon, Samuel (1)	1614
Hamon, Samuel (2)	1693
*Hamson, John	?
*Hamson, Samuel	d. 1615
Hancock, Samuel	1689, 1714
Hand, Samuel	c. 1675
Hands, James	1718
Hands, Richard	1717
Handy, J.	1754
Handy, Thomas	1784
Handy, William (1)	1728, 1746
Handy, William (2)	1746
Handy, William (3)	1755
Hankinson, J.	1693
Hanns, Edward	1704
Hanns, Richard	1727
Harbridge, William	1774
Hardeman, William	1610
Hardin, Jonathan (1)	1693
Harding, Jonathan (2)	1722
Harding, Robert	1668
Hardman, John	?
Harendon, —	1664
Harford, Henry (1)	1676
Harford, Henry (2)	1715
Harper, Edward	1572
Harper, J.	1709
Harraben, William	1712 (Dublin)

Harris, Daniel	1708–1729 (Cork)
Harris, Jabez	1694, 1734
Harris, John	1709
Harris, Richard	1763
Harris, William	1746
Harrison, John (1)	1651–1684 (York)
Harrison, John (2)	1677–1697 (,,)
Harrison, John (3)	1741–1749 (,,)
Harrison, Rufus	? (London)
Harrison, William	1748
Hartshorne, Michael	1676, 1693
Hartwell, Abraham	1591, 1595
Hartwell, John	1736
Hartwell, Peter (1)	1670
Hartwell, Peter (2)	1688
Harvey, William	1712 (Dublin)
Harvie, James	1654 (Edinburgh †)
Harvie, John	1643 (,, †)
Harvye, John	1555
Haryson, Thomas	1483
Haslam, William	1734
Hasselborne, Jacob	1691, 1722
Hassell, Baptist	1599
Hassell, Thomas	1554, 1566
Hastings, James	1614
Has(s)ell, James	1792
Has(s)ell, Thomas	17—
Hatch, Henry	c. 1680
Hatheld, William	1627
Hathaway, James (1)	1734
Hathaway, James (2)	1754
Hathaway, John	1725
Haveland, Miles	1664, 1668
Havering, John	1699
Haward, Thomas (1) (Howard)	1658, 1666
Haward, Thomas (2)	1667
Hawclif, Simon	1568
Hawk(e), Thomas	1579, 1588
Hawkes, Edward	1667
Hawkesford, Roger	1601
Hawkins, John	1738
Hawkins, Richard	1727
Hawkins, S.	1536
Hawkins, Thomas	1742

LIST OF THE NAMES OF PEWTERERS

Hawkins, Thomas	1756
Haws, J.	1791
Haycroft, Charles	1756
Hayes, Hugh	1697
Hayes, Thomas	1746
Haynes, John	1688
Haynes, William	1556, 1560
Hayton, John	1743, 1748
Healey, William	1752
Heaney, John	1767–1798 (Dublin)
Hearman, William	1801
Heath, Edward	1652
Heath, John (1)	1618
Heath, John (2)	1694
Heath, Lancelot (1)	d. 1584
Heath, Lancelot (2)	1688
Heath, Richard	1696, 1699
Heath, Samuel	1715
Heath, Thomas (1)	1709
Heath, Thomas (2)	1714
Heath, William	1670
Heatley, Alexander	1700
Henley, William	1723
Henning, Thomas	1693
Henson, Thomas	1614
Herne, Daniel	1756, 1767
Hernie, James	1651 (Edinburgh †)
Herrin, John	1693–1740 (Edinburgh †)
Herring, James	1692 (Edinburgh †)
Hesketh, Henry	1698
Heslopp, Richard (Heslop)	1700
Hewett, Joseph	1670
Hewitt, J.	1723
Heydon, Samuel	1715
Heyford, William	1698
Heythwaite, Michael	1553
Hickes, Daniel	1690
Hickes, P.	1706
Hickingbotham, Francis	1693
Hickling, Thomas (1)	1685, 1698
Hickling, Thomas (2)	1717
Hicks, Thomas	1698
Hide, Benjamin	1741
Higdon, Joseph	1683
Highmore, William	1742

Higley, Samuel	1775
Hill, Hough (Hugh)	1625
Hill, Jonas	c. 1714
Hill, Thomas	1696
Hill, Thomas	1741 (Dublin)
Hill, Robert	1724
Hill, Roger	1791
Hill, Thomas	1795
Hill, Walter (Hyll)	1583, 1601
Hill, Wm.	1672
Hill, William	1808–1829 (Dublin)
Hills, William	1636, 1641
Hilton, John de	c. 1350
Hinde, John (1)	1776, 1796
Hinde, John (2)	1800
Hindes, John (?)	1760
Hinman, Benjamin	1715
Hitchcock, Evan	1708
Hitchcock, John	1690
Hitchens, James	1744
Hitchins, John	1758, 1786
Hitchins, William (1)	1705
Hitchins, William (2)	1732
Hitchins, —	1759
Hitchman, James	1701, 1716
Hitchman, Robert	1737, 1761
Hoare, Richard	1672
Hoare, Thomas	1718, 1728
Hobson, Thomas	1614 (Bristol)
Hockley, Richard (1)	1715
Hockley, Richard (2)	1725
Hodge, Joseph	1667
Hodge, Robert Piercy	1772, 1802
Hodge, Sampson	1707 (Tiverton)
Hodge, Thomas	1720 (,,)
Hodge, Thomas Bathurst	1810
Hodgert, William	1690 (Dublin)
Hodges, John	1804–1808 (Dublin)
Hodges, Joseph (1)	1670
Hodges, Joseph (2)	1693
Hodges, Joseph (3)	1718
Hodgkin, Thomas	c. 1768 (London)
Hodgkis, Arthur	1635
Hogg, William	c. 1800 (Newcastle)
Hollas, —	?

LIST OF THE NAMES OF PEWTERERS

Holl(e)y, John	1689, 1706
Hollford, Stephen	1664, 1668
Hollinshead, William	1687
Holloway, Richard	1745
Holman, Ary	1767, 1791
Holman, Edward	1688
Holmes, George	1746
Holmes, Joshua	1759
Holmes, Joseph	1755
Holmes, Mary Elizabeth	1751
Holmes, Thomas	1709
Holstock, John	1571
Home, John	1749, 1771
Hone, John	1732
Hone, William	1688, 1713
Hooper, J.	1765
Hooper, Thomas	1784
Hopkins, Joseph	1667
Hopkins, Thomas	1700
Hoppey, G.	1777
Horrod, Thomas	1693
Horton, William	1725
Hoskins, J.	1735
Hoskins, Thomas	1763
Hoskyn, Henry	? (Barnstaple)
Hoskyn, John	(Truro)
Houldsworth, Thomas	1653–1680 (York)
How, John	1670
How, Josiah	1713
How, J.	1760
How, Thomas	1714
Howard, William (1)	1700, 1702
Howard, William (2)	1745, 1779
Howe, J.	1711
Howell, Ralph	1623
Hubbard, Henry	1731
Hubbard, Robert	1690, 1717
Hubert, Isaac	1755
Hudson, John	1770, 1804
Hudson, Thomas	c. 1679
Hudson, William	1729
Hughes, James	1691
Hull, J. (1)	1776
Hull, J. (2)	1799
Hull, Thomas	1639, 1650

Hulls, John	1705, 1709
Hulls, Ralph	1682
Hulls, S.	1693
Hulls, William	1718, 1744
Hulse, Charles	1690
Hume, George	1700
Hume, Robert	1790
Hummerstone, Wm.	1591
Hunt, James	1699
Hunt, John	1701
Hunt, Samuel	1742
Hunt, Thomas	c. 1670
Hunter, Alex.	1682 (Edinburgh †)
Hunter, William	1749 (,, †)
Hunton, Nicholas	1667, 1670
Hurdman, William	1620, 1625
Hurst, Richard	1774, 1826
Hurst, William	c. 1677
Husband, William	1712
Hussey, Thomas	1727
Hustwaite, Robert	1571
Hustwaite, Thomas	1521, 1523
Hustwayte, William	1538, 1559
Hutchens, James	1744
Hutchins, William	1732
Hutchinson, Katharine	1684 (York)
Hutchinson, William (1)	1663–1684 (York)
Hutchinson, William (2)	1698–1738 (,,)
Hux, Elizabeth Gray	1763
Hux, Thomas	1723, 1739
Hux, William (1)	1700, 1728
Hux, William (2)	1751
Hux, William (3)	1784
Hyatt, Humphrey	1681
Hyatt, John	1670
Hynge'stworth, N. de	1364
Ianson, John	?
Iempson, Solomon	1696
Iles, John	1704, 1709
Iles, Nathaniel	1702, 1719
Iles, Richard	1697
Iles, Robert	1691, 1735
Ingles, Arthur	1710
Ingles, John	1723

LIST OF THE NAMES OF PEWTERERS

Ingles, Jonathan	. .	1678
Ingles, Thomas	. .	1707
Inglis, Robert	. .	1663 (Edinburgh †)
Inglis, Thomas (1)	. .	1616 (,, †)
Inglis, Thomas (2)	. .	1647–1668 (,, †)
Inglis, Thomas (3)	. .	1686 (,, †)
Inglis, Thomas (4)	. .	1719–1732 (,, †)
Ingole, Daniel	. .	1667, 1688
Ingram, Roger	. .	1648 (Cork)
Ireland, Ann	. .	1690
Irving, Henry	. .	1750
Isade, Roger	. .	1569
Ives, Richard	. .	1688
Jackman, Nicholas	. .	1699, 1735
Jackson, Henry (1)	. .	1723
Jackson, Henry (2)	. .	1757
Jackson, John (1)	. .	1566, 1589
Jackson, John (2)	. .	1689, 1712
Jackson, John (3)	. .	1731
Jackson, John (4)	. .	1763
Jackson, J.	. .	1735
Jackson, Michael	. .	1757
Jackson, Robert	. .	1781, 1801
Jackson, Samuel	. .	1673, 1714
Jackson, Samuel	. .	1669 (Dublin)
Jackson, Startup	. .	1635
Jackson, Thomas (1)	. .	1647, 1660
Jackson, Thomas (2)	. .	1717
Jackson (Jaxon), William (1)		1512
Jackson, William (2)	. .	1668
Jacob, Richard	. .	1670
Jacobs, John	. .	1663
Jacomb, Josiah	. .	1669, 1675
James, Anthony	. .	1685, 1713
James, Daniel	. .	1691
James, Lewis	. .	c. 1670
James, John	. .	1772 (Dublin)
James, Patten	. .	1744
James, Richard	. .	1709
James, Thomas	. .	1726
James, William (1)	. .	1689
James, William (2)	. .	1749
James, William (3)	. .	d. 1783 (Dublin)
Jameson, James	. .	1680

Jann, Thomas	1520, 1535
Jaques, J.	1724
Jardeine, Nicholas	1573
Jarrett, John	1649, 1656
Jarrett, John	1738
Jeffery, Thomas	1670
Jeffereys, Benjamin	1731
Jeffereys, Joseph	1757
Jeffereys, Samuel	1734, 1739
Jefferies, George	1689
Jeffin, Thomas	1709
Jenkins, Edward	1805
Jenner, Anthony	1754
Jennings, Theodore (1)	1713, 1741
Jennings, Theodore (2)	1757
Jerome, William	1759
Jersey, William de	1744, 1773
Jeyes, John	1763
Jobson, Matthew	1645–1661 (York)
Johns, John	1688 (Cornish)
Johnson, Alexander	1688, 1695 (Dublin)
Johnson and Chamberlain	c. 1735
Johnson, Gabriel	1785
Johnson, John (1)	1666
Johnson, John (2)	1715
Johnson, Luke	1713
Johnson, Richard	1688
Johnson, Samuel	1711 (Dublin)
Johnson, Thomas	1722
Johnson, William	1698
Johnston, James	1688–1719 (Dublin)
Johnston, Thos.	1724 (Dublin)
Jolly, John	1714 (Edinburgh †)
Jones, Charles	1786
Jones, Christian	1709
Jones, Clayton	1746
Jones, James	1628
Jones, John (1)	1700, 1745
Jones, John (2)	1707, 1758
Jones, John (3)	1763
Jones, Joseph	1748
Jones, Mary	1719
Jones, Nicholas	1608
Jones, Owen	1647
Jones, Philip	1733

LIST OF THE NAMES OF PEWTERERS

Jones, Robert	1667
Jones, Richard	1728
Jones, Samuel	1687
Jones, Seth	1719
Jones, Thomas (1)	1632
Jones, Thomas (2)	1755
Jones, William	1666, 1676
Jordan, John	1727
Jordan, Thomas	1732
Jordon, James	1691
Joselyn, William	1734
Joseph, Henry	1736, 1771
Joseph, Henry and Richard	1775
Joseph, Sarah	1780
Joseph, Richard	1785, 1806
Judson, Farshall	1755
Jupe, Elizabeth	1781
Jupe, John	1735, 1761
Jupe, Robert	1691, 1737
Keersey, —	c. 1605
Kelk, James	1677, 1688
Kelk(e), Nicholas	1663, 1686
Kelke, William	1670
Kellingworth, —	cf. Killingworth
Kellowe, Robert	1715 (Edinburgh †)
Kelsall, Arnold	1740
Kempster, John	1670
Kendale, John	1451
Ken(d)rick, John	1739, 1754
Kent, Edward	1689
Kent, John	1749
Kent, Stephen	1766
Kent, William	1623
Kentish, Simon	1693
Kenton, John	1694, 1717
Kerslake, —	? (Crediton)
Keyborne, William	1758 (Cork)
Keyte, Hastings	1730
Killingworth, Clement	1553
Kimberley, Francis	c. 1628
Kimpton, Nathaniel	1697
King, Abraham	1669, 1693
King, Anthony	1745–1763 (Dublin
King, Charles	1830 (,,)

King, Denis	. . .	1618 (Dublin)
King, James	. . .	1716
King, John	. . .	1632 (Dublin)
King, John (1)	. . .	1694
King, John (2)	. . .	1757
King, Joseph	. . .	1691, 1709
King, Richard (1)	. . .	1580
King, Richard (2)	. . .	1714, 1746
King, Richard (3)	. . .	1745
King, Robert	. . .	1698, 1711
King, Thomas (1)	. . .	1686
King, Thomas (2)	. . .	1746, 1798
King, Thomas (3)	. . .	1719
King, William (1)	. . .	1715
King, William (2)	. . .	1732
King, William Harrison	.	1786
Kinge, John	. . .	1632 (Dublin)
Kinnear, Andrew	. .	1750 (Edinburgh †)
Kinnieburgh and Sons	.	1823 (,, †)
Kinnieburgh, Robert	.	1794 (,, †)
Kinnieburgh (Sheriff)	.	1803 (,, †)
Kirke, Joseph	. .	1728
Kirby, Thomas	. .	1722
Kirke, Thomas	. .	1728
Kirt(on), John	. .	1699
Knight, Alex.	. .	1696 (Dublin)
Knight, Francis	. .	1685, 1692
Knight, James	. .	1704
Knight, Richard	. .	1730
Knight, Robert	. .	1770
Knight, Robert Benjamin	.	1808
Knight, Samuel	. .	1703
Knipe, Stephen	. .	1718
Knowles, Tobias	. .	1664
Kymbley, Francis	. .	c. 1614
Lackford, John	. .	1664
Laffar, John	. .	1706, 1714
Lake, Richard	. .	1692
Lamb, Catherine	. .	1737
Lamb, James	. .	1737 (Dublin)
Lamb, Joseph	. .	1708, 1738
Lamb, Penelope	. .	1734
Lambert, John	. .	1739
Lancaster, Alexander	.	1711

LIST OF THE NAMES OF PEWTERERS

Langford, John (1)	1719, 1757
Langford, John (2)	1780
Langford, Thomas	1751
Langford, William	1679
Langley, Adam	1667, 1680
Langley, John (1)	1692
Langley, John (2)	1716
Langley, John (3)	1788
Langtoft, Robert	1499, 1520
Langtoft, Thomas	1472
Langton, John	1731
Lansdown, William	(Bristol)
Lanyon, Thomas	(Bristol)
Large, William	1455, 1477
Larkin, Francis	1685
Lasas, Lewis de	1696
Lather, James	1691 (Dublin)
Latomes, George	1737
Laughton, John	c. 1690
Law, John	1660 (Edinburgh †)
Law, John	1759
Law, Samuel	1768
Lawe, Richard	1670
Lawlor, John	1770 (Carlow)
Lawrance, Edward	1713
Lawrence, John (1)	1691, 1723
Lawrence, John (2)	1726, 1749
Lawrence, Stephen (1)	1667, 1684
Lawrence, Stephen (2)	1708
Lawson, Daniel	1749
Lawson, John	1713
Lawton, Richard	1453
Lay, Henry	1724
Laycock, John	1755
Layton, William	1729
Lea, Francis	1664
Leach, Jonathan (1)	1732
Leach, Jonathan (2)	1742
Leach, Thomas (1)	1691
Leach, Thomas (2)	1736, 1747
Leach, William	1770
Leadbetter, Edmund	1699
Leadbetter, John	1763
Leak, William	1703
Leapidge, Edward	1702, 1724
Leapidge, John	1737, 1763

Leapidge, Thomas	1696
Lee, Benjamin	?
Lee, Edward	1689
Lee, Thomas Charles	1785
Leeson, John	1675, 1680
Leeson, Robert	1626, 1648
Leeton, Robert	1691
Leggatt, James	1755
Leggatt, Richard (1)	1722, 1746
Leggatt, Richard (2)	1746
Leigh, James	1655 (Dublin)
Lester, Thomas	1763–1775 (Cork)
Lestraunge, Stephen	1348
Le Keux, Peter	1779
Letham, John	1718–1756 (Edinburgh †)
Lethard, James	1745
Letherbarrow, T.	c. 1730
Letherbranch, T.	? (Leatherbranch)
Lewins, Leonard	d. 1624
Lewis, George	1706
Lewis, John	1761
Lewis, William	1670
Lickorish, Joseph	1697
Liggins, Robert	1733
Limberley, Francis	c. 1608
Lin(coln)e, Thomas (1)	1718
Lin(coln)e, Thomas (2)	1740
Lindsey, Greenhill	1708
Linnum, J. (Lindum)	1701
Litchfield, Francis	1697
Litchfield, Joshua	d. 1745 (Dublin)
Litchfield, Vincent	1716
Litchfield, William	1745 (Dublin)
Little, Ann	1765
Little, Henry	1738, 1755
Littlefare, Thomas	1705
Loader, Charles William	1784
Loader, Jeremiah	1670
Lobb, William	1612
Lock, Robert	1692
Lockwood, Edward	1768, 1790
Lockwood, George	1616 (York)
Loftus, James	1661–1701 (York)
Loe, Gilbert	1668–1678 (Dublin)
Loftus, Jane	1684 (York)

LIST OF THE NAMES OF PEWTERERS

Loftus, Ralph	1684 (York)
Loftus, Richard	1684–1707 (York)
Long, Sefton	1680, 1692
Long, William	1707 S.
Lord, William	?
Loton, William	1558, 1571
Lovell, John	d. 1742 (Bristol)
Lovell, Robert	? (,,)
Lovely, John	1734
Lowe, S.	1850 ? (Glasgow)
Lowes, George	? (Newcastle)
Lowrie, Thomas	1675 (Edinburgh)
Lucas, Francis	1684 (York)
Lucas, John	1746
Lucas, Robert	1651, 1667
Lucas, Samuel	1734
Lucas, Stephen	1804, 1825
Lucas, William	1779
Ludgate, Nicholas	d. 1348
Luddington, Paul	1736
Lupton, Robert	1775
Lussum (?) Henry	1760
Luton, Thomas	1742
Lydiatt, Samuel	1670
Lyford, Nathaniel	1725
Lyndsay, Alexander	1648 (Edinburgh)
Lyon, William	1747 (Cork)
Mabberley, Stephen	1675
Mabbott, George	1670
Mabbott, William	1659
Mabb(e)s, Samuel	1685
Mabor, Richard	1706
Macdonnel, John	1820 (Limerick)
Machyn, Thomas	1539
Mackenzie, William	1794
Madder, William	1775
Maddox, Thomas	1727
Maitland, James	?
Major, John	1638, 1657
Major, Thomas	1726
Makepeace, Thomas	1670
Makyns, Walter	1554, 1559
Mallum, Lawrence (Mallam)	1503, 1545
Mander, William	1757

Manley, William	1813
Mann, James	1793
Mann, John	1667, 1688
Manning(e), Richard (Mannynge)	1574
Mansell, Richard	1769
Mansworth, Thomas	1585
Manwaring, Philemon	1766
March, Richard	1635
Markham, Richard	1669, 1671
Markland, John	1770
Marriott, Harris	1710
Marsey, William	1753
Marsh, Ralph (1)	1662
Marsh, Ralph (2)	1669, 1671
Marshall, Thomas	1722
Marston, Nathaniel	1671
Marston, Samuel	1670
Marten, Robert	1655, 1674
Martin, John	1766
Martin, William (1)	1670
Martin, William (2)	1726
Masham, Hugh	1713
Mason, Daniel	1673
Mason, John	1695, 1713
Mason, Joseph	1721
Mason, Richard	1679
Mason, Samuel (2)	1720
Mason, Samuel (3)	1798 (Dublin)
Massam, Robert	1740
Mastin, George	1749
Mastin, William	1748
Mathew(e), John	1556, 1569
Mathew, John	1695
Mathews, Abraham	1721
Mathews, Edward	1695, 1728
Mathews, James	1722, 1746
Mathews, Peter	1632
Mathews, Philip	1736
Mathews, Robert	1721
Mathews, Thomas	1711
Mathews, Thomas, jun.	1736
Mathews, William (1)	1676, 1689
Mathews, William (2)	1699
Mathews, William (3)	1721, 1741

LIST OF THE NAMES OF PEWTERERS

Matson, John	1570
Matteson, Thomas	1684 (York)
Mason, Samuel (1)	1670
Mattinson, —	1711
Maundrill, Richard	1693
Maw, —	*c.* 1810
Mawman, John	1710 (Cork)
Maxey, Charles Puckle	1750
Maxted, Henry	1731
Maxwell, Stephen	(London)
May, William	*d.* 1398
Maynard, Josiah	1772
Maynard, Thomas	1767
Mayo, Daniel	1709
Mayors, Anthony	1667
McCabe, Owen	*d.* 1769 (Dublin)
McCulla, James	1719–1729 (Dublin)
Mead, Thomas	1720
Meadows, William	1724
Meakin, Nathaniel (1)	1726, 1768
Meakin, Nathaniel (2)	1741, 1768
Meakin, Nathaniel	
Mearcer, Robert	1709
Meare, —	*c.* 1565
Meares, John	1657
Mear(s), John	1750
Mear(s), Ralph	1643
Mears, William	1571, 1598
Meddom(s), Richard	1672
Meggott, George	1637, 1655
Megre, John	*d.* 1420
Menzies, Alexander	1675
Meriefield, Edward	1716
Meriefield, Robert	1705
Merriott, John	1718
Merrit, Jonathan	1743
Merriweather, John	1718
Merriweather, John C.	*c.* 1747
Merry, Lawrence	*c.* 1850 (Dublin)
Merry, Lawrence and Richard	*c.* 1850 (,,)
Merry, Martin	1824 (,,)
Merry, Richard	*c.* 1850 (,,)
Michael, John	1670
Michell, James	1688 (Cornish)

Middleton, Charles	1690
Middleton, Leonard	1752
Middleton, Thomas	c. 1673
Miles, William	1715
Miles, Samuel	1726
Millett, Richard (Mellett)	1660, 1665
Millin, William	1776, 1786
Mills, Nathaniel	1668
Mills, Nicholas	1529, 1538
Mills (Mylls), William	1557, 1571
Millward, William	1711
Milton, Wheeler	1650
Mister, Richard	1802
Mister, William	1820
Mitchell, Humphrey	c. 1614
Mitchell, John (1)	1619
Mitchell, John (2)	1744, 1755
Mitchell, Paul	1721, 1739
Mitchell, Thomas	1704 (Edinburgh †)
Mogg, Christopher	1708
Moir, Alex.	1675 (Edinburgh †)
Molton, John	1667
Momford, Edward	1712
Momford, John	1630, 1641
Monk, George	1731
Monk, Joseph	1757
Monkhouse, Edward	1715
Monroe, James	1728 (Dublin)
Monteith, James (1)	1634 (Edinburgh †)
Monteith, James (2)	1643 (,, †)
Monteith, James (3)	1778 (,, †)
Moody, J. B.	1816
Moor, Samuel	1704
Moore, Bryan	1691
Moore, Joseph	1700
More, Benjamin	1707
Morgan, William	1614
Moring, Randall	1780, 1821
Morris, Henry	1749
Mors(e), William	c. 1695
Morse, Robert	1702, 1709
Morton, William	1795
Moser, Roger	1806
Morrison, John	1661 (Dublin)
Mortimer, J. H.	? (Exeter)

Moulins, Robert (1) (Mollins)	1678, 1689
Moulins, Robert (2)	1688
Moulins, Robert (3)	1696, 1704
Mountford, Benjamin	1691
Mountford, John	c. 1624
Mourgue, Fulcrand	1807
Mourton, Peter	1688 (Cornish)
Moxon, Samuel (1)	1766, 1799
Moxon, Samuel (2)	1771
Moyes, James	1875 (Edinburgh)
Mudge, Walter	1769, 1793
Mulcaster, John	1792
Mullens, John	1805
Mullins, John	1818
Mullins, Robert	1647
Mumford, Edward	1712
Mumford, Joseph	1670
Munday, Thomas	1758, 1767
Munden, William	1764, 1771
Munns, Nathaniel	1667
Munroe, Andrew	1677 (Edinburgh †)
Murray, William	1734
Napier, Archibald	1666 (Edinburgh †)
Napier, John	1700 (,, †)
Nash, Edward	1717, 1738
Nash, John	1749
Nash, Peter	1670
Nash, Thomas (1)	1485
Nash, Thomas (2)	1729
Neaton, John	1714
Neave, Robert	1690
Needham, Thomas	1665
Nelham, Thomas	1795
Nelham, William	1815
Netherwood, Charles	1716
Nettleford, William	1785
Nevill, Joseph	1762
Newell, Samuel	1689
Newbolt, Edward	1670
Newes, Robert	1578
Newham, John	1699, 1731
Newham, William (1)	1708, 1727
Newham, William (2)	1730, 1745

Newland, Charles	1758
Newman, Michael (1)	1629, 1652
Newman, Michael (2)	1653, 1670
Newman, Ralph	1670
Newman, Richard	1753
Newman, Thomas (1)	1660
Newman, Thomas (2)	1768
Newnam, —	1642
Newson, Thomas	1670
Newth, Elijah	1722
Newton, Hugh	1604, 1621
Newton, Thomas	1725
Nicholl, Thomas	1765, 1786
Nicholls, Henry	1696
Nicholls, James	1670
Nicholls, William	c. 1685
Nichols, John	c. 1685
Nichols, Robert (1)	1692, 1725
Nichols, Robert (2)	1720
Nichols, Samuel	1688 (Cornish)
Nichols, Thomas	1566
Nicholson, James	1730
Nicholson, Robert	1690, 1725
Nisbett, Samuel	1730
Nixon, Robert	1589
Nodes, John	1756, 1778
Nogay, Thomas	1562, 1580
Norfolk, Joseph	1764
Norfolk, Richard	1726, 1776
Norgrove, John	1722
Norris, William	1771
North, George	1690, 1703
North, John	1824 (Dublin)
Northcote, Henry James	1808
Norton, John	1573, 1583
Norwood, William	1727
Nowell, Simon	1731
Nutt, Jacob	1689
Oakford, Michael	1698
Oakford, Nicholas	1699
Oliphant, George (1)	1798
Oliphant, George (2)	1826
Oliver, John	1687
Oliver, Robert	1706

Oliver, William	1689
O'Neal, Richard	1722, 1728
Only, William	*c.* 1675
Orme, Robert	*c.* 1679
Ormiston, John	1769–1796 (Dublin)
Orton, Joseph	1694
Osborn, John	1715
Osborn, Thomas	1719
Osborne, John (1)	1701
Osborne, John (2)	1713
Osborne, Robert	*c.* 1622
Osborne, Samuel	1693
Osborne, Thomas (1)	1670
Osborne, Thomas (2)	1729
Osborne, William	1733
Osgood, Edward	1670
Osgood, Thomas	1679
Otway, Thomas (1)	1733
Otway, Thomas (2)	1786
Oudley, Robert	1708
Outlawe, Thomas	1504
Overend, George	d. 1733 (Dublin)
Owens, Robert	1741 (Dublin)
Oxden, William	1687
Paddon, Thomas	1699, 1705
Page, John	1692
Page, Thomas	1456, 1470
Page, Thomas	1747 (Bristol)
Page, William	1748
Paine, —	1661
Paine, Edward	1716
Painter, John	1718
Palmer, Ebenezer	1818
Palmer, John (1)	1702
Palmer, John (2)	1725
Palmer, John (3)	1749
Palmer, John	1763
Palmer, Richard	1759–1773 (Dublin)
Palmer, Richard (1)	1771
Palmer, Richard (2)	1803, 1822
Palmer, Roger	1634, 1642
Palmer, Thomas	1757
Palmer, William (1)	1724
Palmer, William (2)	1743

Paltock, John	1627
Paradice, Francis	c. 1675
Pargiter, William	1670
Paris, Henry	c. 1683
Park, Thomas	1743
Parke, Peter	1666
Parker, Daniel	1686, 1710
Parker, John	1768 (Limerick)
Parker, Joseph	1679
Parker, Thomas	1695
Parker, William	1809
Parker, William Thomas	1802
Parr, Norton	1742–1773 (Cork)
Parr, Robert	1703, 1767
Parrett, Thomas (Parrat)	1609
Parsons, —	1670
Partridge, John	1688 (Cornish)
Partridge, Richard	1715
Parys, John	1457, 1484
Paskin, George	1730
Paskin, Jeremiah	1752
Paskin, Robert	1757
Paskin, William (1)	1695
Paskin, William (2)	1724
Paterson, Walter	1710 (Edinburgh †)
Patience, Robert (1)	1727
Patience, Robert (2)	1734, 1772
Patrick, William	1697
Pattinson, Simon	1715, 1733
Pattison, Peter	d. 1715 (Dublin)
Paul, Peter	1791
Pauling, Henry	1659–1660
Pawson, Richard	1752
Paxton, James	1698
Paxton, John	1717
Paxton, Richard	1738
Paxton, William	1676, 1696
Payne, John (1)	1725
Payne, John (2)	1706
Pea, Francis	1798–1808 (Dublin)
Peacock, Samuel	1771, 1785
Peacock, Thomas	1783
Peacock, Thomas	1506, 1518
Peacock, Wm. (Pecok)	1492, 1511
Peake, George	1759

LIST OF THE NAMES OF PEWTERERS

Peake, Richard	1750
Pearce, James	1802
Peck, Daniel	1720
Peck, Thomas	1704
Pecke, Nicholas	1548
Peckham, Richard	1761
Peckitt, George	1655 (York)
Peddie, Andrew	1766 (Edinburgh)
Pedder, Henry	1748
Pedder, Joseph	1727
Peel, Thomas	1740 ?
Peircy, Robert	1749, 1760
Peirson, Thomas	1464–1493
Peisley, George (1)	1719
Peisley, George (2)	1738
Peisley, Thomas (1)	1693
Peisley, Thomas (2)	1732
Pelham, John	1698
Pellett, Joseph H.	1817
Pellett, Joseph R.	1788
Pellitory, Mathew	d. 1609
Pender, Charles	169–
Penman, David	1693–1715 (Edinburgh †)
Peppercorn, Thomas	1728
Perchard, Hellier (Hilary)	1709, 1745
Perchard, Samuel	1743, 1749
Perkins, Arthur	1734
Perkins, John	1713
Perkyns, Richard	1593
Perris, Henry	1662, 1678
Perris, James	1772
Perry, John (1)	1743, 1773
Perry, John (2)	1765, 1808
Perry, Richard	1757
Peters, Isaac	1725
Pett, Henry	1783
Pettit, John	c. 1685
Pettiver, Samuel	1695
Pettiver, William	1674, 1679
Phelan, Philip	1755–1767 (Kilkenny)
Philips, James	1632, 1651
Phillips, John (1)	1670
Phillips, John (2)	1784, 1815
Phillips, Thomas (1)	c. 1622
Phillips, Thomas (2)	1727

Phillips, Thomas (3)	1795, 1817
Phillips, William (1)	1719
Phillips, William (2)	1744
Phillips, William (3)	1759
Phillips, William (4)	1783
Phillips, William (5)	1787
Phillips, William (6)	1823
Phillips, William Augustus	1815
Phipps, Joseph	1722
Phipps, Robert	1738
Phipps, William (1)	1693
Phipps, William (2)	1743
Pickard, Joseph	1691
Pickering, Daniel	1723
Pickering, John	1727
Pickever, Benjamin	1773 (Dublin)
Pickever, William	1778 (,,)
Pickfat, Thomas	c. 1680
Piddle, Joseph	1685
Pidgion, John	1785
Pierce, Francis	1784
Pierce, James Henry	1798, 1825
Pierce, Tristram	1702
Pierce, William	1783
Piercy, Thomas	d. 1747 (Dublin)
Piggenitt, Bertrand	c. 1685 (,,)
Piggott, Francis (1)	1736
Piggott, Francis (2)	1741, 1770
Piggott, John	1738
Piggott, Thomas	1698, 1725
Pight, Henry	1678
Pight, John	1693
Pilkington, John	1714
Pilkington, Robert	1709
Pistoll (? Pistelly, Pistolet) Benjamin	1703
Pitcher, John (1)	1744
Pitcher, John (2)	1779
Pitt, Richard	1749, 1781
Pitt, Thomas	1778
Pitt & Dadley	c. 1780
Pitt & Floyd	c. 1780
Pixley, Joseph	1706
Platt, Thomas	1619
Plivey, William	1697

LIST OF THE NAMES OF PEWTERERS

Plumber, Daniel	1720
Plummer, John	1684 (York)
Plummer, John	1717
Plummer, Robert	1689
Pole, Robert	1717
Pollard, John	1684 (York)
Ponder, Simon	1555
Ponton, John	1708
Ponty, James	1732 (Dublin)
Poole, John	1747
Pool(e), Richard	1748
Poole, Robert	1740 (Dublin)
Poole, Rowland	1717
Pope, John	1688
Port, Richard	1723
Porter, John	1691
Porter, Luke	1722
Porter, Thomas	c. 1683
Porteus, Robert	1765, 1790
Porteus, Robert & Thomas	c. 1770
Postgate, Thomas	1765
Postgate, William	1679–1691 (York)
Potten, William	1729
Potter, George	1814
Potter, Thomas	1783
Potterill, George	1715
Potts, Isaac	1723
Potts, John	1753–1772 (Dublin)
Powell, Ralph	1612, 1621
Powell, Robert (1)	1728–1769 (Cork)
Powell, Robert (2)	1787 (,,)
Powell, Thomas	1684, 1707
Poynton, Towndrow	1684 (York)
Pratt, Alfred	1763
Pratt, Benjamin	1730
Pratt, Cranmer	1761
Pratt, Henry	c. 1670
Pratt, James	1724
Pratt, John	1709
Pratt, Joseph	1691, 1720
Pratt, Thomas (1)	1670
Pratt, Thomas (2)	1714
Prentice, Robert	1781 (Edinburgh)
Price, Benjamin	1784
Price, James	1784

Price, John	1755, 1781
Price, Thomas	1768–1807 (Dublin)
Prichard, Polydore	1649
Pridden, William	1807
Priddle, Samuel	1773, 1798
Priest, Peter	1667
Priestley, Thomas	c. 1693
Prince, John	1697
Prior, William	c. 1607
Probert, William	1688
Proctor, Francis	1631
Proctor, John	1752
Prosser, Peter	1755 (Cork)
Pruden, James	1759
Puddiphatt, Joseph	1670
Pugh, Rowland	1763
Puleston, James	1752
Puller, Samuel	1709, 1714
Purcell, Balthazar	1640 (Dublin)
Purcell, L.	c. 1800 (Dublin)
Purle, Richard	1822
Pycroft, Walter (? Ry—)	1624
Pypond, John	1461, 1464
Quick, Edward (1)	1708
Quick, Edward (2)	1714, 1756
Quick, Edward (3)	1735, 1772
Quick, Hugh	1704, 1708
Quick, John	1699
Quissenborough, Samuel	c. 1680
Rabson, Thomas	1732
Rack, Charles	1691
Rainbow, J.	c. 1690 (Edinburgh †)
Rainbow, William	1743
Rait, James	1718
Ralphs, Henry	1778
Ramsden, John	1795
Rance, Robert	1771
Randall, Charles	1699
Randall, Edward (1)	1692, 1711
Randall, Edward (2)	1715
Randall, John	1723
Randall, Lewis	1609, 1613
Randall, Robert	1748
Raper, Christopher	1694, 1696

LIST OF THE NAMES OF PEWTERERS

Ravenhill, Thomas	1699
Rawlins, William	1652, 1668
Rawlinson, Benjamin	1749
Rawlinson, James	1749
Rawlinson, John	c. 1675
Rawlinson, Thomas	1756
Rawson, James	1774
Raymond, Benjamin	1749
Raymond, James	1749
Raymond, John	1691
Raymond, Thomas	1756
Rayne, Joseph	1893
Raynolde, Anthony	1623 (Dublin)
Raynolde, Thomas	1545–1551 (Dublin)
Read, Isaac	1743
Read, Joseph	1727
Read, Samuel	1688
Read, Thomas	1753
Reade, Simon	1660
Reading, Roger	1675
Reading, Theophilus (Ridding)	1679
Redfearn, Thomas	1756
Redhead, Anthony	1684, 1695
Redhead, Gabriel	1667
Redknap, Peter	1713, 1720
Redman, William	1569, 1574
Redshaw, John	c. 1674
Redworth, John	1635 (Dublin)
Reech, Charles	1723
Reeve, Isaac	1754
Reeve, John	1818
Reeve, Joseph (1)	1786, 1807
Reeve, Joseph (2)	1810
Reeve, William	1815
Reeves, John	1714
Reid, H.	1850 (Glasgow)
Reid, Robert	1718 (Edinburgh †)
Relfe, Edward	c. 1680
Rendale, John (? Kendale)	1451, 1462
Rendall, Hugh	1670
Render, Charles	1699
Renston, John	1527, 1532
Renton, John	1687
Reo, Edward	1560, 1588
Rewcastle, Morgan	1687

Reymers, James	1703
Reynold, Thomas	1716
Reynolds, Henry	1746–1796 (Kilkenny)
Reynolds, John	1616–1639 (Dublin)
Reynolds, Robert (1)	1704
Reynolds, Robert (2)	1761, 1767
Reynolds, Thomas	1669
Reynoldson, John	1693
Rhodes, Thomas	1730, 1746
Rice, Joseph	1719
Rice, Matthew	1719
Rice, Richard	1595 (Dublin)
Rich, Charles	1812
Rich, George	1812
Rich, Robert	1781
Rich, William	1820
Richards, Richard	1709
Richards, Timothy	1699
Richards, William	1768
Richardson, Charles	1668
Richardson, Edmund	1542, 1576
Richardson, J.	1709
Ridding, Joseph	1701, 1735
Ridding, Theophilus (Reading)	1679
Ridding, Thomas (1)	1685, 1697
Ridding, Thomas (2)	1699
Ridge, Gabriel	1698
Ridgley, William	1691, 1731
Ridgeway, William	1691
Righton, Samuel	1737
Riley, Nathaniel	1670
Rind, Thomas	1675
Road, Nicholas	d. 1609
Roaffe, George	1600
Roaffe, Jasper	1600
Roane, George	d. 1759 (Dublin)
Roberts, Edward	1685
Roberts, George (1)	1722
Roberts, George (2)	1801
Roberts, James	1714, 1725
Roberts, John	c. 1614
Roberts, Oliver	1627, 1644
Roberts, Philip	1742, 1753
Roberts, Richard	1733

Roberts, Thomas (1)	1688
Roberts, Thomas (2)	1693
Roberts, Thomas (3)	1727
Roberts, William (1)	1618
Roberts, William (2)	1727
Roberts, William (3)	1762
Robeson, Richard	c. 1598
Robins, James (1)	1718, 1725
Robins, James (2)	1776
Robins, John	1614, 1638
Robins, Joseph (1)	1754
Robins, Joseph (2)	1819
Robins, J. Henry	1802
Robins, Luke	1761
Robins, Obedience	?
Robins, Thomas	1740
Robinson, Christopher	d. 1759 (Dublin)
Robinson, George (1)	1783, 1808
Robinson, George (2)	1819
Robinson, John	1717
Robinson, John	d. 1758 (Dublin)
Robinson, William	d. 1652 (Newcastle)
Robinson, William, jun.	1819 (? London)
Roden, John	1696
Rodwell, Henry	1665–1683 (York)
Rodwell, Thomas	1697 (,,)
Rodwell, William	1677–1684 (,,)
Roe, Thomas	1749
Rogers, John	1703
Rogers, John	d. 1762 (Cork)
Rogers, John Smith	1764–1779 (,,)
Rogers, Thomas	1774 (,,)
Rogers, Philip	1708
Rogers, William	1758–1780 (Cork)
Rogers, William	1783
Rolls, Thomas (1)	1690
Rolls, Thomas (2)	1713
Rolt, John	1716
Rooke, George	1670
Rooke, Richard	1748, 1777
Rooker, Joseph	c. 1685
Rose, Edward	1691
Ross, Edward	1803
Rothwell, John (1)	c. 1670
Rothwell, John (2)	1756

Rouse, G.	1668
Rowe, Anthony	c. 1700
Rowe, Francis	1691
Rowe, Wm.	1507
Rowell, William	1726
Routledge, John	1670
Rowlandson, Stephen	1550, 1563
Rowles, Thomas	1732
Royd(en), Elizabeth	
Royedon, John (Roysdon, Rowdon)	1519, 1532
Royse, Lawrence	1742
Royston, —	1620
Royston, Ambrose	1597, 1609
Rudd, Anthony	1629
Ruddock, Philip	1690
Rudsby, Andrew	1712
Rudsby, John	1712
Ruffin, Thomas	1790, 1808
Rumball, John	1670
Rumball, Robert	1691
Rumbold, John	1694
Russell, Francis	1766 (Limerick)
Russell, John	1747 (,,)
Russell, Thomas	1611
Russell & Laughton ?	(London)
Rutland, Robert	1806
Rydge, William	1612
Ry(e)croft, Walter (Pycroft ?)	1614
Rymill, Thomas	1691
Rymott, William	?
Sadler, Robert	1684–1692 (York)
Sall, George	1775 (Dublin)
Sall, John	1771
Salmon, Ferdinando	1699
Salmon, Thomas	1742
Sanders, Simon	? (Bideford)
Sanderson, John	1684 (York)
Sandys, William (Sands)	1690, 1703
Sankey, Humphrey	1710
Sansby, John	1810
Sarney, Richard	1745
Saunders, Henry	c. 1680

LIST OF THE NAMES OF PEWTERERS

Saunders, John (1)	c. 1675
Savage, John (1)	1714, 1739
Savage, John (2)	1746, 1758
Savage, Silvester	1788–1827 (Dublin)
Savell, Jacob	1748
Savidg(e), John	1683
Sayers, Roger	1672
Scarlet, Samuel	1744, 1756
Scatchard, Robert	1756, 1761
Scattergood, John	1732
Scattergood, Thomas (1)	1700, 1733
Scattergood, Thomas (2)	1736, 1775
Schleicher, J. H.	1802
Scott, Benjamin	1656
Scott, James	1708
Scott, John	1629 (Edinburgh)
Scott, Richard	1562
Scott, S.	1670
Scott, Samuel	1705
Scott, William (1)	1779 (Edinburgh †)
Scott, William (2)	1794 (,, †)
Seabright, Charles	1685
Seabright, White	1707
Seabroke, Robert	1776, 1794
Seabrook, John	1812
Seager, James	1706 (Dublin)
Seaman, Timothy	1764
Seare, William	1705
Seaton, —	1689
Seawell, Edward	1779, 1797
Secker, James	1663–1692 (York)
Seddon, Charles	1669
Sedgwick, Giles	c. 1690
Sedgwick, John	? (Leeds)
Seears, Roger	1651
Seeling, John	1656
Selby, Richard	1571
Selby, Robert	1712
Sellman, Thomas	1612
Sellon, John	1740
Sepper, Robert	1692
Sewdley, Henry	1706, 1738
Sexteyn, Wm.	1476, 1503
Seymour, George	1754–1795 (Cork)
Seymour, Henry	1793–1817 (,,)

Seymour, John	1779	(Cork)
Seymour, Nicholas (1)	1739–1763	(,,)
Seymour, Nicholas (2)	1790–1817	(,,)
Seymour, William	1817	(,,)
Seymour, W. & Son	1820	(,,)
Shaboe, Thomas	1773	
Shackle, Thomas (1)	1680, 1686	
Shackle, Thomas (2)	1701	
Shakle, John	1685	
Shakle, Tobias	1685	
Sharle, Christopher	1670	
Sharp, Durham	1754	
Sharp, John	1692	
Sharrock, Edmund	1742	
Sharwood, James	1748, 1776	
Shath (?), Thomas	1680	
Shaw, James (1)	1693	
Shaw, James (2)	1785	
Shaw, James (3)	1796	
Shaw, John (1)	1726	
Shaw, John (2)	1776	
Shayler, William	1734	
Shearman, Francis	1772 (Dublin)	
Sheffield, —	c. 1603	
Shelton, Ellis	c. 1614	
Sheve, John	1768–1796 (Dublin)	
Shephard, Andrew	1692	
Shepherd, David	1810 (Cork)	
Sheppard, Robert	1602, 1619	
Sheppard, Thomas	1704	
Shercliffe, Hector	1786 (Dublin)	
Shermar, Joseph	1767	
Sherstone, Thomas	1693	
Sherwin, Joseph	1726	
Sherwin, Stephen	1709	
Sherwood, William (1)	1700	
Sherwood, William (2)	1731	
Sherwood, William H.	1774	
Sherwyn, John (1)	1528, 1547	
Sherwyn, John (2)	1572, 1578	
Shirley, James	1818–1840 (Dublin)	
Shorey, Bartholomew	1721, 1749	
Shorey, John (1)	1692, 1720	
Shorey, John (2)	1708, 1711	
Shorey, John (3)	1738	

LIST OF THE NAMES OF PEWTERERS

Short, John	1694
Shortgrave, N.	1689
Shoswell, James	1736
Shryve, Thomas	1591 (Dublin)
Shurmer, Richard (Shermar)	1693
Shygan, Nicholas	1640 (Dublin)
Shypwaysshe, Arnold	d. 1350
Siar, William	1633, 1641
Sibbald, Alexander	1605 (Edinburgh)
Sibbett, James	1600 (,, †)
Sibley, Henry	c. 1690
Sibthorp, Joseph	1699
Sidey, Edward	1772
Silk, John (1)	1652, 1658
Silk, John (2)	1694, 1700
Silk, Vincent	1663
Silver, David	1744
Silvester, William	1746
Simkin, James	1659
Simpkin, James	1639 (Dublin)
Simpkins, Thomas	1670
Simpson, James	1536–1567
Simpson, John (1)	1760
Simpson, John (2)	1771
Simpson, Ralph	1512–1538
Simpson, Robert	1631 (Edinburgh †)
Simpson, Thomas	1728 (,, †)
Simpson, George	1757–1796 (Dublin)
Singleton, Leonard	1619
Sisson, —	1754 (Dublin)
Sivedall, Henry	1699
Skepper, Robert	1692
Skin(n), John	1679
Skin(n), Thomas	c. 1673
Skinner, John	1679
Skinner, Richard	1738
Skinner, Robert	o. 1735
Slacke, John	1522
Slade, Charles	d. 1754 (Dublin)
Slade, William	1754 (,,)
Slaughter, Nathaniel	1781
Slaughter, Richard	1732, 1742
Slow, Joseph	1702
Slow, William	1716
Smackergill, William	1610

Smalley, John	1691
Smalley, Samuel	1695, 1701
Smalman, Arthur	1713
Smalpiece, Richard (*Smallpece*)	c. 1685
Smalpiece, William	1710
Smallwood, William	1462, 1469, 1486
Smart, John	1768
Smile, Thomas	1674
Smite, George	1672
Smith, Anthony (1)	1702
Smith, Anthony (2)	1708
Smith, Benjamin (1)	1714
Smith, Benjamin (2)	1730
Smith, Carrington	1801
Smith, Charles	1765, 1789
Smith, Christopher	1730
Smith, Daniel (1)	c. 1620
Smith, Daniel (2)	1731
Smith, Emmatt	1683 (York)
Smith, George (1) (? John)	1623
Smith, George (2)	1712
Smith, George (3)	1768, 1795
Smith, Henry	1724
Smith, Isaac	1795, 1813
Smith, James	1732
Smith, James Edward	1764
Smith, John (1)	1656
Smith, John (2)	1702, 1709
Smith, John (3)	1716
Smith, John (4)	1724
Smith, John (5)	1765
Smith, John (6)	1770
Smith, Joseph (1)	1699, 1706
Smith, Joseph (2)	1811
Smith, Laurence	1810 (Dublin)
Smith, Maurice	1770
Smith, Richard	1684, 1705
Smith, Richard	1733
Smith, Robert	1675 (York)
Smith, Rowland	1734
Smith, Samuel	1728, 1753
Smith, Thomas (1)	1669
Smith, Thomas (2)	1684, 1689

LIST OF THE NAMES OF PEWTERERS

Smith, Thomas (3)	1705
Smith, Thomas (4)	1709
Smith, Thomas (5)	1731
Smith, Thomas (6)	1739
Smith, Thomas (7)	c. 1754
Smith, Thomas (8)	1761
Smith, William (1)	1691
Smith, William (2)	c. 1712 (Edinburgh)
Smith, William (3)	1732
Smith, William (4)	1799
Smith & Leapidge	c. 1760
Smithe, Thomas	1616, 1632
Smithy, Richard	17—
Smyth, George	1660
Smyth, Humphrey	1678
Smyth, William	c. 1610
Smythe, Anthony	1587
Smythe, Nicholas	1538
Smythe, Thomas	1460
Smyther, George	1612
Snape, Elias	1724
Snape, William	1764
Snell, Samuel	1670
Snow, Samuel	1681
Snoxell, Edward	1706
Snoxell, John	c. 1670
Snoxell, Richard	1709
Sogrove, John	1451
Somers, Robert	1571
Somerton, William	1730
Somervell, James	1616 (Edinburgh)
Southey, William	1811
Southwell, Charles	1713
Spackman & Grant	1731
Spackman, James (1)	1704, 1742
Spackman, James (2)	1781
Spackman, John	1723
Spackman, Joseph (1)	1749, 1761
Spackman, Joseph (2)	1784
Spackman, Joseph & James	c. 1790
Spackman, Joseph & Co.	c. 1780
Sparling, Joseph	1714
Sparrow, Francis	1746
Spateman, John	1755
Spateman, Samuel	1719, 1750

Spencer, Thomas	1702
Spicer, John	1699
Spicer, Richard	1735
Spiller, Joseph	1818
Spilsbury, James	1773
Spinks, John	1815
Spinks, Thomas	1793
Spooner, Richard	1726, c. 1748
Spring, Pentlebury	1717
Spring, Thomas (1)	1714, 1720
Spring, Thomas (2)	1756
Squires, Benjamin	1815
Squires, Nicholas	1716
Stacey, Edward	1715
Stafford, Edward	? 1718
Stafford, George	1730, 1740
Stanbrow, John	1694
Stanbrow, Samuel	1728
Stanley, Francis (1)	1690
Stanley, Francis (2)	1722
Stanton, James	1815
Stanton, Robert (1)	1773
Stanton, Robert (2)	1810, 1818
Stanton, William	1810
Staples, Henry	1817
Staples, Richard	1618, 1623
Staples, William	1698
Starkey, Benjamin	1753
Starkey, James (1)	1708
Starkey, James (2)	1748
Statham, Robert	1690
Steel, Peter	1797
Steevens, James	1753
Stent, John	1709
Stephens, John	1771
Stephens, Lawrence	?
Stevens, James (1)	1748
Stevens, James (2)	1753, 1774
Stevens, John (1)	1724
Stevens, John (2)	1756
Stevens, John (3)	1821
Stevens, Jonathan	1744
Stevens, Philip	1709, 1716
Stevens, Thomas	1716, 1732
Stevens, William (1)	1697, 1710

Stevens, William (2)	1729
Steventon, Richard	1603, 1614
Steward, John (1)	1590, 1608
Steward, John (2)	1634
Steward, John (3)	1641
Steward, Moses	1712
Steward, Rowland (1)	1694
Steward, Rowland (2)	1720
Steward, Thomas	1694
Steward, Toby (Tobias)	1626, 1630
Stewart, Thomas	1781 (Edinburgh)
Stiff, William	1790
Stiles, Henry (1)	1688
Stiles, Henry (2)	1760
Stile(s), John	1696, 1730
Stock, John	1616 (York)
Stode, John (Stood)	1527, 1537
Stizzeken, Thomas	1726
Stone, Edward	1695
Stone, Edward	d. 1702 (Dublin)
Stone, Isaac	1736 (,,)
Stone, John	1768 (,,)
Stone, Thomas	1684, 1692
Stoneley, William	1766
Stout, Alexander	1733
Stray(e), Ralph	1578, 1594
Stribblehill, John	1722
Stribblehill, Thomas (1)	1693
Stribblehill, Thomas (2)	1704
Stribblehill, Thomas (3)	1742
Street, Robert	1742
Street, Thomas	1750
Strickland, John	1703
Stringfellow, William	1756
Strong, Francis (1)	1736, 1746
Strong, Francis (2)	1759
Sturt, Walter	1679
Sturton, Anthony	1702
Styan, Henry	1723
Sullivan, Thomas	1820 (Waterford)
Summers, John	1697, 1747
Sutton, William	1697 (Cork)
Swaine, Lawrence	1670
Swan, R.	?
Swanborough, Thomas	1741

Swanson, John	1766
Swanson, Thomas	1753, 1777
Sweatman, John	1766
Sweatman, Nicholas	1698
Sweatman, Samuel (1)	17—
Sweatman, Samuel (2)	1728
Sweatman, Samuel (3)	1803
Sweeting, Charles (1)	1658
Sweeting, Charles (2)	1685
Sweeting, Charles (3)	1688, 1717
Sweeting, Charles (4)	1716
Sweeting, Henry	1631, 1646
Sweeting, John (1)	1659, 1661
Sweeting, John (2)	1707
Swift, Cornelius	1770, 1814
Swift, William Cornelius	1809
Swindell, Thomas	1705
Swingland, Joshua	1723
Swinnerton, Richard	c. 1608
Swinton, Thomas	1713
Syde, John	1680 (Edinburgh †)
Sykes, Anthony	1610
Symmer, David	1692 (Edinburgh †)
Symontoun, James	1694 (,, †)
Symons, Robert	1570
Syward, John	1350
Syward, William	d. 1368
Tabe, Matthew	1729 (Cork)
Tabor, Richard	1706
Tait, Adam	1747 (Edinburgh †)
Tait, John	1700 (,, †)
Talbut, Elisha (1)	1748
Talbut, Elisha (2)	1776
Tallent, William	c. 1599
Taudin, Jacques (or James) (1)	1663–1679
Taudin, James (2)	1680
Taudin, James (3)	1688
Tanner, William	1702
Taylor, Abraham	1651
Taylor, Anthony	1614
Taylor, Cornelius	1610 (Edinburgh †)
Taylor, Ebenezer	1819
Taylor, George (1)	1722

LIST OF THE NAMES OF PEWTERERS

Taylor, George (2)	1764, 1783
Taylor, James	1666
Taylor, John	1783
Taylor, Richard (1)	1509, 1529
Taylor, Richard (2)	1670
Taylor, Robert	1535, 1551
Taylor, Samuel	1734, 1748
Taylor, Thomas (1)	1704, 1716
Taylor, Thomas (2)	1737
Taylor, Timothy	1760
Taylor, William (1)	1670
Taylor, William (2)	1728
Taylor, William Gardiner	1819
Teale, John	1685, 1690
Tedder, Richard	1688 (Cornish)
Templeman, Thomas	1667, 1697
Tennent, George	1706 (Edinburgh †)
Terrall, Francis	1712
Terry, Leonard	1684–1708 (York)
Terrys, Charles	c. 1610
Theobald, John	1723
Theobald, William	1764–1791
Thickness, Samuel	1736
Thomas, John	1695
Thomas, Josiah	1717
Thomas, Philip	1731
Thomas, Walter	1756
Thomas, William	1722
Thomings, Samuel	1760
Thompson, Benedictus	1674
Thompson, Gilbert	1668 (Edinburgh)
Thompson, Paul	1733
Thompson, Robert	1643–1663 (Edinburgh)
Thompson, Thomas	1755
Thompson, William	1738
Thorndell, Richard	1752
Thorogood, Nicholas	1634
Thurgood, John	1497, 1529
Thursby, Thomas	1684 (York)
Thurston, Thomas	1738
Tibbing, William	1685
Tidmarsh, Ann	1728
Tidmarsh, James (1)	1701
Tidmarsh, James (2)	1734, 1750
Tidmarsh, John	1713, 1752

Tidmarsh, Richard	1714
Tidmarsh, Thomas (1)	1691, 1721
Tidmarsh, Thomas (2)	1709
Tilyard, Thomas	1702
Tinsley, Thomas	1695
Tisoe, James (1)	1733, 1764
Tisoe, James (2)	1764
Tisoe, John	1738, 1774
Titerton, Robert	c. 1698
Tolley, Edward	1805
Tomkins, James	1708
Tomlin, Daniel	1735
Tomlin, William	1765
Tompson, R.	1576
Toms, Edward	1744, 1783
Tonkin, Matthew	1749
Topliff(e), Richard	1684 (York)
Torbuck, Peter	1739
Tough, Charles (1)	1667
Tough, Charles (2)	1689
Toulmin, George	1797, 1805
Tovey, William	1787, 1801
Towers, John G.	1809
Towers, Robert	1771, 1807
Towers, William	1781
Towgood, George	1764–1797 (Cork)
Towns, William G.	1808
Townsend & Compton	1770–18—
Townsend, Benjamin	1744
Townsend, Edward	1730
Townsend, Geo. Herbert	1810
Townsend, John (1)	1748, 1784
Townsend, John (2)	1778
Townsend, J., and Reynolds, R.	c. 1760
Townsend, Richard	1670
Townsend, William	1699
Trahern(e), Edward	1685, 1718
Trapp, John	1695
Travers, Henry	1720
Treasure, John	1758
Tredaway, William	1710
Tregian, Alexander	1688 (Cornish)
Tregian, Richard	1688 (,,)
Trenchfield, William	1696

LIST OF THE NAMES OF PEWTERERS

Trew, James	c. 1675
Trewalla, Charles	1689
Trewallon, Charles	1731
Triggs, John	1763 (Cork)
Triggs, Nathaniel	1688 (Cornish)
Tristam, Robert	1757
Trout, John	1689
Tubb, John	?
Tunwell, Richard	1804
Turberville, Daubeny	1703, 1714
Turner, Benjamin	1765
Turner, Nicholas (1)	1561
Turner, Nicholas (2)	1606
Turner, Peter	?
Turner, Samuel	1790
Turner, Stephen	1694
Turner, William	1702
Turner, William Robert	1815
Turnour, John	1453
Turnour, Robert	1498
Twiddell, Nicholas	1741
Twist, John	1611
Twogood, —	179– v. Towgood
Tylsh, Nicholas	1581 (Dublin)
Ubly, Edward	1716, 1727
Ubly, John (1)	1722
Ubly, John (2)	1748
Ubly, Thomas	1741, 1751
Underwood, George	1712
Underwood, Jonathan	1698
Underwood, Matthew	1752
Urswyke, Thomas	1516, 1540
Usher, Thomas	c. 1739
Vallat, Richard	1637 (Cork)
Vaughan, John	1753, 1792
Vaughan, T.	
Vaughan, Walter	c. 1603
Vaughan, William	1773
Venables, William	1772
Veitch, Robert	1725 (Edinburgh †)
Verdon, Thomas	1751
Vernon, Richard	1650
Vernon, Samuel	1674

Vickers, T.	176–? (Sheffield)
Vile, Thomas	1669, 1675
Villers & Wilkes	1818–1825 (Birmingham)
Villers, William	1720–1825 (,,)
Vincent, John	1685
Virgin, George	1817
Viveash, Simeon	1756
Vokins, B.	c. 1670
Vooght, James	1774
Waddle, Alexander	1714 (Edinburgh †)
Waddoce, Thomas	cf. Woodhouse
Wade, William	1785
Wadsworth, William	1780
Waid, Jane	1684–1699 (York)
Waidson, George	1709
Waight, Thomas	1702
Waite, John	1706
Wakefield, John	1809
Wakefield, Richard	1720
Waldby, Dionysius	1759
Walker, James	1643 (Edinburgh)
Walker, James	1745
Walker, John (1)	1617
Walker, John (2)	1713
Walker, John (3)	1748
Walker, Nicholas	1465, 1473
Walker, Patrick	1607 (Edinburgh †)
Walker, Patrick	1631 (,,)
Walker, Ralph	1614
Walker, Richard	1616 (York)
Walker, Samuel	1660 (Edinburgh †)
Walker, William (1)	1739
Walker, William (2)	1787
Wall, Christopher	1704
Wallbank, Miles	1670
Wallden, Thomas	1797
Waller, Robert	1779
Wallis, John	?
Wallis, Robert	1739
Walmsley, John	1702
Walmsley, John	c. 1712 (Gainsborough)
Walmsley, Simon	1716
Walsh, Piers	1685 (Dublin)
Walsh, Walter	1483, 1489

LIST OF THE NAMES OF PEWTERERS 215

Walter, John	c. 1603
Walter, Thomas	1620 (Huntingdon)
Waltham, Thomas	1669
Wandsworth, Thomas	1575, 1585
Waple (?), Thomas	1698
Ward, Edward	1670
Ward, James (1)	1693
Ward, James (2)	1711
Wardrop, J.	? (London)
Wardman, Baldwin	1743
Wareing, John	1698
Wareing, Samuel	1714
Warham, Peter	1759
Waring, John	1555
Warkman, Richard	1697, 1727
Warkman, William	1713
Warrener, Richard (Waryner)	1561
Wass, Robert	1712
Wastell, Clement	c. 1655
Waterman, Henry	1693
Watkins, William	1738
Watmouth, William	1704
Watson, David	1660–1679 (Dublin)
Watson, George	1697
Watson, John	1671 (Edinburgh)
Watson, Joseph	1713
Watt, William	1783
Watterer, Thomas	1686, 1709
Watts, James	1749
Watts, John (1)	1725, 1760
Watts, John (2)	1749
Watts, John C.	1779, 1780
Watts, Thomas	1744
Watts & Harton	c. 1800
Waylett, Samuel	1691
Waylett, William	1701
Weaver, William	1801
Webb, Christopher	1669
Webb, George	1641 (Dublin)
Webb, Isaac	1705
Webb, Joseph	1695, 1726
Webb, Richard	1692, 1699
Webb, Thomas	1714
Webb, William (1)	1600

Webb, William (2)	1751
Webber, I.	(Barnstaple)
Weir, John	1701 (Edinburgh †)
Weir, Robert	1646 (,, †)
Weir, Thomas	1631 (,, †)
Welford, James	1727, 1754
Welford, John	1760, 1788
Wells, Edmund	1772
Wells, James	1777
Wentworth, Moses	c. 1675
Wescott, Abel	1670
Wescott, Henry	1640
Wescott, John	c. 1670
Wescott, Wilson	1752
Westcott, Thomas	1761
Westcott, William	1667
West, John	1729
West, Moses	c. 1680
Westwood, Joseph	1706
Wetwood, Humphrey	1602
Wetwood, Katharine	1633
Wharram, Ralph	1756
Wharton, Arthur	1684 (York)
Wheeler, George	1732
Wheeler, Thomas	1692
Wheeler, William	1701
Wheeler, William	1728
Wheelwright, Francis	1683–1686 (Dublin)
Wheely, Robert	1666
Whitaker, Benjamin	1695, 1712
White, John (1)	1670
White, John (2)	1755
White, John	1684–1726 (York)
White, John	1468 (Dublin)
White, Joseph (1)	1658
White, Joseph (2)	1747
White, Philip	1778
White, Richard	1695, 1729
White, Richard	1477–1487 (Dublin)
White, Samuel (1)	1696
White, Samuel (2)	1729
White, William	(Rotherham)
White, William (1)	1640
White, William (2)	1702
White, William (3)	1736, 1743

LIST OF THE NAMES OF PEWTERERS

White, William (4)	1751, 1772
White & Bernard	c. 1715
Whitear, William	1749
Whitebread, James	1735
Whitehead, Joseph	1721
Whitehede, John	1463, 1475
Whiteman, Benjamin	1692
Whiteman, William	1758
Whitfield, Charles	?
Whiting, John	1480
Whiting, Thomas	1701
Whittington, Robert	1757
Whittle, Francis	1715, 1731
Whittle, William	1760
Whittorne, John	1701
Whitwood, Humphrey	1592
Whyt, George	1676 (Edinburgh)
Whyt, John	1619 (Dublin)
Whytbe, Thos.	1551
Whyte, Robert	1805 (Edinburgh)
Widdowes, J.	1672
Wiggin, Abraham	1707
Wiggin, Henry	1690
Wiggin, John	1738
Wigginton, Thomas	c. 1730
Wigley, John	1713
Wigley, Thomas	1699
Wikelin, William	1758
Wilb(e)y, Wm.	1467, 1498
Wildash, George	1820
Wildman, Richard	1728
Wilkes, Edward Villers	1825–1835 (Birmingham)
Wilkes, Matthew	d. 1642 (Cork)
Wilkes, Richard	1708
Wilkinson, George	1742
Wilkinson, John	1764 (Dublin)
Wilkinson, John	1764–1775 (Dublin)
Wilkinson, Oliver	d. 1762 (Dublin)
Willey, Allen	1670
Willey, Mary	c. 1750
Willett, Edward	c. 1684
Willett, Richard	1666
Williams, A.	n.d. (Bideford)
Williams, —	1750 (Falmouth)
Williams, Anthony	1608

Williams, Edward	1697
Williams, John	1688 (Cornish)
Williams, John (1)	1697
Williams, John (2)	1719
Williams, John (3)	1724
Williams, John (4)	1729
Williams, Robert	1689
Williams, Roger	1755 (Cork)
Williams, Thomas (1)	1670
Williams, Thomas (2)	1698
Williams, Thomas (3)	1741
Williamson, Charles	1715
Williamson, James	1647–1677 (York)
Williamson, Richard	1677–1700 (,,)
Williamson, Richard	1553
Willis, Nicholas	1529
Willison, Thomas W.	1795
Wills, William	1733
Willshire, T.	1795 (Bristol)
Willson, Edward	1684 (York)
Wilmore, Edward	1670
Wilmore, Samuel	1758
Wilmotte, B.	——
Wilson, Daniel	1690
Wilson, George	1773 (Lurgan)
Wilson, Henry	1749
Wilson, John	1502
Wilson, John	1732
Wilson, Joseph	(——)
Wilson, John	1732 (Edinburgh †)
Wilson, Thomas	1801
Wilson, William	1758
Winchcombe, Thomas	1691, 1697
Wingod, John	1748, 1766
Wingod, Joseph (1)	1721, 1767
Wingod, Joseph (2)	1811
Winter, George	1701
Wintle, Charles	1785
Wiseman, Robert, jun.	1747
Withebed, Richard	1670, 1678
Withers, Benjamin	1719, 1730
Withers, William	1667, 1692
Witte, Ludwig	1815
Witter, Samuel	1676, 1682
Wittich, J. Christian	1820

LIST OF THE NAMES OF PEWTERERS

Wood, Henry	1768, 1786
Wood, John	1612, 1618
Wood, Robert	1551
Wood, Robert	1678, 1701
Wood, Robert	1700
Wood, Thomas (1)	1580, 1596
Wood, Thomas (2)	1705
Wood, Thomas (3)	1792
Wood, Tobias	c. 1598
Wood, William (1)	1589
Wood, William (2)	1726
Wood, William (3)	1736
Wood & Hill	(1067)
Wood & Michell	c. 1735
Woodehouse, Nicholas	c. 1541
Woodeson, John	1708
Woodford, John	1669
Woodhouse, Thomas	1549, 1565
Woodley, Thomas	1743
Woodnoth, Benjamin	1670
Woods, Samuel	1820–1840 (Waterford)
Woodward, Robert	1699
Wooldridge, Robert	1749
Wooldridge, Robert	1795
Wormlayton, Joseph	1691
Wormlayton, Fulk Humphrey	1701
Wormlayton, Richard	1749
Wratten, Robert	1718
Wright, Alexander	1732 (Edinburgh †)
Wright, Harman	1766
Wright, James	1780 (Edinburgh †)
Wright, John	1717, 1743
Wright, Nicholas	c. 1630
Wright, Richard	1712
Wright, Thomas	c. 1700
Wright, Thomas S.	1803
Wright, William	1764, 1772
Wroghan, Edward	1645–1665 (York)
Wyatt, John	1718
Wyatt, Thomas	1723
Wyatt, William	1688 (Cornish)
Wycherley, Thomas	1613, 1627
Wyer, Daniel	1754 (Dublin)
Wyeth, William	1733

Wylls, Charles	1734
Wylie, J.	1852 (Glasgow)
Wynder, Richard	1474–1499 (York)
Wynn, Jacob	1687
Wynn, John	1746, 1763
Wynslaye, John (Wynsley)	1525
Yalden, George	1732
Yalden, Martin	1691
Yates, James	1826 (Birmingham)
Yates, James Edward	1802
Yates, John	1741
Yates, Lawrence	1738, 1757
Yates & Greenways	(Birmingham)
Yates, Richard (1)	1777, 1783
Yates, Richard (2)	1803
Yates & Birch) Yates, Birch & Son)	(London)
Yeates, George Allinson	1763
Yewen, John	c. 1700
Yorke, Edward	1735, 1772
Yorke, James Samuel	1773
Youle, John	c. 1691
Young, Thomas	1693
Young, William	c. 1590
Younghusband, John	d. 1700 (Newcastle)

CHAPTER XIII

THE TOUCH PLATES

(Thoroughly revised, from the originals impressed on the 5 Touch Plates preserved at Pewterers' Hall.)

NOTE.—Names, dates, and parts of names and dates in parentheses are conjectural, for the most part being supplied from the Lists of Freemen and Yeomen, the lists of Officials of the Pewterers' Company, articles in museums and collections, and from various rubbings. L. = Took up his livery; M. = Master of the Company; S. = Steward; W. = Warden of the Company; Y. = became a Yeoman of the Company; s. b. c. = small beaded circle; v. s. b. c. = very small beaded circle; p. c. = plain circle; b. o. = beaded oval; l. p. o. = large plain oval; p. o. = plain oval; p. l. = with sprays of palm-leaves at the edges of the punch; p. l. c. = palm-leaves crossed; p. l. c. t. = palm-leaves crossed and tied; b. p. = between pillars. The horizontal lines are inserted to show the lines of touches on the touchplates, and so to facilitate reference.

It would be possible to hazard conjectures as to many more of the initials in these touches, but it had only been done when there was some peculiarity in the combination coupled with corroborative evidence from the initials of the names of the Liverymen and of the Yeomanry, or from other sources. In some cases where earlier conjectures have been proved to be correct, the brackets have been omitted.

Touch Plate I. (Dimensions $19\frac{1}{2} \times 13\frac{3}{8}$ in.)

1. R. L. in an oval; a comet between the letters. (Robert Lucas. M., 1667.)
2. JOHN SILKE in b. c.; below an indistinct device. Is it meant for a leaf and silkworms? (W., 1652, '55; M., '58.) (Struck twice.)
2a. Illegible except 10s.
3. A. M. in v. s. b. c.; device, two pewter pots with date between, [16]63. (? Anth. Mayors. W., 1667, '68.)
4. [TH]EOPHILUS READING; device, a winged caduceus with two stars above (p. l.)

5. N. K.' in b. c.; a hand grasping a slipped rose. (? Nicholas Kelk. W., 1663; M., '65, '81, '86.)
6. T. H. in b. o.; with a crowned heart. (P. b. c.) (? Thomas Howard or Haward. W., 1658; M., '66.)
7. R. M.; beaded circle with bird and [16]63.[1] (? Ralph Marsh. W., 1657, '62; M., '65. Or Rich. Millet or Mellet. W., 1660.)
8. W. G.; device, a dolphin (?) in b. c.
9. I. F. in s. b. c.; a harp.
10. A. F. in s. b. c.; harp rising out of a crown.
11. S. I. in s. b. c.; a lamb and flag. (? Samuel Jackson.)
12. T. D. in b. c.; a griffin's head erased, on a torse, with crown above. (? Thomas Dickinson. L., 1667.)
13. N. H. in s. b. c.; a talbot, with date 1662.
14. I. B., with crowned rose-en-soleil. (? James Bullevant. L., 1667.)
15. I. L. in s. b. c.; six flowers between the rays of an estoile. (? John Lackford. 1664.)
16. In l. p. o., at the top E. SONNANT[2] in a label; below this, in a cartouche between two palm-branches, a rose with large crown above it; and on a scroll above, I. TAUDIN [JAQUES TAUDIN]. (This man was a Frenchman, naturalized, who became a freeman in 1657.) His name is often misspelled. (Cf. No. 344 and 557.)
17. T. H.; in a p. o. a fleur-de-lys, with a palm-spray on either side; at the top a crown, with the letters T. H. (Thomas Hudson).
18. FRA. LEA; a pomegranate with p. l. (He seems to have had two similar punches, but of different sizes.) (Cf. No. 39.) (L., 1664.)
19. JO. INGLES in a b. o. on a scroll in the upper part of a cartouche; below this 1671 and two hands grasped (p. l.). (A large manufacturer of pewter.)
20. W. A. in a very small touch. (? William Austin or William Ayliffe.)
21. I. H. (?) in v. s. b. c., with a mermaid.

[1] "It was ordered by the Court Dec. 11th 1662-3 that all Laymen doe alter there tutches within fourteene dayes wth ye date of 1663," and on the 17th it was ordered that "all tutches bee ... registered in a booke at ye hall wthin a month." (Welch, ii. 130.)

[2] It is probable that TAUDIN inserted E. SONNANT in order to show the quality of his pewter. Later TAUDINS, and also JONAS DURAND, did the same, and the E is often badly stamped and looks like H or R.

22. C. S. in s. b. c., with a spray of rose.
23. I. L., with date [16]63.
24. W. C. in b. c., with date 1663. (? William Cross. L., 1659.)
25. W. A. in b. c.; a female figure, with anchor, W. A., and date [16]63. (Vide No. 20.)
26. W. I. in b. c.; with a bush in the centre.
27. R. I. in c.; with a shepherd's crook surmounted by a crown, and date 1657.
28. R. H. in b. c.; two naked boys (? the sign Gemini) holding hands; above them a sun in splendour; between them [16]64.
29. H. P. in b. o., with foliage; below it an interlaced knot and a letter, very indistinct. (? Henry Perris. S., 1662; W., '68, '73; M., '78.)
30. I. F. in b. c.; with a cardoon on a stalk, and 166(?). (? John Finch.)
31. T. C. in s. b. c., with an eel, and date [16]63.
32. I. C., with a griffin's head erased in a 12-pointed star.
33. G. (? A.) in b. c.; a unicorn gorged with a mural crown and a rose near the forefeet.
34. S. A. in b. c.; a griffin's head erased, two stars, and [16]66.
35. B. B. in b. c., with 1664 and a star.
36. T. F. in b. o., and a fountain. (Thomas Fontaine or Fountain. L., 1670.)
37. R. M. in b. c.; with a wheatsheaf with R. M. (? Robert Moulins. M., 1676.)
38. WILLIAM BURTON in b. c.; a hand holding a sceptre. (W., 1675, '80; M., '85.) (Cf. No. 354.)
39. F. L. in s. b. c.; a pomegranate. Probably Francis Lea. (Cf. No. 18.)
40. (Close to this is a smaller touch, giving a pomegranate, without initials. This was probably F. Lea's smaller touch; he had also a larger one with the same device.)
41. P. D. in s. b. c.; an hour-glass with P. D. (? Peter Duffield. L., 1657. W., '64; M., '72, '88.)
42. P. B. in b. c., with a leaf.
43. W. A. in s. b. c., with hand grasping a dagger. (? Wm. Archer. W., 1646, '49; M., '53.)

Here follows an almost indecipherable touch. Part of it shows a hand and a retreating figure.

44. I. H. in b. c.; a crown, two crescents, and I. H.
45. T. B. in b. c., with a bell. (? Thomas Bell, 166–).

46. R. H. in b. c.; also a locust or grasshopper, with three stars and date [16]56. (Ralph Hulls. W., 1671, '77; M., '82.) (Cf. No. 208.)
47. N. M. in an octagon, with a windmill and 1640 (over it is scratched 1640). (? Nathaniel Mills.)
48. T. S. in b. c.; a portcullis, crowned, with T. S. Each initial is also apparently crowned. (? Thomas Stone. L., 1667; W., '87, '90; M., '92.)
49. . . . C. in b. c.; a cock with a crown above. (? Humphrey Cock. L., 1679.)
50. G. R. in s. b. c., with a double-headed eagle and date [16]63.
51. I. C. in b. c.; a head (? the king's head), crowned.
52. D. I. in b. c., with the lion and the lamb lying down together.
53. W. W. in b. c.; a cock and date [16]55. (William Withers.)
54. H. B. in b. c., between three pears.
55. L. in s. b. c.; and a talbot.
56. E. A. in b. c., with a hand grasping an anchor.
57. C. T. in s. b. c., with a lion rampant.
58. W. M. in s. b. c., with two voided lozenges, one over the other, with date 1666.
59. W. A. in l. b. c. (badly punched); a man under a tree.
60. H. C. in b. o., with a crown and a sword, also portcullis and two stars of five points, and [166]6.
61. E. H. in s. b. c.; device, a ploughshare (?) and a star.
62. E. H. in s. b. c.; device, a sword surmounted by a crown. E. H.
63. Peter Braile[s]for[d]; in oval; a shield charged with cinquefoil berries, with palm-spray on either side; above, a ducal crown with the name; p. l. c. t. below. (L., 1667.)
64. T. C. in b. c.; device illegible.
65. F. G. in b. c., with a crescent.
66. W. B. in b. c., with a pegasus and date.
67. I. B. in s. b. c., with a boar and [16]65.
68. W. I. in v. s. b. c., with 1665 (or ?6).
69. W. M. in circle, with crescent and trace of a star.
70. T. S. in v. s. b. c., with a pellet and 1663.
71. Vincent Silk in b. c.; for device a bale of silk (?).
72. W. W. in v. s. b. c., with a sword.
73. W. P. in v s. b. c., with spray of leaves and [16]63.
74. W. P. in b. c., with spray as a background, but date 1655. (Probably an earlier touch of the same pewterer.)

THE TOUCH PLATES

75. W. E. in l. b. o.; Father Time with hour-glass and scythe. (Cf. No. 201).
76. C. in s. c. b.; winged male figure, to waist only.
77. W.; a pelican in her piety, dated 164(?). (?1664.)
78. W. W.; two thistles in s. b. c., with date [16]66.
79. A. W. in s. b. c., with three roses. (Vide No. 154.)
80. T. V. in s. b. c., with a spray of stalks and fruit.
81. W. D. in b. o., with an antelope's head within a crown.
82. T. B. in s. b. c., with talbot's head erased on a torse.
83. S. M. in s. b. c., with a dolphin.
84. R. A. in b. c., with a squirrel.
85. T. H. in b. c.; on a torse an arm erect with a heart held in the hand. (Each initial seems to be crowned.)
86. T. B. in s. b. c., with a bird flying; above, a sun or star.
87. I. N. in b. o.; device illegible (? a hydra erased); (? 66).
88. F. M. in s. b. c., with two crossed keys, with star above.
89. T. L. in s. b. c., with a knot.
90. I. I. in s. b. c., with a key.
91. A. L. in b. c.; a hand grasping a hammer, with, above it, the word GRADATIM. (? Adam Langley. L., 1667.)
92. I. H. in v. s. b. c., with two keys erased, and the date [16]63.
93. R. S. in oval, with cockatrice on a cap of estate (?).
94. R. M. in b. c., with a rabbit or a hare, and a wheatsheaf.
95. B. C. in b. o., with crowned thistle below, and a pegasus' head and wings above.
96. A. R. in b. c.; device, a sleeved arm holding a bundle of rods with date in full, 1646.
97. JOHN BULL; a bull's head in b. c., with two stars.
98. H. H. in oval (no rim), with three hearts (one and two), surmounted by a crown (p. l. c. t.). (? Henry Hartford.)
99. I. H. in b. c.; a strake, with fret (? or a checker-board); double punched, and therefore indistinct; date 1663.
100. ? P. or S. P. in b. c.; a cardinal's hat.
101. E. H. in a s. shield, with two keys crossed.
102. R. I.; a diamond, small, with two rods crossed.
103. I. I. in a shield, with a key; date [16]68.
104. P. P. in p. c., with beacon; 1668. (? Peter Parke, or Peter Priest.)
105. W. L. in shield, with beaded edge and date 1668.
106. T. V. in an oval, with an anchor with legend SPES EST, all contained in a frame of two palm-sprays, twice crossed. (? Thos. Vile. L., 1669.)

107. W. D. in v. s. b. c., with date 1668. (Wm. Daveson, or Wm. Dyer. L., 1667.)
108. B. B. in v. s. b. c., with a peacock and [16]68.
109. G. R. in s. b. c., with a two-headed eagle, and [16]68. (? Gabriel Redhead. L., 1668.)
110. T. S. in s. b. c., with rose and 1668.
111. W. P. in s. b. c., with spray of leaves and [16]68.
112. I. H. in pointed shield, with a crook and a key, and [16]68.
113. W. A. in a diamond, a hand grasping a crook or hook, and [16]68. (? William Aylife. L., 1667.)
114. W. D. in b. c., with fleur-de-lys and [16]68. (? Wm. Daveson. L., 1667. Or Wm. Dyer. L., 1667.)
115. S. A in b. c.; a lion rampant. (? Sam. Attley. L., 1667.)
116. I. I. in b. c., with a crowned hammer and 1666.
117. T. R. in b. c.; a woolsack (?), and [16]63.
118. W. . . . (?) in b. c., with slipped rose and two stars.
119. T. S. in s. b. c., with sun or star and 1663.
120. I. A. in p. c., with a lion and a thistle and three stars.
121. R. H. in s. b. o., with a portcullis and [16]66.
122. THOMAS TEMPLEMAN in o.; a temple and a man (p. l. c. t.) (S., 1667; W., '95; M., '97.)
123. S. L.; a crowned knot (p. l.). (? S. Lawrence on Touchplate II. Cf. No. 357.) (S. Lawrence. L., 1667.)
124. H. F. in s. b. c., with 1668.
125. T. E.; a limbeck on a stand.
126. E. N. in s. b. c., with a bird-bolt.
127. R. T. in b. c., with a stag's head couped, and [16]68.
128. WILLIAM HALL, with a globe and the signs of the zodiac.
129. I. T. in b. c., with a pair of scissors or shears.
130. I. H. in p. o., with an owl between in two palm-sprays.
131. RICHARD COLLIER in b. c. (? as rebus, a collier bearing a sack.) (L., 1669.)
132. I. C. in s. b. c., with a thistle.
133. L. D. in b. c., with a heart transfixed by two arrows, and 1668.
134. R. M. in b. c., with a closed helmet.
135. L. DYER; a shield with three anchors upon it; palm-spray on either side; on a scroll the name Dyer; on a scroll above this LONDINI. (L., 1668; W., '69; M., '75. Cf. No. 691.)
136. I. H. in p. c., with a wheatsheaf and [16]63.
137. In tiny square-pointed shield a crown and [16]77.
138. F. P. in b. c., with a pelican in her piety.
139. W. P. in b. c., with a pear, or fig.

THE TOUCH PLATES

140. CHRIS: RAPER in circle, with a dagger between three castles (p. l. c.). (L., 1676; W., '88, '92; M., '94.) (Repeated.)
141. C. H. in b. c.; a swan with wings raised. The same device was used later by Samuel Burch, whose touch is not in the Touch-plates.
142. JOHN BURTON in o., at the top; below, a dog and a crown (p. l. c. t.).
143. NICH. HUNT[ON]; beneath, a crown; below this (p. l. c. t.) on a torse, a demi-lion holding a stag's head in his paws. The touch is very indistinct. (L., 1667; S., '70.)
144. C. C. H. in s. b. c., with two cinquefoils.
145. The next touch is illegible, except a shield with a greyhound's head erased, on a torse; above, a crown and the word LONDON.
146. T. D. in s. b. c.; and castle.
147. T. A. in p. o.; beneath, a crown; below, a plough (p. l. c.).
148. F. C. in b. c.; a maidenhead, crowned.
149. R. A. in p. o., over an anchor between a harp and a crown; all between palm-branches.
150. C. R. in s. b. c., with lotus-flower. The same touch repeated later on with [16]74.[1]
151. I. M. in b. c., on either side of a fat boy's face, and date [16]68. (? John Mann or John Molton.)
152. G. ROOKE; device, a bird on a trumpet (p. l.).
153. In b. o. a ship in full sail, with initials I. C. This touch is stamped sideways.
154. A. W. in s. b. c., with three roses. (Repeated from above. Cf. No. 79.)
155. I. G. in s. b. c., with bugle-horn and a star. (J. Cooper, 465.)
156. IERE. LOADER in b. c., with a sun in splendour on an anchor. (Jeremiah Loader. Y., 1670.)
157. E. G. in pointed shield, with star and fleur-de-lys.
158. R. P. in s. b. c., with bird and [16]71.
159. H. N. in s. b. c., with Neptune and a trident, riding on a sea-horse.

---

[1] In 1674 " a new pewter plate to strike touches on " was bought for 6s. 6d. This may be the second plate now at Pewterers' Hall, but it is doubtful, as there are touches on the first plate later than 1674; one at least is dated 1680, and there are several for 1676, 1677.

160. R. B. in an oval, with skull surmounted by a crown; both initials crowned.
161. W. H. in oval, with St. George and the dragon (p. l. c.).
162. R. W. in s. b. o., with female dancing figure and date [16]69 (? Venus on a shell on the waves). (? Robert Wheeley.)
163. DAVID BUDDEN in large b. c., with device of a hand grasping a scroll. (Y., 1670.)
164. G. C. in p. o., with ostrich (p. l.).
165. R. S. in v. s. c.; device illegible (? a hook); date [16]69.
166. R. I. in b. c., with windlass and well.
167. W. SMITH; below this LONDINI (?); as device, Prince of Wales' feathers (p. l. c.).
168. WILLIAM PAXTON in p. o.; below, a crown; on a shield a sun crowned (p. l. c. t.). (L., 1676; M., '96.)
169. T. W. in shaped octagonal punch, [16]70, with four stars.
170. I. I. in b. c., with two hands clasped, 1670.
171. IOHN WESTCOTT on two scrolls; on a crowned shield three crowns (p. l.). (J. W., probably a son of Henry Wescott or Westcott. S., 1640.)
172. I. C. in b. c.; an open left hand, crowned.
173. T. H. in b. c.; crossed sceptres, with a bird perched above, a crown above, and 1670 below.
174. E. H. in diamond-shaped touch divided into four compartments.
175. ROGER READING in plain oval; device on a shield, a mermaid (?) crowned (p. l. c. t.). (Y., 1675.)
176. I. S. in s. b. c., with the worm of a stile.
177. R. G. in b. c., with a crown. (? Robert Gibson, c. 1668.)
178. THOMAS TAYLOR in two scrolls; on a shield a lion passant (p. l.). (An earlier touch of his bore the word LONDON. M., 1704.)
179. I. C. in b. c.; a sun in splendour, rising from clouds.
180. IOSEPH PARKER on a crown, above two hands, each with a hammer (p. l. c.). (S., 1679.)
181. D. B. in small pointed shield, with a helmet; date 1670. (Daniel Barton. Cf. No. 298 and 573.)
182. B: VOKINS in large b. c.; name on a scroll, with a crown above, and below, three fleurs-de-lys (p. l.). (c. 1670.)
183. L. R. in b. c.; device, a roebuck.
184. LEWIS IAMES on scrolls in p. o.; device, a hand grasping a thistle (p. l.).
185. B. E. in b. c.; a hawk, with raised wings.
186. I. H. in b. o.; a harp with a hammer above it.

187. I. G. in b. c., with three trees.
188. E. D. in eight-foiled stamp, with four large pellets and twelve smaller ones, and 1672.
189. S. W., with a crescent and a bird; all defaced.
190. I. B. in s. b. c.; a flaming heart, crowned.
191. I. WIDDOWES in l. b. c.; a crown above, and a mitre below (p. l. c. t.).
192. R. H. in spider's web.
193. W. R. in b. c.; a shepherd with crook, sheep and dog.
194. THO. HUNT in l. b. c.; a greyhound running (p. l. c. t.).
195. JOHN ROTHWELL; a hand holding fleur-de-lys (p. l. c. t.).
196. S. W. in b. o., with harp.
197. JOHN ALLEN, Anno 1671; device, the eagle and child (p. l.). (L., 1679; W., '97.)
198. E. L. with palm tree; nearly illegible owing to double stamping.
199. S. I. in b. c.; a dove with olive-branch in its beak; [16]71.
200. RO: WOOD in l. b. c.; above the scroll a crown; below, a man with a bow, and a child; palm-leaves. (L., 1678; W., '91, '98; M., 1701.)
201. I. P. in b. c., with Father Time and an hour-glass and scythe. (For similar device see Touch No. 75, with letters W. E.)
202. EDWARD RELFE, LONDON; device, a child playing with a dog (p. l. c.).
203. W. M. in b. c.; a crowned heart (p. l.).
204. WILL: HOWARD; a leopard's head, ducally crowned; (p. l.). (W., 1693, 1700; M., '02.)
205. ... ADKINSON; a cupid with bow and arrow (p. l. c.).
206. C. C. interlaced, with a dolphin embowed, crowned; 1672.
207. L. W. in b. c., with a large pellet, crowned.
208. RALPH HULLS in p. o.; a grasshopper (p. l. c.). (Similar device in touch No. 46, dated 1656. W., 1671, '77; M., '82.) The name is given HULL in Welch.
209. MABBERLE[Y]; an eagle perched on a knotted snake (p. l.). (? Stephen Mabberley. Y., 1675.)
210. T. R. in b. c.; in exergue Charing Crosse; Queen Eleanor's Cross; 1672.
211. P. I. in b. c., with spray of flowers (? a pink) and [16]72.
212. RIC. MEDDOM on scroll and crown; device on shield, a nowed snake (p. l. c.). (Y., 1672.)
213. S. Q. in beaded heart, with an arrow and a key; [16]73. (? Sam. Quissenborough.)

214. DANIEL MASON in a double floral border; with device, Samson (or Hercules) between two pillars.
215. ROBERT GREGGE; device on a crowned shield, a slipped trefoil; 1673.
216. T. H.; in s. b. c. a negro's head.
217. G. H. in p. o., three hearts with a crown above (p. l. c. t.). Same device as H. H., No. 98, above.
218. M. W. in pointed shield, with a hand grasping a crook; [16]73.
219. IOHN REDSHAW; device, a running greyhound.
220. C. R. in b. c., with tulip-flower and [16]74.
221. W. S. on shield with three fleurs-de-lys; above, a crown on a cushion. The whole in a l. b. c. (p. l.).
222. B. T. in p. c., with crown and crossed sword and sceptre (p. l. c. t.). (? Benedictus Thompson.)
223. THO: SKIN (LONDON), in a scroll at the top with crown; below (p. l.), an angel with palm-branch; [16]73.
224. I. W. in s. b. c., with pair of scales.
225. In b. c. an alembic and a bell.
226. On two touches, THO: M[I]DDLET[ON]; device (p. l.), a man standing behind a tun holding a bunch of grapes and a hammer.
227. IAMES TREW; device, a scallop-shell and five pellets (p. l.).
228. EGERTON BRYAN; device, the arms of Bryan, three piles (p. l. c. t.). (A device used by W. Tibbing in No. 334.)
229. EDWARD [MUMF]ORD; device, a griffin's head erased and a crown (p. l. c. t.). (Y., 1712.)
230. H. Q. in s. b. c., with cross paty and 1674. (Hugh Quick.)
231. I. S. in s. b. c., with fruit-tree and [16]74.
232. SAMUEL HAND on a circular band; device, a crown, two stars and a hand.
233. THOMAS RIDDING in two scrolls; device, a pelican in her piety in a shield, crowned (p. l.). (L., 1685; W., '97.)
234. FRA. DURNFORD in oval; device, a seal with a fish on his back (p. l.).
235. N. ? M. in b. c., with a mill and wheel. (Nathaniel Mills.)
236. I. IACOMB, or IACOMBE; device, a dove with an olive-branch (p. l. c. t.). (Josiah Jacomb. L., 1669; S., '75.)
237. IOHN IOHNSON . LONDINI; device, the moon and seven stars (p. l.). (S., 1666.)
238. HENRY PRATT; device, a cat (p. l.).

239. I. SAUNDERS; device, an elephant's head erased (p. l.).
240. W. A. and an acorn in a beaded octagon, crowned.
241. H. H. in b. o. (LONDON); a ship and an anchor. (? Humphrey Hyatt.)
242. H. F. in s. b. c.; and boar's head.
243. In l. o.; device, a running hare, and S.F. Above in a label, LON[D]ON.
244. I. E. in b. c.; a duck and [16]75.
245. GEORGE HALE. 1675; device, a running hare.
246. R. W. in s. b. octagon, [16]75; device, a tun.
247. C. T. in diamond-shaped touch with beaded edge, and [16]75.
248. WILL. ONLY; a phœnix (p. l. c. t.).
249. IOHN RAWLINSON . . . LONDINI; device, a mitre (p. l.).
250. I. K. in s. b. c., with two stars.
251. IOHN SNOXELL; device, a globe. 1675.
252. IOHN SMITH; device, two hearts point to point; 1675 (p. l.).
253. H. I. in circle with three horseshoes; [16]75.
254. . . . TON, LONDON; device, a stag tripping (p. l. c. t.).
255. IOHN TEALE. CHARING CROSS; device, a man on horseback (? Charles I). (L., 1655, '90.)
256. IOHN HULLS, LONDINI; three Prince of Wales' feathers encircled by a crown (p. l. c. t.). (W., 1705; M., '09.)
257. E. I. in circle, with ram's or antelope's head couped.
258. { T. S. in s. b. c., with pomegranate; 1675.
     { T. S. in s. b. c., with pomegranate; 1675. (Both are presumably touches by the same pewterer.)
259. THO: KING in large oval; two hands holding an anchor, crowned; date 1675 (p. l. c. t.).
260. O. R. in b. c., with a wrench and [16]76. (? Obedience Robins.)
261. FRA: KNIGHT; device, a beehive. (L., 1685; S., '92.) (Vide No. 3451.)
262. I. COX, LONDINI; device, two cocks respectant, with a crown above (p. l.). (L., 1679.)
263. T. R. in b. c., with three tulips; [16]75.
264. A. R. in small shield, with lozenge; [16]76.
265. [EN] MORSE; device, a winged griffin (p. l. c. t.). (? Badly struck for HEN :)
266. G. C. or C. C., with crown and horseshoe (p. l. c. t.); 1676.
267. T. G. in b. c., with key and four lozenges.
268. H. B. in crowned shield, with lion's head erased (p. l. c. t.); 1676.

269. D. H. in shield with key; [16]76.
270. I. G. in b. c.; on a shield, the arms of the City of London (p. l.).
271. P. H. in b. c., with a monkey (?); [16]76.
272. Tho. Deacon in l. o. with moulded rim; a flaming beacon (p. l. c.). (Cf. No. 364.)
273. G. V. in s. b. c., with anchor and a heart.
274. [Ralp]h Benton, London, [16]76; device, three nutmegs (?) (p. l.) (L., 1681.)
275. I. R. in s. b. c.; a castle with star above, with 6 quatrefoiled flowers; [16]76.
276. T. Cutl[er]; three fleurs-de-lys and three small stars, in shield, crowned (p. l. c.).
277. H. L. in b. c., with three trees.
278. Will. Hurst; device, a peacock (p. l. c.).
279. H. P.; a dexter hand holding a quill pen; 1677. (? Henry Perrin.)
280. Wil. Adams; device, a unicorn's head erased (p. l. c.)
281. T. H. in p. c., no rim, with beacon; 1676.
282. I. I. in diamond-shaped touch and [16]77; device (?).
283. Robert Morse, London; in a band; device, a cloven skull with a bone in the cleft of a pipe in the mouth; on the band a porcupine. (Y., 1702; L., '09.)
284. I. H. in b. c., with two keys in saltire.
285. Moses West, London, over a shield with a chevron, and three leopards' heads (p. l).
286. R. T. in b. c.; a goat with nine stars. London.
287. To. Shakl[e] in b. c., with a crown between two plumes of ostrich feathers, crossed. (For the name cf. No. 416.)
288. Sa: Mabbs, London, with a fleur-de-lys issuing from a rose (p. l.). (L., 1685.)
289. W. W., with an elaborate double knot (two trefoils joined by a loop) and [16]77. (William Westcott, L., 1667.)
290. I. P. in b. c.; a maidenhead.
291. W. K. in b. o., with mullets and an illegible date. (? Wm. Kelke.)
292. R. D. in diamond, with star; 1677.
293. Io. Castle, Londini; a lion issuing from a castle (p. l.).
294. Ed. Groves; device, a man in a grove; below, a label with London.
295. I. Dove in plain oval; a dove perched on a nowed serpent. (W., 1703.)
296. T. T. in shield with beaded edge; a crown and [16]77.

297. I. L. in s. b. c.; a two-handed pot and 167[8].
298. DA. BARTON; device, a helmet and [16]78 (p. l. c.). (W., 1692, '99.) (Cf. No. 573.)
299. I. W. in s. c., with four stars; 1678.
300. IOHN STRIBLEHILL; stamped double; device, a mitre between two palm-branches. (Another of this name became a liveryman in 1693.)
301. RICHARD SMITH in b. c. with three roses. (W., 1696, 1702; M., '05.) (Cf. No. 860.)
302. HENRY HATCH in label over earl's coronet; below a shield with dog (or lion) (p. l. c.).
303. ROB. LOCK, 1678; device, a padlock or fetterlock (p. l. c.). (L., 1692.)
304. THOMAS LEACH; a two-headed eagle, with a crown above (p. l.). (Cf. No. 725.)
305. I. C. in b. c., with fox carrying off a goose.
306. FRA. PARADICE in exergue of octagon; device, two angels with flaming swords guarding the Tree of Life.
307. IONAT. BONKIN; device, two cardoons or teazles (p. l. c.). (Y., 1699.) (Cf. No. 722.)
308. WILLIAM MORS; device illegible[1] (? a trivet); p. l. at sides. (? for MORSE. Cf. No. 265.)
309. F. L. in b. c., with skull and crossbones; on top of circle a porcupine.
310. W. V. in b. c. with [16]78 and a monumental pillar (? the Monument or Duke of York's Column).
311. I. N. in shield, with [16]78 and fleur-de-lys.
312. R. F. in b. c., with windmill.
313. W. G. in b. c., with winged Pegasus.
314. F. (?) P. in b. c.; a horse with a crown over its hind-quarters; 1678.
315. C. B.; device, a building (? the Royal Exchange); badly punched.
316. IER: COLE; device, a maidenhead with a dagger below (p. l.). (L., 1692.)
317. I. P. in b. c., with three roundels.
318. R. B. in lozenge, with scalloped edge with flory cross; [16]78.
319. A monogram, indecipherable, badly punched; above, a lion passant (p. l.). (? Thomas Kirk.)
320. DAN. BLACKWELL in b. c.; device, a bell with seven roses upon it.

[1] Mr. R. C. Hope describes it as a scorpion stinging itself.

321. T. F. in b. c.; a bird on a torse, a belled hawk, with a crown above, and [16]79.
322. W. P. in b. c., with fleur-de-lys and [16]79.
323. J. B. in a framing of two feathers, crossed and tied.
324. I. GRIMSTED; device, a wheatsheaf, crowned (p. l. c.).
325. T. W. in b. c., with handbell; 1679. (Thos. Wright. Cf No. 399.)
326 T. C. in b. c.; within a coiled snake (?)
327 LUKE PORTER; device, a porter (?); [16]79 (p. l. c.).
328 WILL FLY.; device, a fly (p. l. c.). (L., 1691.)
329 I. H., with thistle, crowned, a bird perched on each leaf.
330. A. R. in bordered c., with three crosses paty. (? Anthony Redhead.)
331. N. R. in foliated lozenge, with 1679.
332. N. I. in b. o., with three lozenges and [16]79.
333. RANDALL ANDREWS; device, a face (?)
334. WILLIAM TIBBING; device, a pheon (p. l.).
335. W. N. in s. shield, with crescent and two stars; [16]87.
336. E. T. in b. o., with three cranes, one and two.
337. I. S. with mermaid.
338. WILLIAM HALL in l. b. c., with a dexter arm grasping some object in the hand.
339. B. C. in b. c.; a bird on a torse and 165(1?) [? 1687].
340. F. P. in b. c., with plough; 1680.
341. THOMAS BETTS in b. c.; device, an ass's head erased, with a bugle-horn.
342. Below this is a tiny punch upside down, with W. H. and [16]87.
343. H. T. in b. c., with a hammer, a pair of shears and [16]80 (badly punched).
344. IAQUES TAUDIN; on another scroll E. SONNANT; a rose and crown (p. l.). (Cf. Nos. 16 and 557.)
345. FRACIS KNIGHT; device, a spur. (Cf. No. 261.) (p. l.).
346. RIC. SHURME[R] on a shield, crowned; a cinquefoil ornament (p. l.).
347. THOMAS CLARKE; in centre a two-tailed merman with hands uplifted (p. l. c. t.). (W., 1699, 1706; M., 1711.)
348. ? G. [EVERI]TT in b. c.; a hand holding a thistle. (c. 1680.)
349. I. P. in b. c.; a fleur-de-lys and 1680.
350. T. PICKFAT LONDINI; device, three lions rampant; below, four roundels (p. l.).
    Two stamps follow which are only partly legible. One has the initial T . . . and a crowned rose-en-soleil;

the other WILLIAM . . .LL and a shield of arms, a fess indented and three crosslets fitchy.

351. WILLIAM CROOK[ES]; device, two swords in saltire (p. l. at sides).

The above are the names on the first of the existing touch-plates at Pewterers' Hall.

Touch Plate II (Dimensions, 17 in. × 12⅞ in.)

352. R. P. Old P[arr] Aged 152; in centre an old man; R. P. at the sides. Robert Parr, a descendant of Old Parr, was Warden in 1767.
353. G. SMITH in oval, with a plough and three roundels.
354. WILLIAM BURTON; device, a hand holding a sceptre (pl. l.). (Cf. No. 38.)
355. C. R. in b. c.; a dexter hand grasping a mace.
356. WILLIAM [HO]NE; device, a snail, large ducal coronet above (p. l.). (Y., 1688.)
357. S. LAWREN[CE], with a crown; in centre, a knot with S. L. (p. l.). (Cf. No. 123.)
358. M. C. in s. b. c., with sugar loaf and [16]76.
359. W. H. in s. b. c., with goat's head erased and gorged with a coronet.
360. F. D. (or H. D. ?) in s. b. c., with spray of oak-leaves and acorn.
361. An indistinct touch with figure of St. George and the dragon, and a name IOHNSON. (Probably RICHARD JOHNSON. Y., 1688.)
362. T. S. in s. b. c., with tankard.
363. I. M. in s. b. c., with key.
364. IOS: GARDINER; same touch as that of Tho. Deacon, No. 272; device, a beacon (p. l.).
365. EDWARD [RAND]ALL; device, a grasshopper, with crown over (p. l.). (W., 1711.)
366 IOHN BONVILE; device, a crown and six five-pointed stars (p. l.).
367. IOSEPH ROOKER; device, a unicorn's head erased (p. l.).
368. T. R. in b. c., with a Saracen's head.
369. I. SAVIDG[E]; device, Gog and Magog and a bell.
370. T. WATTERER, LONDON; device, a hand supporting a crowned anchor (p. l.). (L., 1686; W., 1709.)
371. GILES SEDGWICK in b. c.; a skull, crowned.
372. HENREY SIBLEY; device, a Catharine wheel, crowned (p. l.), with four letters (probably BLEY) beneath the wheel.

373. H. Wiggin in b. c., with a dagger. (L., 1690.)
374. N. (?) Gosle[r]; three cinquefoils (p. l.). (? Gosling, a name found later in the list of Yeomen. Cf. No. 794.)
375. Samuell [Hancoc]k; a cock upon a hand (p. l.). (L., 1689; W., 1704, 1714.)
376. [Nich] Hunton, London; device, on a torse a demi-lion holding a stag's head couped on a wreath (p. l.). (Cf. No. 143.)
377. W. A. in b. c., with [16]82; device, a man-at-arms bearing a boar's head on a pike.
378. I. C. in b. c., with floral ornament and 1683.
379. I. K. in b. c., with crescent and two stars.
380. E. C. in p. c.; a figure with a crook; 1681.
381. R. H. in b. c. and 1682; device, a right-hand glove (?).
382. B. C. in heart-shaped punch, with a mullet in base.
383. I. C. in a spiral, in a b. c.
384. I. P. in b. c., with a heart and an orb (?), and [16]83.
385. Edw. Kent, London; a unicorn leaping and a wheat-sheaf. (Y., 1688.)
386. Will—— ——; an eagle; below, a bugle-horn (p. l. c. t.).
387. Samvel [Mars]ton; device, a sea-horse (p. l.).
388. T. S., London, with a rose (p. l.).
389. R. S. in b. c.; Londini, with stirrup.
390. I. S. in shield, with four-petalled flower; [16]85.
391. —— James; device, a squirrel (p. l.). (? Anthony James. L., 1685; W., 1708; M., '13.)
392. James Carter in b. o.; device, a horse and cart.
393. I. I. in c.; device, hen and chicks.
394. T. P. in b. c.; a winged figure.
395. Hen[ry Ha]rford; an animal with large crown above it.
396. R. G. in b. c., with daisy.
397. Richard Smalpiece; a bust, crowned (p. l.).
398. P. M. London; device, a man with bow and arrow (p. l.).
399. Tho. Wright; device, a hand-bell (p. l.).
400. Will. Long; a shield, crowned; on the shield a thistle and a lion (p. l. c. t.). (S., 1707.)
401. G. G. in b. c.; a bust of a girl. (? Gabriel Grunwin, L., 1693.) (Cf. No. 677.)
402. ——; two thistles in p. l. c. t.
403. A figure kneeling on a pyre (?); 1684, with D. V. below.
404. H[enry] Saunders; device, a sun in splendour; between each pair of rays a roundel.
405. F. F. in s. c.; device, a lantern (?)
406. Thomas Marshal; device, a crowned tulip (p. l.).

407. IOSEPH PIDDLE; device, a rhinoceros and six roundels. (L., 1685.) It is wrongly spelled in the touch.
408. ——; device, Adam and Eve and the Temptation; in scroll, BRAH probably for ABRAHAM.
409. ED. WILLETT; a bird rising, perched upon a crown (p. l.).
410. Two children beneath a tree picking fruit, with initials I. C. At the foot in a scroll, CORMELL.
411. T. L. in b. c., with lock and key and [16]84.
412. E. D. WILLETT, repeated.
413. C. O. in s. shield, with a dagger.
414. A confused mark composed of the same touch struck twice; device, a winged angel or flying cupid (p. l. c. t.).
415. JOHN PETTIT; device, a unicorn (punch repeated).
416. IOHN SHAKLE in b. c. and date 1685; device, a star of many points, each alternate point bearing a six-pointed star. (For the name cf. No. 287.)
417. WILLIAM NICHOLLS; a fleur-de-lys issuing from a castle (p. l.).
418. E. A. in s. c.; device, a worm from a still.
419. S. S. in s. c., with a shepherd with a crook and some sheep.
420. I. S. in s. b. c., with a tankard and date [16]85.
421. I. M. in s. b. c., with [16]85.
422. I. D. in s. b. c., with a dexter hand holding a seal between the thumb and forefinger, and 1685.
423. C. R. in b. c., with a griffin passant.
424. I. NICHOLLS in oval, with dragon's head erased (p. l. c.).
425. EDWARD ROBERTS; device, a portcullis (p. l. c.).
426. JOHN LAWRANCE; device, a figure in Roman costume. (W., 1710, '19; M., '23). It is given as LAWRENCE in Welch.
427. I. S., in s. b. c.; a . . . (?) between two stars and 1685.
428. THO. [S]MITH, LONDON, 1675; device, a seeded pomegranate, and date 1675 (p. l.). (This punch seems ten years out of its place.)
429. THO. CARY; device, a dexter hand grasping a key, crowned (p. l. c.).
430. IOHN CO[UR]SEY; device, a cock with large crown and [16]86.
431. HEN. ADAMS, PICKADILLY; device, Adam and Eve and the Temptation. (L., 1692; W., 1713, '21; M., '24.)
432. I. D. in b. c., with flower-spray and [16]86.
433. THO. PDADON, LONDON. In a shield a bend between three fruits (?) (p. l.). (S., 1705.)

434. W. B. in b. c.; on a torse a lion sejant holding a key; date [16]85.
435. N. M. in v. s. b. c.; an inkstand, or mortar, and 1687. (? Nathaniel Munns.)
436. THOMAS SMITH; device, a salamander, with crown (p. l.). (S., 1689.)
437. In l. b. o., a shield of arms, ermine, a bend, and closed helmets on the bend; no name.
438. W. W. in b. c., with cock and [16]85. (William Withers.)
439. I. W. in b. c., with alembic and worm; [16]86.
440. D. S.; a figure (? S. Stephen) being stoned by three others.
441. DANIELL PARKER in b. o.; two hands grasping hammers, above, an earl's coronet. (L., 1686; W., 1710.) (Cf. 180.)
442. CHARLES ——; device, a winged arrow; [16]86 (p. l.).
443. THOMAS ROBERTS; device, a lion rampant, a crown and two stars above (p. l.).
444. W. B. in b. c., with a cinquefoil, a star, and two roundels.
445. E. W. in b. c., with a lily, crowned.
446. T. B. in diamond, with triangular ornaments in border, with two stars.
447. WILL. HALL, LONDON; in b. c., a palmer (?). (Y., 1687.)
448. RICHARD WHITE; device, a pelican in its piety, and date 89 (p. l.). (L., 1696; W., 1717, '25; M., '29.)
449. IAMES TISOE; device, a portcullis (p. l. c. t.). (W., 1764.) (Cf. No. 854.) (Above this touch is No. 450.)
450. H. I. in b. c., with a rose and two roundels.
451. E. O. or E. Q. LONDON in b. o.; device, a wheel of Fortune.
452. N. SHORTGRAVE; device, a demi-boar on a torse. (Below this touch is No. 453.)
453. Io. STILE; device, a dove perched on a nowed snake (p. l. c.). (W., 1719, '27; M., '30.)
454. E. or Z. (?) H. in b. c.; a lion rampant to sinister, holding a harp, over both a crown; date 1689. (Above this is No. 455.)
455. I. V. in s. c.; a wheatsheaf within a crown. (? John Vincent, 1685 L.)
456. IOHN FRENCH, 1687, LONDON; device, a harp (p. l. c. t.).
457. A. C. in b. c.; device, a dexter hand holding a rose. (This punch is repeated.) (? Alexander Cleeve. Y., 1688.) (Cf. No. 791.)
458. RICHARD [F]EBBA[RD]; device, a sovereign (Queen Elizabeth?) throned and crowned (p. l.). (Y., 1690.)

459. T. P. in p. c., with three horseshoes, three small pellets and [16]89.
460. IOHN CAMBRIDGE; device, a heart with palm-leaves surmounting a clasped book; 1687 (p. l.).
461. IOHN HOLLY, LONDON; device, a comet and various roundels. (Y., 1689.)
462. ROBERT NICHOLS;[1] an eagle on a globe (p. l.).
463. F. CASTLE, LONDON; a castle (p. l.).
464. IOHN TROVT; a trout and a crown above (p. l.).
465. IO: COOPER, LONDON; a ship in full sail (p. l.).
466. CHARLES HVLSE, [16]90; device, three fleurs-de-lys and five small roundels (p. l.). (Y., 1690.)
467. E. S., LONDON; a rose. (p. l. c.).
468. E. S. in s. c.; a rose and [16]90
} (Probably both are touches of the same maker.)
469. SAMUEL [HUME]; device, an interlaced knot with a wheatsheaf. (Cf. No. 598.)
470. W. E. in s. b. c., with hour-glass and six roundels.
471. T. A. O. B. (?) in monogram in s. b. c.
472. E. M. in b. c.; two busts facing, affronté, with a crown between them at the top.
473. THOMAS COWDEROY; a swan with wings addossed (p. l.). (Y., 1689.)
474. IOHN BASKERVILE; device, a rose and thistle, dimidiated and crowned. (L., 1695.)
475. E. W. in s. shield, with a triangle.
476. F. C. in b. c., with a nude figure of Venus standing in a shell on the waves. (? Francis Cliffe. Y., 1687.)
477. IAMES BRETTELL; device, three pears and three roundels (p. l.). (Y., 1688.)
478. IOHN OLIVER, LONDON; device, a seven-branched candlestick and [16]89.
479. SAMUELL JACKSON; device, a shield of arms, a chevron indented and three griffins' heads. (W., 1673, '78; M., '84, '87, '90, 1700, '14.)
480. IOHN LAUGHTON in b. o.; device, a vase of flowers.
481. DANIEL WILSON; device, a shield of arms; three coiled snakes (p. l.).
482. R. W. in b. o., with five stars; below, a cock and a fox sejant, facing; 1692.

[1] Probably a mistake for NICHOLSON whose touch I have seen as here given. ROBERT NICHOLSON was a Yeoman in 1690, Warden n 1714 and 1722, and Master in 1725. There is no ROBERT NICHOLS in any list that I have examined before 1720.

483. WILLIAM BRAVELL, a crowned beacon and [16]92, (p. l .c.).
484. WILLIAM CLARKE; device, a rose and two buds (p. l. c.). (Y., 1695.)
485. BENJAMIN WHITAKER; device, a shield of arms, three voided lozenges. (Y., 1691.) (In the list of the Yeomanry it is given Whiteacre.)
486. I. G. in b. c.; a lion rampant bearing an orb, and date [16]92.
487. I. COOKE, LONDON; a stag tripping, similar to the indistinct touch on Plate II, No. 254, between those of PRATT and TEAPE (p. l. of archaic type).
488. IOHN DONNE; device, a hand with a pawn and two smaller objects. (L., 1694; W., 1716, '23.)
489. I. S. in b. c.; a fox or cat; [16]92.
490. IOHN KENTON; device, two large six-rayed stars, I. K. (p. l. c. t.). (W., 1702, '11; M., '17.)
491. WILLIAM SANDYS; on a torse a griffin rampant. (L., 1703.)
492. THOMAS LEAPIDGE, LONDON; device, a goat and a wheatsheaf (p. l.). (L., 1696.)
493. IAMES HUGHES; device, a goat (ibex) and ducal coronet (p. l.). (Y., 1691.)
494. IOHN PAGE; device, a lion passant under a tree, and two roundels (p. l.). (Y., 1692; L., 1697.)
495. PHILLIP [RUDDY]CK; device, a duck; 1690. (Y., 1690.)
496. I. B. in b. c.; device, a bee; [16]93.
497. WILLIAM SMITH; device, three Prince of Wales' feathers and a crown above; [16]92 (p. l. c. t.).
498 IOHN FRYER in b. o.; device, a two-headed eagle surmounted by a crown and two crossed staves; at each side a rose. (Y., 1692; L., '96; M., 1710, '15.)
499 I. S. in b. c.; a lion lying down with a lamb (p. l.).
500. I. P. in b. c., with hammer; [16]93.
501. ROBERT TITERTON, dated 1698; device, a sun in splendour (p. l.).
502. W. C. in b. c.; a syringe and a worm; [16]93.
503. E. M. in b. c.; device, a giant; [16]93.
504. WILLIAM [RID]GLEY; device, Atlas supporting the world. (p. l.). (Y., 1691; W., 1731.)
505. F. B. in b. o.; arms of Bainbrigge; on shield of arms a chevron and three battle-axes.
506. H. M. in p. o.; a marigold between two ears of barley flanked by two palm-branches; in chief H. M. and six pellets with a sun or star above.

THE TOUCH PLATES

507. IOHN ELDERTON, 169–; three tuns (p. l.). (L., 1696; W., 1720, '28; M., '31.)
508. CHARLES CRANLEY; a tent and a lion of England, the arms of the Merchant Taylors' Company; on the field nine pellets (p . l. c. t.). (Y., 1692.)
509. T. WINCHCOMBE; a demi-lion (p. l.). (Y., 1691.)
510. HARRY GOODMAN; a hen and chickens. (Y., 1693.)
511. BENJAMIN BOYDEN; a figure of Justice, with a sword and a pair of scales (p. l.). (Y., 1693.)
512. I. C. in b. c., with a cock. (Above this is No. 513.)
513. I. R. in b. c.; a fox leaping over a heart.
514. IOSIAH [CLA]RK, within a l. b. o. band inclosing seven stars. (Y., 1690.)
515. GEO. HAMMOND in b. c.; a dexter arm and hand holding a two-edged dagger. (Y., 1693.)
516. SAMUELL NEWELL; device, a rose ensigned by a mitre. (Y., 1689.)
517. MARTIN BROWNE in shaped oval; a boat with spread mainsail, with moon and seven stars above.
518. GEORGE CANBY; device, a blazing castle or gatehouse and [16]95. (Y., 1694.)
519. JOHN HEATH in b. o.; a child or dwarf bearing palm-leaf.
520. R. I. in b. c.; a spray of acorn; [16]96. (? Robert Iles. Y., 1691.)
521. D. I. in centre of a dial face; [16]94 (obviously out of its place). (? Daniel James. Y., 1691, or Daniel Ingole.)
522. JOSEPH SMITH in l. p. o. with a wreath of leaves as a border; in centre the Monument. (Y., 1695.)
523. THOMAS SPRING; device, a fountain with two small birds (p. l.). (Y., 1710.)
524. C. M. in s. c., and a barrel or tun. (? Charles Middleton. Y., 1690.)
525. L. H. in small shield, with a rose and some animal.
526. L. C. in s. b. c.; a doll or puppet (?), crowned; [16]95. (? Lawrence Child. L., 1702.)
527. S. B. in a wheel inside a s. b. c. (Stephen Bridges. Y., 1692.)
528. HENRY FEILD; a mailed arm holding out a sphere (p. l.). (Y., 1693.)
529. W. CLARK, LONDON; device, a naked boy holding a heart and a pansy; [16]96 (p. l.).

Q

530. I. R.[1] in b. c., with a crescent, surmounted by a rainbow.
531. WILLIAM DIMOCKE; device, a squirrel beneath a crown.
532. GEORGE EVERARD in p. c., within a small b. c.; three stars; [16]96. (Y., 1696.)
533. W. ATLEE; device, an anchor, a rose, and two stars above (p. l.). (Y., 1696.)
534. H. BRASTED in b. o.; a sun in splendour, crowned (p. l. c.). (Y., 1692.)
535. RICHARD CLARKE; a crown, with a dolphin beneath; [16]96.
536. IOHN GISBVRNE; device, arms barry [. . .] and ermine, a lion rampant. (Y., 1691.) (The name of a Robert Gisberne occurs in the roll of Masters and Wardens. He was Master in 1691.)
537. I. C. or G. in s. b. c.; a wheel; 1697.
538. IABEZ HARRIS; a leopard's head jessant-de-lys (p. c.). (Y., 1694; W., 1734.)
539. GEORGE NORTH in b. o.; crest, on a torse a griffin's head ducally gorged. (Y., 1693.)
540. WILLIAM ELLWOOD; the King's head; [16]97 (p. l.). (Y., 1693; L., '97; W., 1722, '30; M., '33.)
541. SOLOMON IEMPSON; a lion rampant (p. l.). (Y., 1696.)
542. IOSEPH BOWDEN; a cherub's head and wings (p. l.). (Y., 1701.)
543. IOHN SVMMERS; two keys in saltire, with a crown at the crossing (p. l.). (Y., 1697; L., 1734; W., '37.)
544. A. W. in lozenge with beaded edge; 1698.
545. I. T. in lozenge with beaded edge, with a star and two cinquefoils; 1698.
546. R. W. in c., with lion rampant.
547. EDWARD STONE, [16]98; for device, London Stone. (Y., 1695.)
548. W. P. in b. c., [16]98, with two hearts.
549. THOMAS TILYARD; device, a spur and —— (?); with [16]98. (Y., 1698; L., 1702.)
550. WILLIAM GILLAM; device, a sword, point downwards (p. l.). (Y., 1698.)
551. W. M. in b. o.; a crowned heart and eight pellets (p. l.). (? Wm. Mathews. Y., 1698.)
552. W. S. in b. c., with a hand outstretched grasping a tulip or lily.

[1] Probably an ancestor of WM. RAINBOW, in Yeomanry list of 1740.

THE TOUCH PLATES

553. I. I.; an ox, with an open book above; 1700. (? John Jones. Y., 1700.)
554. IOHN BARLOW; a tulip on a plough. (Y., 1698.)
555. ROBERT DAKEN; a unicorn rampant and arms of City of London (p. l.). (Y., 1698.)
556. WILLIAM HEYFORD; device, a bull (p. l.). (Y., 1698.)
557. IONAS DURAND; device, a rose; above the rose 1699, and a label with E. SONNANT (p. l.). (DURAND was a nephew of JAMES TAUDIN, whose touch is twice given on Touch-plate I, (*a*) No. 16, and (*b*). No 344, in each case with E. SONNANT in small extra scrolls. W., 1718, '26. Another JONAS DURAND was Warden in '63.)
558. RICHARD DYER in b. o.; device, a crown. (Y., 1699.)
559. W. R. in s. b. c.; above, a sword and a pistol in saltire; below, a star.
560. BASILL GRAHAM; a hand grasping a cup or chalice (p. l.). (Y., 1699.)
561. NICHOLAS S[WEA]TMAN; device, a tree-top (?) and a crown. (Y., 1698.)
562. I. B. in s. b. c., with a gull; [16]99.
563. I. C. in b. c.; a girl's head, wreathed.
564. T. B. in b. c.; a tankard or measure; [16]99.
565. THOMAS COOKE; a bird in a hand, and a bush below; (p. l.).
566. I. W. in b. c.; a fleur-de-lys, crowned, and date 1699.
567. P. C. in b. c.; a handcart; [16]99. (? Peter Carter.)
568. EDW. LEAPIDGE, LONDON; device, a goat and a wheatsheaf. (Y., 1699; W., 1724.)
569. WILLIAM DIGGES; device, a cinquefoil (p. l.). (Cf. No. 492.) (Y., 1699.) Surmounted by a marquis's coronet.
570. CHARLES RENDER; device, a horse's head, couped. (Y., 1699.)
571. F. L., in floral wreath. (? Francis Litchfield. Y., 1697.)
572. CHARLES RANDALL; device, seven stars and a crescent (p. l.).
573. DA. BARTON, LONDON; device, a helmet; over it a hand grasping a dagger (p. l. c.). (Y., 1700. Another Daniel Barton was L., 1678; W., '92, '99.) (Cf. No. 298.)
574. W. H. in b. c., with a fleur-de-lys; 1700.
575. ANT. ROWE; a crescent, crowned (p. l.).
576. T. P., in b. c., with a stag's head, crowned; 1700.

577. BERNARD BABB; arms, a cross crosslet and three crescents (p. l.). (Y., 1700.)
578. I. E. in b. c., with a bird; [16]86.
579. THOMAS PARKER; device, a lion rampant, and seven stars, with a coronet above. (Y., 1695.)
580. THOMAS BENNET; crest, on a torse a demi-lion holding a crown (p. l.). (Y., 1700.)
581. IOHN NEWHAM; a lion passant; above, a globe (p. l. c. t.). (Y., 1699; L., 1703; W., '31.)
582. ROBERT DEANE; a statue like that of Charles I at Charing Cross. (Y., 1692.)
583. JOHN PRINCE; a dexter arm, mailed, issuing from a coronet, and grasping three ladles, or flowers. (Y., 1697.)
584. THOMAS HOPKINS; a bear and ragged staff; (p. l.).
585. IOHN YEWEN, LONDON; a hand holding out a crowned thistle (p. l.).
586. IOHN CHILD; a naked boy holding up a sceptre and a sword. (Y., 1700.)
587. I. C. in s. b. c., with a hand grasping a battle-axe; 1701.
588. In plain circle, a two-headed eagle, with two crescents. In a label portion of the name WORMLAYTON.[1]
589. SAMUELL BOSS; a tulip, crowned; 1701 (p. l.). (Y., 1695.)
590. IOHN CALCOTT; device, St. George and the dragon. (Y., 1699.)
591. I. Q. in s. b. c., with harp and a star. (John Quick. Y., 1699.)
592. THO. BUCKBY; a buck's head erased. (L., 1716.)
593. I. H. in b. c., with a lion holding a key.
594. ROBERT BORMAN; a boar's head couped; 1701. (BORDMAN in the list of Yeomanry.)
595. THO. BURGES, LONDON; a gunner and cannon (p. l.). (Y., 1701.)
596. NICHOLAS O[AKFORD]; device, a man's head (p. l.). (L., 1699.)
597. IOHN KIR[TON], 1702; a shield with five ermine bars (p. l.). (Y., 1699.)
598. GEORGE HUME; an interlaced knot and a wheatsheaf. (Y., 1700.) (Cf-. No. 469.)
599. ANTHONY STURTON; a rose and a mitre; 1702 (p. l. c. t.).

---

[1] There were two pewterers of this name: JOSEPH, Yeoman in 1691, and FULK HUMPHREY, Yeoman in 1701. The latter was probably the owner of the touch here given.

THE TOUCH PLATES

600. T. S., 1702; shield of the arms of Spencer: quarterly 1 and 4 argent, 2 and 3 gules fretty or, over all a bend sable, and three escallops or on the bend. (Thos. Spencer. Y., 1702.)
601. THOMAS FRITH; device illegible (? a kettle). (Y., 1693.)
602. THOMAS ———; device, bust of Queen Anne (p. l.).
603. N. GRANT; the arms of the Cinque Ports: the three leopards of England dimidiated with the hulls of three ships (p. l. c. t.).
604. D. B. in b. c.; a woolsack, crowned.
605. DAVID BUDDEN; a hand grasping a staff (p. l.).
606. WILLIAM ELLIS; device, a man's bust with letters P. G. (Y., 1702.) (p. l.). (Cf. No. 778.)
607. TRISTRAM PIERCE; device, a rose and thistle dimidiated and crowned. (Y., 1702.)
608. GEORGE WINTER; a star, a heart, and a marquis's coronet (p. l.). (Y., 1701.)
609. W. S. in s. b. c.; a skull surmounted by an eye.
610. THOMAS SCATTERGOOD; two hands with hammers and a rose (p. l.) (Yoo., 17; W., '33. Another Thomas Scattergood was W., 1760 and '73, and M., '74, '75.)
611. THOMAS BECKETT; a rose within a monogram. (Y., 1702; W., '31.)
612. NICHOLAS JACKMAN; a man working a handpress or jack. (Y., 1699; W., 1733; M., '35.)
613. IOHN SMITH; a chevron engrailed and six crosslets fitchy, with three fleurs-de-lys on the chevron.
614. I. S. in b. o., with a flower and sun, and a date [1]703.

This is the end of the second touch-plate. Many of the last two rows of touches are almost illegible owing to their having been carelessly punched.

Touch Plate III.[1] (*Dimensions, 18 in. × 13⅝ in.*)

615. I. T. in s. b. c., with a pear and [1]704.
616. S. P. in b. c., with heart and flowers issuing from it
617. B. C. in small stamp, with a flying bird.
618. R. R. in b. c., with fox running off with a goose, and date 1704. (? Robt. Reynolds. Y., 1704.)
619. ——— ———; a man grasping a boy by his hair and about to punish him; in the exergue PATER FIDE[LIS].

---

[1] This plate is probably the one referred to in Welch, ii. 174, as follows: "Paid John ffrith for a plate to Strike Touches on 8ˢ. 9ᵈ."

620. IOHN SAVAGE; crest, a unicorn; a star on the field. (Y., 1699. Another John Savage was Y., 1711.)
621. ROBERT IU[PE]; a rose and a crown.
622. T. H. in s. b. c.; two naked boys (? the sign Gemini) holding up a sun between them, and date 1705.
623. [HOWELL] GWILT; punch illegible, as a hole has been made here to suspend the touch-plate. (L., 1709.)
624. IONATHAN COTTON. A bird between a spray of flowers and a spread eagle; date 1704. (Y., 1704; W., '34; M., '36.) (Cf. No. 866.)
625. ROBERT PILKINGTON; a man carrying a bird on his back. (Y., 1704.)
626. DAW[BENY] TURBERVILE; a lion rampant on a crescent. (Y., 1703) (p. l.).
627. Here follows a small shaped punch, with a grasshopper and 1705 (p. l.).
628. E. H. in s. b. c.; a figure of a man (? a pikeman and his dog).
629. W. B. in s. b. c., with [16]75; crest, an eagle's head, couped, with crescent over its head.
630. GUY, EARLE OF WARWICK. Guy of Warwick as an armed figure holding the boar's head between initials T. W. (This from a rubbing sent to me was Thomas Wigley. Y., 1699.)
631. I. S., with a pear (?) and a heart, 1706.
632. THOMAS SMITH; a seated figure, apparently with a mitre.
633. THOMAS ARNOTT; (? the flower of a leek).
634. W. S., with a small book, crowned, 1706.
635. T. P. in a small touch; no device.
636. IAMES PAXTON; a sun and a marigold.
637. EVERARD GILLAM; a dagger or short sword (p. l.).
638. I. P. with a bear and a ragged staff.
639. BENJAMIN F[OST]ER; arms, a chevron ermine and three phaeons. (Y., 1706.) (Cf. No. 847.)
640. JAMES [? GREEN]; arms, barry ermine and a lion rampant.
641. RICHARD [H]ESLOPP; two sheep with long tails. (Y., 1700.) (p. l.).
642. H. H. in b. c.; a crown and tun, 1707. (Henry Hammerton.[1] Y., 1706; W., '33.)
643. ROBERT MORSE; a lion passant and crown above. (Y., 1702.) (p. l.).

[1] His touches were various. *Vide* Miscellaneous Touches in the Appendix.

THE TOUCH PLATES

644. WILLIAM TOWNSEND; a Neptune (? Father Thames) with a trident. (Y., 1699.)
645. W. F. in top of shaped punch, with star; below, a phœnix surrounded by flames; below, three fleurs-de-lys. (? Wm. Frith. Y., 1700.)
646. ROBERT CROSFEILD in large circular punch; in centre a clock-face; within the rim of the figures of the hours a crescent, a sun, and 1707.
647. TIMOTHY RICHARDS (*fecit* in interior scroll); device, a rose with Prince of Wales's plumes. (Y., 1699.)
648. R. KING in b. o.; device, a horse's head. (? Robert King. Y., 1698.) (A Richard King was W., 1745, and M., '46.) Richard King, Jr., became a Yeoman in 1745.
649. RICHARD COLLIER; arms, three cocks. (Y., 1706 W., W., '42) (p. l.).
650. T. B., in b. c., with a crescent.
651. ABRAHAM WIGGIN; a sword-hilt (?) and a crown. (Y., 1707.)
652. IOHN [BLE]WETT; a lion rampant and a pierced mullet. (Y., 1707.)
653. PHILIP ROGERS; a saltire with a stag above; at each side a rose. (Y., 1708.)
654. THOMAS SHEPPARD; a shepherd, with sheep, piping to a shepherdess. (Y., 1705.)
655. RICHARD WILKS; a lion rampant, leaning against a tree. (Y., 1708) (p. l.).
656. W. K. in s. b. c.; a star in centre with a fleur-de-lys above, a crescent below; in the other spaces two roundels, two smaller stars. (? William King. Y., 1715.)
657. EDWARD QUICK; two heads (William and Mary.) (Y., 1714.)
658. HENRY SEW[DLEY]; a heart pierced by two arrows, crossed; below, an eagle with two heads. (Y., 1706; W., '36; M., '38.) (p. l.).
659. I. P. in b. c.; two matchlocks crossed with a spiral roll or match.
660. JOHN HARRIS; crest, a dog, seated. (Y., 1709) (p. l.).
661. HELLARY PERCHARD;[1] an anchor encircled with a G. and 1709. (Hellary or Hellier P. [Y., 1709) was W., 1738, and M., '40) (p. l.).

[1] His touches were various.

662. SPACKMAN & GRANT; a fleur-de-lys, with a cross paty on either side of it; below, a crown, with a cross paty under it. (A James Spackman was W., 1732, and M., '42; E. Grant was W., '31, '40, and M., '41) (p. l. c. t.).
663. W. H. in b. c.; two hands clasped with a crown above, 1709.
664. PHILIP STEVENS; a grasshopper; above, two keys cross-wise, with a roundel between them (p. l.).
665. ROBERT OUDLEY; a rose with an acorn-spray above it. (Y., 1708) (p. l.).
666. R. I. in shaped punch; a small boat in full sail.
667. RICHARD DALE; device, a pump, or a beacon, or possibly a still. (Y., 1709.) (Cf. No. 704) (p. l.).
668. WILLIAM COX; crest, a goat's head couped, transfixed with a spear, a crown and a tent behind. (Y., 1708.)
669. I. S. in b. o.; ? an Eleanor Cross, or that in Cheapside, 1710.
670. THOMAS PEISLEY; arms, a lion rampant, with two tails. with a mullet. (*Vide* 709; this is a large stamp. Y., 1693.)
671. THOMAS GOODWIN; crest, a demi-griffin. (Y., 1707.)
672. ARTHUR ENGLEY; two crescents, with a ducal coronet above them (p. l.).
673. HENRY FEILDAR; a spray of rose-tree, with a sun shining thereon, between two pillars. (Y., 1704.)
674. G. LINDSEY; a female figure, seated, with a lance and holding the rose and the thistle;[1] by her side the arms of the City of London, and a coronet over. (? Greenhill Lindsey. Y., 1708.)
675. TIM. FLY; device, a fly (p. l.). (W., 1737; M., 1739.)
676. GEORGE SMITH; a bust of Queen Anne, facing left. (Y., 1712.) (p. l.).
677. RICHARD GRUNWIN; a portrait, full face. (Y., 1713; W., '29.) (Cf. No. 401.)
678. PETER REDKNAP; St. Peter bearing two keys. (Y., 1713) (p. l.).
679. IOHN WALMSLEY; a heart, crowned. (Y., 1702.)
680. T. I.; a rose, 1713. (? Theodore Jennings. Y., 1713.)
681. THOMAS GIFFIN; a crown, a heart and a hammer, and six stars. (W., 1751; M., '53, '57.)

[1] The rose and the thistle were the badge of Queen Anne, and they occur on many of the touches.

682. Ric. Drinkwater; a bird bearing an olive-branch on a wheatsheaf; at the sides, a snake tied in a knot, and a lion passant. (Y., 1712.)
683. W. Beamont; a lion on a cap of estate. (Y., 1706) (p. l.).
684. I. Laffar; Atlas, supporting the world, between two mullets. (Y., 1706.)
685. William Newham; b. p. a rose and a thistle on the same stem. (W., 1745.) (Y., 1708.)
686. G. V. in p. o.; a female, nude, skipping, and date 1712. (? George Underwood. Y., 1712.)
687. Iohn Osborne in large punch; a crown; and below, rose and thistle on same stem; at the bottom *Semper Eadem*.
688. A small touch is stamped at the side of No. 687, with I. W., and date [17]07.
689. Samuel Knight; b. p. an arm holding a dart. (Y., 1703.)
690. I. Wooddeson; a wood with the sun shining upon it. (Y., 1708.)
691. Law. Dyer; three anchors (p. l.). (Y., 1704; W., '26, and '28.)
692. Thomas Wheeler; Queen Anne with sceptre and orb, standing up. (Y., 1692.)
693. In° Palmer, 1714; three horseshoes (p. l.). (Y., 1702.)
694. I. E. in b. c.; a hand with a heart in it, 1714.
695. I. W. in b. c., 1715; a man walking (? a Walker).
696. In a l. p. o. without a rim, a lion's head, issuing from a marquis's coronet.
697. John Tidmarsh; a ship in full sail. (Y., 1713; W., '39, '50; M., '52.)
698. Tho[mas] Cart[wrig]ht; crest, a bird on a torse. (W., 1742; M., '43.)
699. John Ne[aton] in b. c.; a crescent and two mullets. (Y., 1714.)
700. Richard Partridge; three partridges, and a large mitre above. (Y., 1715.)
701. Thomas Webb; two swords crosswise, with a crown and three fleurs-de-lys in the under spaces. (Y., 1713.)
702. Thomas Mathews; a mermaid, with six roundels (p. l.). (Y., 1711.)
703. I. S. in b. c.; a stork with wings displayed, 1716.
704. William Meadows. This touch resembles that of Richard Dale, No. 667 (p. l.). (Y., 1714.)
705. A. C.; in plain stamp a saltire between fruit and flowers.

706. WILLIAM MILES; b. p. a wheatsheaf and a sun. (Y., 1715.)
707. THOMAS CLARIDGE; a griffin's head, erased, and two frets.
708. I. A. in a small shaped punch, with a bunch of grapes and two mullets.
709. GEORGE PEISLEY; a shield with a right hand bearing a dagger. (Y., 1718.) (Cf. No. 670.)
710. IOHN ROLT; a dolphin; above, crest: a griffin's head, couped. (Y., 1716.)
711. {IO. GRAY / IA. KING} a pelican in her piety. (John Gray. Y., 1712.) (James King. Y., 1716.)
712. In p. o., a griffin's head couped, with a snake in its mouth.
713. JOHN LANGFORD; a hand with hammer, and below, a barrel. (Y., 1719; W., '55; M., '57.)
714. SETH JONES; the Archangel Michael, crowned with scales and a sword (p. l.) (Y., 1719.)
715. FRANCIS WHITTLE; a dove with an olive-spray; below, an olive-tree (p. l.). (S., 1731.)
716. THOMAS LIN[COLN]E; a rose and a leaved thistle above it. (Y., 1718.)
717. ABRAHAM FORD; b. p. a sun in splendour shining on a wheatsheaf. (Cf. W., ii, 185, and punch of J. Blenman, p. 241). (L., 1719.)
718. IOHN CARPENTER; with globe and compasses (p. l.). Below this are
719. W. W. in small lozenge, 1721.
720. I. M. in shaped punch, with a sheep and 171-. (? 1721). (? John Merriott, or John Merrieweather.)
721. IOHN OSBORNE; a lion rampant, holding a rose or other flower (p. l.). (Cf. No. 917.) (? John Osborne, Jun. Y., 1713.)
722. IONATHAN BONKIN; a shepherd on foot with a crook and a dog; in his left hand a rose. (Cf. No. 307.)
723. RICHARD KING; a demi-ostrich with outspread wings and horseshoe in its beak. (Y., 1714; W., '45; M., '46.)
724. PEN^{RY} SPRING; a fountain with three basins; on the top a sun (p. l.). (Pentlebury Spring. Y., 1717.)
725. THOMAS LEACH; arms of London, with two swords (p. l.). (Cf. No. 304.)
726. ARTHUR SMALMAN; two nude figures holding up a crown. (Y., 1713.)

727. JOHN LANGLEY; a fleur-de-lys and two roundels, with a crown above (p. l.). (Y., 1716.)
728. W. N. in shaped punch, with fleur-de-lys and a sun in splendour. (? Wm. Nicholson. Y., 1720.)
729. BENIAMIN [WITH]ERS; a cock, and a small crown above. (Y., 1719.)
730. COLLYER in oblong label, above which is a globe on a stand. (Somewhat similar to that of J. Watts, No. 801.) (? Richard Collier. Y., 1706.)
731. IOHN TRAPP; a dove with olive-branch. (Y., 1695.)
732. IOS. WATSON in b. o.; a soldier (? a grenadier), with a musket. (Y., 1713.)
733. W. CLARKE; an artichoke with a mullet (p. l.). (Y., 1695; M., 1750, '51, '55.)
734. THOMAS RHODES; b. p. a sun in splendour shining on a dove with olive-branch. (W., 1746.)
735. IONATHAN BRODHURST; b. p. a stag and a bell. (Y., 1731.)
736. JOHN KENT; a lion holding up a crown (p. l.). (Y., 1718.)
737. RICHARD WRIGHT; a peacock in his pride (p. l.). (Y., 1712.)
738. ROBERT POLE; a cock, pecking at a wheatsheaf. (Cf. No. 762.)
739. I. W., each with a mullet above; a wheatsheaf and a rose.
740. T. H. with a lamp, in a plain circle.
741. EDWARD LAWRENCE; b. p. St. Lawrence with his gridiron, and a sun. (Y., 1713.)
742. I. E. in shaped punch; a crown and pear (?) (p. l.).
743. WHITE AND BERNARD; an eagle issuing from a rose. (p. l.). (? Wm. White. Y., 1714. ? Onesiphorus Bernard. Y., 1722.)
744. JOHN HEATH in moulded oval; three cocks and six mullets. (Y., 1711.)
745. GEORGE TAYLOR; with a figure of Neptune and two mullets (p. l.). (Cf. No. 758.) (Y., 1722.)
746. SAMUEL ELLIS; with golden fleece. The rim contains two panels of very florid ornament. (W., 1737, '47; Master, '48.)
747. IOHN RANDAL; a leopard's head (p. l.). (Y., 1723.)
748. ROBERT WASS; b. p. a crown, a woolsack, a rose. (Y., 1712.)
749. LUKE IOHNSON; a crowned arrow, point downwards, between a 2 and a 3 (i.e. 1723), between two wings (p. l.). (Y., 1713.)

750. ALEXANDER LANCASTER; a swan with collar and chain (p. l.). (Y., 1711.)
751. I. E. in b. c., with a head, wreathed.
752. I. C., with a wheel, crowned, 1723 (p. l.).
753. IOSEPH PRATT; Time, with scythe and hour-glass (p. l.). (Y., 1709.)
754. T. HUX, in a guilloche border; a fleur-de-lys within a crescent. (Y., 1723.)
755. EDWARD NASH; three fleurs-de-lys (p. l.). (Y., 1717.)
756. CATESBY CHAPMAN; a ship in full sail (p. l.). (Y., 1721.)
757. THOMAS STEVENS; a dexter hand holding a small globe, also a star or sun (p. l.). (Y., 1716.)
758. GEORGE TAYLOR; Neptune, with a trident. (Also struck badly, above, cf. No. 745.) (Y., 1722.)
759. EDWARD UBLY; a stag trippant. (Y., 1716.)
760. HENRY IACKSON; b. p. three beehives, with eleven bees volant. (Y., 1723.)
761. T. W. in small shaped punch, with crown; rest illegible; below it vertically an oblong punch, LONDON, with beaded edge.
762. IOHN NORGROVE; a cock pecking at a wheatsheaf. (Similar to Robert Polc's touch, No. 738.) (Y., 1722.)
763. RICHARD COX; a cock perching on a helmet. (Y., 1712.)
764. R. S. in s. c., and a worm from a still.
765. IOHN COLE; a bull (p. l.).
766. P. M. in s. b. c., with scallop-shell. (? Paul Mitchell. Y., 1721.)
767. SIMON PATTINSON; three crowns. (Y.. 1715.)
768. THOMAS BACON, with a boar. In interior scroll, the word FECIT (p. l.). (Y., 1717.)
769. IOHN PAXTON; sun shining on a marigold. (Y., 1717.)
770. EDWARD MERRIEFIELD; a hand, sleeved, holding a marigold or daisy. (Y., 1716.)
771. RICHARD LEGGATT; a horse walking. (Y., 1722.)
772. THO. STRIBBLEHILL; David slaying Goliath. (Y., 1704.)
773. TO. KIRKE; a bonnet with strings and an upright feather in front. (? Tho. Kirke. Y., 1728.)
774. IOSEPH WINGOD; b. p. a beadle leading away an offending child. (Y., 1721; W., '66; M., '67. His name is given as WINGARD in the List of the Yeomanry.)
775. HENRY ELWICK; a fountain between two dolphins, all spouting water. (Y., 1707.)
776. SAMUEL MILES; b. p. a sun in splendour and a wheatsheaf. (Y., 1726.)

777. THOMAS JAMES; a squirrel sejant (p. l. c.). (Y., 1726.) (HENRY ELWICK [No. 775] repeated.)
778. WILLIAM ELLIS; b. p. a lion rampant bearing a heart in its paws. (Y., 1726.) (Cf. No. 606.)
779. IOHN SHAW; a fleur-de-lys with crown above, between two roundels (p. l.). (Y., 1726.)
780. IAMES MATTHEWS; crest, two arms holding up a plate. (Y., 1722.)
781. IAMES BISHOP; a bishop's bust between two crossed crosiers and a mitre. (Y., 1724.)
782. ROWLAND COLE; two hands interlocked, with a crown above.
783. R. M. in oval; a large daisy, with a sun and six roundels (p. l. c.).
784. THOMAS PHILLIPS; a cock perched on a rose. (Y., 1727.)
785. [EDWARD] BRADSTREET; the name at the top and also at the bottom. For device, the star of the Order of the Garter. (For the name cf. Welch, ii, 186; Y., 1720.)
786. MARK CRIPPS; b. p. a sun shining through a cloud on a wheatsheaf. (Y., 1727; W., '51, '60; M., '62.)
787. HENRY SMITH; a rose ensigned by a mitre. (Y., 1724.)
788. I. SMITH; a rose (p. l. c.). (Y., 1716.)
789. IOHN PAYNE; b. p. a crescent or moon and seven stars. (Y., 1725.)
790. IOHN HATHAWAY; a crown, with two sceptres through the crown. (Y., 1724.)
791. ALEX. CLEEVE; a hand grasping a rose spray, and one mullet. (Y., 1688; W., 1705, '15; M., '20, '27.)
792. IOHN CATER, LONDON; b. p. a lion issuing from a crescent. (Y., 1725; L., '52.)
793. IOHN ROGERS; a sun in splendour. (Y., 1717.)
794. THOMAS GOSLING; b. p. a gosling. (Y., 1721.)
795. I. P.; Time, with scythe and hour-glass; above, a crown (p. l.). Below these follows a half-line of touches:
796. SAMVEL SMITH; b. p. a holy lamb and flag. (Y., 1727; W., '41, '53.)
797. IOHN BLENMAN; a sun in splendour shining on a wheat-sheaf. (Welch, ii. 185; Y., 1726.)
798. JOSEPH CARTER; a carter with his cart, and date 1726.
799. Here follows a small punch, very indistinct, with initials W. M.
800. THOMAS PIGGOTT; device, a Roman. (Cf. No. 809.)

801. In° Watts in oblong punch; upon it a globe, mounted in a stand. (Somewhat similar to the stamp of — Collyer, No. 730. There was a John Watts Y., 1725; W., '58; M., '60; and another, W., 1779; M., '80.)
802. Th[omas] Swindell; crest, a mitre. (Y., 1705.)
803. Ann Tidmarsh; a ducal coronet. (Y., 1728.)
804. Ios^ph Donne; a hand holding a seal between the finger and the thumb (p. l. c.). (Y., 1727; L., 1727.)
805. R. B. in s. shield, with a flower and a wheel and four roundels.
806. T. K. in oblong punch; a heart surmounted by a rose, with three stars, and date 1799 (?).
807. Ios^ph Donne (No. 804) repeated, but defaced.
808. Smith & Leapidge in a square touch; b. p. a goat (?) and a wheatsheaf. (A Samuel Smith, whose touch is given, No. 796, was W., 1753, with John Leapidge. The latter was W., 1762, and M., '63.)
809. Ioseph Sherwin; same device as Thomas Piggott, No. 800. (Y., 1726.)
810. Ioseph Claridge; a hand grasping a dove with olive-branch. (Y., 1724.)
811. Daniel [Picker]ing; a lion rampant, and below, a dolphin. (Y., 1723.)
812. W. H. in p. c.; a Bacchus astride a barrel.
813. Samuel Cooke; a lion rampant holding a crown in its paws. (Y., 1727.)
814. Benjamin Browne; arms, a two-headed eagle, and above the crest, a hand grasping a bird's foot and a wing (?). (Y., 1726.)
815. William Norwood; a hammer, crowned, between two fleurs-de-lys (p. l.). (Y., 1727.)
816. William Rowell; arms, two chevrons engrailed, and on each three roundels. (Y., 1726.)
817. William Stevens; a hand, with a tulip (p. l.). (Y., 1729.)
818. Below this, Richard Bradstreet; two naked figures supporting a crown. (Y., 1727.)
819. Iohn Williams in b. o., with a crescent; in a border, the signs of the Zodiac. (Cf. No. 903.)
820. George [Staffo]rd; a hand holding a seal. (Y., 1730.)
821. Ioseph Pedder; a cock, standing over two crossed keys. In the margin four mullets.

822. I. Iones, London ; an angel. (Y., 1720 ; W., '35, '44 ; M., '45. Another J. Jones was Y., 1707 ; W., '56 ; M., '58.
823. Andrew Rudsby ; b. p. a dove with olive-branch, perched on a wheatsheaf. (Y., 1712.)
824. Cooke and Freeman ; no device, merely two scrolls. (? White Cooke. Y., 1720. ? William Freeman. Y., 1727.)
825. Samuel Sp[ateman] ; a sun, with a wheatsheaf and a cock below. (Y., 1719.) In the list of Yeomen it is spelled Spademan.
826. I. F. in b. o., with a bit within a horseshoe.
827. W. Sandys ; a griffin rampant.
828. Jo. Jordan ; a dove perched on a snake. (p. l. c. t.). (Y., 1727.)
829. William [Smith] ; device, a tankard or possibly a lantern.
830. Simon Halford ; crest, a griffin. (Y., 1726.)
831. Richard Wildman ; Hercules and his club. (Y., 1728.)
832. Giles Cleeve ; b. p. three griffins' heads erased. (Y., 1706.)
833. John de St. [Croix] ; three leopards. (Y., 1729.)
834. Richard Hands ; a shepherd with a crook and a dog. (Y., 1717.)
835. Thomas Barnes ; a unicorn rampant, with collar and chain and two mullets. (Y., 1726.)
836. E. D. ; in p. o , a mermaid, with comb and mirror
837 Richard Brown 1731 ; a lion sejant affronté, with one paw on a lamb (Y., 1729.)
838. I. C. in b. c., with a worm.
839. Alexander Hamilton ; St. Andrew, holding a cross ; at the sides a thistle and a rose. (Y., 1721.)
840. Iames Smith, a rose and acorn (p. l.). (Y., 1732.)
841. William Phillips ; a hand holding a gillyflower. (Y., 1744.)
842. W. C. in square touch with corners cut off, with rose and thistle on one stem.
843. TD. NM. 1732 ; a snake coiled like the worm of a still, crowned.
844. William Cooch ; a wyvern above a star of eight points within a crescent. (? Wm. Couch in list of Yeomanry, 1731.)
845. Sam. Guy, London ; device, a kilted figure holding a grotesque animal (Warwick). (Cf. No. 630.) (Y., 1729.)

846. WILLIAM [FOX]; a fox. (Wm. Fox, Y., 1670.)
847. BEN FOSTER, LONDON; arms, a chevron engrailed ermine and three pheons, with a label of three points. (Cf. No. 639.)
848. EDWD. YORKE; on a cross, five lions rampant. (L., 1735.)
849. W. S., an earl's coronet; above, a mullet within a crescent.

This is the end of the third touch-plate.

Touch Plate IV. (*Dimensions,* 21⅜ × 14 *in.*)

850. SAMUEL TAYLOR; a cock on a plough. (Y., 1731.)
851. SAMUEL RIGHTON; a cock, two crossed sprigs of olive below. (Y., 1732.)
852. I. T. with a pear and 17 . . , very indistinct.
853. IOHNSON [AND] CHAMBERLAIN; the Prince of Wales's feathers, crowned.
854. IAMES TISOE; portcullis. (Y., 1733; W., '64.) (Cf. No. 449.)
855. IOHN IACKSON; an hour-glass and three fleurs-de-lys. (Y., 1689; W., 1712.)
856. SAMUEL JEFFERYS; a rose and two fleurs-de-lys above. (p. l.) (Cf. No. 986.)
857. WILLIAM MURRAY; a crested bird on nowed serpent, a star above. (Y., 1734.)
858. R. P. in the centre of a clock-face. (? R. Parr or R. Pitt.)
859. IOHN SCATTERGOOD; two hands with hammers and a rose (p. l.). (Y., 1716.)
860. RICHARD SMITH; device, a plough and a star. (Y., 1733.) (Cf. No. 301.)
861. HENRY MAXTED;[1] b. p. a sun (in part) shining on a rose. (Y., 1731.)
862. THOMAS COLLET; b. p.; a crown above, a woolsack and a rose below. (Y., 1735.)
863. An illegible punch follows here, being an attempt at the next.
864. W. D. and a star above.
865. A crowned rose-en-soleil. No name or letters are in this touch.

[1] With this punch the series begins with pillars at either side, of ever-varying forms, the palm-leaves becoming somewhat more scarce.

866. IONATHAN Co[TT]ON, 1705; an eagle displayed, a crescent, a hand with flower-spray, and dove. (W., 1734; M., '36.) (Cf. No. 624.)
867. ROBERT MASSAM; three fleurs-de-lys and a rose below (p. l.). (Y., 1735.)
868. IOHN PIGGOTT; a figure of a Roman. (Y., 1736.)
869. P. M. in b. o., with a boy naked to the waist, holding a popgun and a rattle. (? Philemon Mathew. Y., 1736.)
870. I. W. in p. c., with a star and a bell.
871. DANIEL GRENDON; crest, on a torse a bird (p. l.). (Y., 1735.)
872. ALEXANDER STOUT; a cock on a globe mounted on a stand (p. l.). (Y., 1733.)
873. THOMAS SCATTERGOOD; arms, two bars and three hands, with helm and mantling; and crest, an open hand. (Y., 1736; W., '60, '73; M., '74, '75.) (Cf. No. 610.)
874. FLY AND THOMPSON in oval; device, a fly. (Timothy Fly was W., 1737; M., '39. Paul Thompson became Yeoman in 1733.)
875. HENRY LITTLE; b. p. a cock, with crown above. (Y., 1734; W., '55.)
876. THOMAS GROCE; b. p. three crowns. (Y., 1737.)
877. ROBERT HITCHMAN; b. p. a lion rampant bearing a key.
  (Y., 1737; W., '52 and '61.)
878. IOHN IUPE; a fleur-de-lys issuing from a rose (p. l.). (Y., 1731; W., '50, '59; M., '61.)
879. SAMUEL GRIGG; a sun in splendour and a snake. (Y., 1734.)
880. PATRICK GARIOCH; two leopards' heads point to point, one above, the other below; a curious saltire device. (Y., 1735.)
881. EDMUND SHARROCK; arms, a chevron and three human heads. (Y., 1737.)
882. R. P. in p. c., with a cock and a pheasant.
883. ROBERT PATIENCE; a standing figure of a queen. (Y., 1734; W., '71; M., '72.)
884. WILLIAM HANDY; device, a hand and a weight (?) or little book above. (Y., 1728.) (Cf. No. 984.)
885. IOHN KENRICK; b. p. a stork. (Y., 1737; W., '54.)
886. FRANCIS PIGGOTT; a teazle and a crescent above. (Y., 1736; W., '69; M., '70.)

887. GEORGE ALDERSON; a lion issuant from a mural crown, looking back and holding an escallop; on the field a crescent and a star. (Y., 1728.) (Other Aldersons bore the same device.)
888. PHILIP ROBERTS; arms, a lion rampant, and a crescent for difference. (Y., 1738.)
889. ROBERT SKYNNER; crest, on a torse a unicorn sejant, and a star.
890. JOHN BELSON; b. p. a bell over a sun. (Y., 1734.)
891. BARTHOLOMEW ELLIOT; a female figure pointing with a sceptre. (Y., 1738.)
892. WILLIAM COWLING, b. p.; crest, on a torse a demi-griffin sejant. (Y., 1737.)
893. WOOD & MICHELL; device, bust of a man in a wig.
894. WILLIAM HIGHMORE; three fleurs-de-lys. (Y., 1741.)
895. V. S. in p. c., with a Britannia.
896. THOMAS UBLY; b. p. a stag holding up a wheatsheaf. (Y., 1741.)
897. IOHN FOSTER; b. p. a crowned book or Bible. (Y., 1742.)
898. T. M.; an oval with demi-mermaid (?) holding up two double balls, the whole surrounded with palm-leaves.
899. THOMAS BOARDMAN b. p.; arms, a lion passant and three stars, impaling a chief ermine with a demi-lion on the chief.
900. EDWARD QUICK;[1] arms, a chevron vair (?) and three griffins' heads erased; crest: a demi-stag. (W., 1744, '54; M., '56.) (Cf. No. 657.)
901. S. S. in oval, with crown, and two small stars beneath it.
902. R° NORFOLK IN LONDON; arms, a lion passant and three fleurs-de-lys. (Y., 1726; W., '75; M., '76.)
903. IOHN WILLIAMS; arms, a stag's head couped, with a crown between the horns. (Cf. No. 819.)
904. IOHN BENSON; arms, a double-headed eagle, with a crown in chief. (Y., 1740.)
905. L. Y. in b. oval; a griffin's head couped, with a crown over. (? Lawrence Yates. Y., 1738.) (Cf. No. 1031.)
906. HENRY IOSEPH; a scallop-shell. (Y., 1736; W., '70; M., '71.)
907. R. C. in b. c.; a lamb with a crook. (? Robt. Crooke. Y., 1738.)

[1] There were three of this name, the dates of their becoming Yeomen being respectively 1708, 1714, 1735.

THE TOUCH PLATES

908. GEORGE HOLMES; arms, a rose and four fleurs-de-lys. (Y., 1742.)
909. I. PERRY; b. p. a female figure, seated. (Y., 1743; W., 1773.)
910. IOHN [B]OTELER; a lion passant and a sun in chief. (Y., 1743.)
911. W. P. in b. c., with a crescent in centre and six stars.
912. EDWARD TOMS; a wheatsheaf and a plough. (Y., 1744; W., '81; M., '83.)
913. AQUILA DACKOMBE; device, a bee or fly. (Y., 1742.)
914. [JOHN] FARMER in b. o.; a bundle of rods tied. (Y., 1725.)
915. I. S. in b. o.; device illegible (? a hippocampus or seahorse).
916. W. T. in b. o.; a crescent.
917. I. G. in p. o.; a tree.
918. IOHN HAYTON; a blazing star with an earl's coronet above. (Y., 1743.) (Cf. No. 939.)
919. IOHN BRUMFIELD; the sun, the moon, and seven stars. (Y., 1745.)
920. WILLIAM HOWARD; a mounted soldier with drawn sword between the letters D. C. (probably for the Duke of Cumberland). (Y., 1745.)
921. GEORGE BACON; crest, on a torse a boar. (Y., 1748; W., '62.)
922. IONATHAN LEACH; a shield of arms: quarterly, (1) a rose; (2) a sprig of laurel; (3) a lamb and flag; (4) illegible; over all a cross. (Y., 1732.)
923. IOHN WYNN b. p.; arms, a lion rampant with three mullets. (Y., 1746.)
924. RICHARD PITTS; a running hare. (Richard Pitt was Y., 1747; W., '80; M., '81.)
925. IOHN HARTWELL; a saltire and four castles, and a compass point on the saltire. (Y., 1736.)
926. RICHARD NEWMAN; b. p. a mitre. (Y., 1747.)
927. IOSEPH WHITE; a man holding a cup, standing in a crescent. (Y., 1755.)
928. IOHN TOWNSEND; a lamb and a flying bird above. (Y., 1748.)
929. BURFORD & GREEN; arms, a cross with two crosslets fitchy in chief, for Burford, impaling three stags tripping, for Green. (Thos. Burford. Y., 1746; W., '48; M., '79. James Green. Y., 1746.)
930. RICHARD POOLE; a rose with spray of leaves on either side, and three fleurs-de-lys above. (Y., 1749.)

931. VILLIAM HARRISSON; an acorn on a stalk with two leaves, one pointing downwards; above the acorn an uncertain object. (William Harrison. Y., 1748.)
932. IAMES LETHARD; a hand holding a mallet. (Y., 1745.)
933. WM. GLOVER ANNISON; arms of Oxford City impaling those of Oxford University. (Y., 1742.) (Cf. No. 947.)
934. IOHN WINGOD; a square and compasses. (Y., 1748; S., '66; M., '67.)
935. IOHN SELLON; a unicorn supporting a classical headpiece. (Y., 1740.)
936. I. M. in a small, plain, oblong touch, with domed top, with a rose, a wheatsheaf and two stars and a rose above.
937. WILLIAM BAMPTON; b. p. a rose and a blazing star. (Y., 1742; W., '74, '83; M., '85.)
938. DANIEL LAWSON; crest, on a torse two arms issuing from a cloud and holding a sun in spendour (p. l.). (Y., 1749.)
939. GEORGE BEESTON; a blazing star and an earl's coronet (the same touch as that of John Hayton; No. 918). (Y., 1743.)
940. ISAAC READ; a man fishing. (Y., 1743.)
941. MATHEW TONKIN; a miner (?) at work. (Y., 1749.)
942. DANIEL LAWSON, repeated.
943. HENRY APPLETON; arms, a fess engrailed, and three apples slipped in the stalks. (Y., 1749.)
944. JOHN UBLY; a stag tripping (p. l.). (Y., 1748.)
945. WILLIAM PHIPPS; arms, a trefoil and an orb of eight mullets. (Y., 1743.)
946. IAMES BULLOCK; crest, a beehive surmounted by a bee. (Y., 1750.)
947. [W. GLOVER] ANNISON; the arms of Oxford City impaling those of Oxford University. (Cf. No. 933.) There is an indecipherable word in the lower scroll.
948. ROWLAND SMITH; a rose and an acorn slipped in the stalks (p. l.). (Y., 1734.)
949. WILLIAM PHILLIPS; a hand holding a clove-pink or gilly-flower. (Y., 1759.)
950. CHARLES MAXEY; b. p. a pelican vulning herself and standing on a globe. (Y., 1750.)
951. BOURCHIER CLEEVE; b. p. a hand holding a slipped rose. (Y., 1736.)
952. The next touch consists of an oval beaded band, with a Latin motto, HAUD ULLIS LABENTIA VENTIS, and the

name, H. IRVING in the exergue, badly punched; and crest, an arm embowed, with the hand grasping a spray of holly. (Y., 1750.)
953. RICHD. PEAKE in b. o.; a lion's head erased. (Y., 1750.)
954. WILLIAM WHITE; b. p. on a torse a demi-stag. (Y., 1751.)
955. ROBERT RANDALL in b. o.; three fleurs-de-lys. Y., 1748.)
956. IAMES BOOST; device, a crescent and six stars. (Y., 1744.)
957. JOHN WALKER in p. o.; a man crowned, walking. (Y., 1748.)
958. MATTHEW UNDERWOOD, 1752; a lion and a lamb.
959. RICHARD ALDERWICK; a falconer or man hawking. (Y., 1748.) (Cf. No. 1035.)
960. WILLIAM HEALEY; arms, a chevron cotised indented and three lions, with three crosses paty on the chevron; crest, a demi-lion holding a cross-paty. (Y., 1752.)
961. IAMES FONTAINE; an elephant. (Y., 1752.)
962. R^D PAWSON; a rose spray with a ducal coronet over. (Y., 1752.)
963. IOHN EDWARDS; a horse. (Y., 1739.)
964. IOHN FASSON; a horseshoe. (Y., 1749.) (Cf. Nos. 977 and 1048.)
965. IOHN HOME; arms, a lion rampant, impaling party per band sinister six martlets. (Y., 1749; W., '71.) (Cf. No. 1037.)
966. WILLIAM HARRIS; crest, on a torse a demi-griffin with expanded wings. (Y., 1746.)
967. BENJ: TOWNSEND; arms, fretty and a cross, and five mullets on the cross. (Y., 1744.) (Cf. No. 1058.)
968. IAMES STEEVENS; a Britannia, seated, 1754. (Y., 1753.)
969. THOMAS LANGFORD; a vase of flowers. (Y., 1751.)
970. WM. DE IERSEY; arms, party per fess azure and gules an eagle displayed. (L., 1744; W., '72; M., '73.)
971. IOHN WHITE; b. p. a man holding a cup, standing in a crescent. (Y., 1755.)
972. I. R. in b. c., with griffin's head erased, and a crown and two stars above.
973. THOMAS BUTTERY; a bee and a rose above it. (Y., 1730.)
974. HENRY BOWLER; b. p. a man bowling. (Y., 1757.)
975. THOMAS HAWKINS; in circle, a hawk perched upon a woolsack. (Y., 1742.)
976. GEORGE GRE[EN]FELL; a griffin standing on a ragged staff (?). (Y., 1757.)

977. WILLIAM F[ASSON]; a rose within a horseshoe. (Y., 1758; W., '76, '85; M., '87.) (Cf. Nos. 964 and 1048.)
978. THOMAS MUNDAY; bust of a man in a wig (1767). (Y., 1754.)
979. BENJAMIN BACON; arms, gules and on a chief two mullets; crest, a boar.
980. ROBERT SCATCHARD; arms, a lion rampant and in chief three mullets (1761); crest, a demi-lion. (Y., 1756.)
981. CHARLES CLARIDGE; an outstretched hand holding a bird bearing a spray (1758). (Cf. No. 810.) (Y., 1756.)
982. JOSEPH SPACKMAN; a ducal coronet between a fleur-de-lys and two crosses paty above; a cross paty and two crossed palm-branches below. (Y., 1749.) (Cf. No. 1045.)
983. JAMES PULESTON; a lion's paw erased, grasping a battle-axe.
984. W. H. in b. c.; two hands interlocked, with a crown above and 1709 below. (? Wm. Handy. Y., 1753.) (Cf. No. 884.)
985. IOHN VAUGHAN; b. p. a holy lamb and a flag. (Y., 1753; W., '91; M., '92.)
986. IOSEPH IEFFERYS; a rose with two fleurs-de-lys above.
987. W. F. in shaped and indented oblong touch; crest, a lion rampant with a crescent between the legs.
988. MARY WILLEY; a rose and four fleurs-de-lys.
989. T. S. in s. b. c., with two hearts, point to point. (Cf. No. 1011.)
990. THO. IONES; in an oval, a gun on a carriage and five mullets. (Y., 1755.)
991. BROWNE & SW[ANSON] THOMAS SWANSON } device in both a talbot. (? John Brown. Thomas Swanson. Y., 1753; W., '77.) (Cf. No. 1008.)
992. W. M. E. C. (?) in square punch, with corners cut off; a rose and a thistle on one stem (a badge of Queen Anne).
993. WILLIAM WIGHTMAN; in an inner circle a cross crosslet between two roses and two stags' heads. (Y., 1758.)
994. BENNETT & CHAPMAN; arms, three demi-lions and a roundel; impaling party per chevron, a crescent and two leopards' heads. (? Wm. Bennett. Y., 1758; and Oxton Chapman. Y., 1760.) (Cf. No. 998.)
995. IOHN KING; a female figure of Hope, draped, with an anchor. (Y., 1757.)

996. RALPH WHARRAM; arms, a fess between a goat's head couped and three scallop-shells in base. (Y., 1756.)
997. THOMAS GREENWOOD; device, a still, with a worm attached, and a sun. (Y., 1759.)
998. WILLIAM BENNETT; arms, three demi-lions and a roundel. (Y., 1758.) (Cf. No. 994.)
999. ROB^T. AND THO. PORTEUS; device, an ostrich. (Robt. Porteus was Y., 1760; W., '78, '90. Thomas Porteus was Y., 1762.)
1000. N. M. in b. c., 1732; a worm, crowned. (? Nathaniel Meakin. W., 1759, '67; M., '68.)
1001. R. E. in b. c.; a nude man with a long scroll (? Hercules and a snake.)
1002. IOHN BROWN, IOHN LEWIS, & IOSEPH BROWN in the exergue of a large circle; device, an angel holding a palm-branch in one hand, the other leaning upon a worm.
1003. IAMES FI[DD]ES; a tun and a hammer. (Y., 1754.)
1004. THOMAS THOMPSON; in the centre a sun in splendour, upon the clouds between the two scrolls, with a thistle on one side, a crown on the other. (Y., 1755.)
1005. THOMAS SMITH; a set of masonic emblems between two masonic pillars. (Y., 1761.)
1006. THOMAS GIFFIN;[1] b. p. a dagger piecing a heart and ensigned with a ducal coronet between six mullets. (Y., 1759.)
1007. CLARK & GREENING; a flower (? a teasle) displayed, surmounted by a star. (J. Clarke. Y., 1756. Richd. Greening. Y., 1756.)
1008. THOMAS SWANSON;[2] the Golden Fleece between four rings and a fleur-de-lys. (Y., 1753; W., 1777.) (Cf. No. 991.)
1009. JOHN PERRY; arms, gules a bend cotised ermine and three leopards on the bend. (Y., 1743; W., '73.)
1010. JOHN ALDERSON; a demi-lion between a crescent and a star, looking back, issuant from a mural crown. (Y., 1764; W., '82.)
1011. CHARLES SMITH; a mailed fist with sword; a lion rampant and three horseshoes. (Y., 1765; W., '89.)

[1] Another Thomas Giffin was L., 1726; W., '51; M., '53 and '57.
[2] *Vide* No. 991. The pewter stamped with the touch No. 1008 was probably made by Samuel Ellis (M., 1745). The two seem to have been in partnership.

1012. I. Townsend & R. Reynolds; a lamb and a dove with olive branch. (J. Townsend. Y., 1748; W., '69, '82; M., '84. Robert Reynolds, Y., 1761.)
1013. William Snape; b. p. a horse. (Y., 1764.)
1014. W. Farmer in b. c., with two muskets in saltire and a powder-flask. (Y., 1765.)
1015. A. Jenner in plain rectangle. (? Anth. Jenner; Y., 1754.)
1016. Thomas Smith: a cock treading a hen.
1017. Stephen Kent Hagger; a hand with hammer and a barrel. (Repeated.) (Y., 1754.)
1018. Pitt & Floyd; a running hare. (R. Pitt was W., 1780; M., '81. John Floyd, W., '87.)
1019. R. P. Hodge in p. o., with a clock-face. (Robert Piercy Hodge was W., 1796 and 1801; M., '02.)
1020. Edward Sidey in b. o., with large hour-glass. (Y., 1772.)
1021. H. Wood in b. c.; two dogs fighting. (Y., 1768.)
1022. Saml. Law in b. c.; a dove with olive-branch. (This punch is repeated.) (Y., 1768.)
1023. Iohn Hudson; arms, quarterly per chevron embattled, or and vert, and three martlets. (Y., 1770.)
1024. Ioseph Monk; crest, a griffin. (Y., 1757.)
1025. Iohn Gurnell, London; a camel with a star. (Y., 1768.)
1026. Iohn Hinde; a female figure of Hope, with an anchor in her left hand. (Y., 1760; W., '90, '91, '95; M., '96.)
1027. Thomas Dodson, 1775; a ship in full sail. (Y., 1769.)
1028. W. Phillips in p. o.; a cock crowing. (Y., 1759.)
1029. William Cooch; a fox running; a star and a crescent above. (This touch is given thrice, the first two being badly struck.) (Y., 1775.)
1030. Joseph Monk (repeated). See above, No. 1024.
1031. Richard Yates; a griffin's head erased, with a marquis's coronet above; at each side, between the scrolls, a star. (Y., 1772.) (Cf. No. 905.)
1032. Jno. Appleton in a l. p. o., with a still and a worm. (Y., 1768; W., '99; M., 1800.)
1033. Samuel Higley; arms, a cross engrailed, and a crescent on the cross; also a crescent in the quarter for difference; crest, an eagle with two heads. (Repeated). (Y., 1775.)
1034. William Barnes; a standing figure of a Queen with orb and sceptre. (Y., 1770.)

1035. RICHARD ALDERWICK; a man hawking. See above, No. 959.
1036. C. SWIFT, on a square punch with regular indentations, with a spray of a thistle and a rose on one stem, the badge of Queen Anne. (C. Swift repeated.) (Y., 1770.)
1037. NATHANIEL BARBER; with the arms of John Home. (Y., 1777.) (Cf. No. 965.)
1038. SAM^L. SALTER BOWLER; a running greyhound; above, a star. (Y., 1779.)
1039. SAMUEL PRIDDLE; in the centre in b. o. a flower displayed and a crescent.
1040. ROBERT JUPE; a rose and a fleur-de-lys. (Y., 1776.)
1041. WILLIAM WRIGHT in exergue of a plain shield-shaped punch; on inner shield, a griffin's head issuing from a crown. (Y., 1764.)
1042. ROB^T. LUPTON; crest, a griffin's head erased, on a torse. (Y., 1775.)
1043. PITT & DADLEY; a running hare. *Id.* (repeated). (E. Dadley was W., 1799, 1803; and M., '04.)
1044. WILLIAM MILLIN; two hearts, point to point. (Y., 1776.) (*Vide* touch of T. S., No. 989.)
1045. JOS^H. AND JA^S. SPACKMAN. (James S. was W., 1797, and had a different touch.) (For touch of Joseph Spackman cf. No. 982.)
1046. ROBERT WALLER; a woman in a gown standing. (Y., 1779.)
1047. JOSEPH FOSTER in exergue of oval; within, a unicorn rampant. (Y., 1757.)
1048. THOMAS FASSON; a horseshoe encircling a heart; above, a dagger (a variant of the touches of John and William Fasson, Nos. 964, 977). (Y., 1783; W., 1802; M., '03.)
1049. RICHARD BACHE; b. p., an angel with a palm branch in the left hand; also a scroll in the right hand. (Y., 1779.)
1050. CHARLES LOADER; in a large shield-shaped punch, a swan swimming. (Y., 1784.)
1051. ROBERT JACKSON; b. p., three beehives and eleven bees volant. (Cf. No. 780.) (Y., 1780; W., '95, 1800; M., '01.)
1052. IOSEPH SPACKMAN & Co.; device as before. (? J. Spackman, Jr., Y., 1784.)
1053. ROBERT KNIGHT; in central oval, a compass and an eight-pointed star. (Y., 1770.)

1054. HENRY & RICHARD JOSEPH; device, a large scallop-shell. (Henry Joseph, Y., 1763; Richard Joseph, Y., 1785; W., 1804; M., '05, '06.) Richard Joseph, Y., 1785.
1055. EDWARD LOCKWOOD; a wheatsheaf and a dove. (Y., 1768; W., '93, '97; M., '98.)
1056. PHILIP WHITE; in a b. c., a lion rampant between two stars. (Y., 1778.)
1057. W. H. KING, 1786; a badger (?). (Wm. Harrison King, Y., 1786.)
1058. RICHARD BAGSHAW; same arms as Benjn. Townsend on touch, No. 967.
1059. ROBERT BARNETT; a rose and a fleur-de-lys (p. l.). (Y., 1783.)
1060. —. WADSWORTH; a rose spray with coronet over. (? Wm. Wadsworth, Y., 1780.)
1061. PETER LE KEUX in attenuated oval; a man on a race-horse. (Y., 1779.)
1062. C. JONES; b. p., a holy lamb with a flag, and LONDON below. (Y., 1786.)
1063. IOHN BROWN; a Pegasus volant, a star above. (Repeated. (?) Coney John Brown, Y., 1786.)
1064. EDWARD SEAWELL; in large circle, a dove (?). (Y., 1779.)
1065. R. M. in small plain oblong. (? Randall Moring, Y., 1794.)
1066. CARPENTER & HAMBERGER; a pair of compasses and a globe. (? Henry Carpenter, H., 1757; John Hamberger, Y., 1794.)
1067. WOOD & HILL; two sheep in a shield without border. (? Thos. Wood, Y., 1792; ? Roger Hill, Y., 1791.)
1068. JOHN GRAY GREEN; a female figure (? Hope) with an anchor and two mullets. (Y., 1793.)
1069. I. M.; a dove, and below, an anchor. (? John Markland, Y., 1770.)

This is the end of the fourth touch-plate.

Touch Plate V. (Dimensions $21\frac{3}{4}$ in. × $14\frac{1}{8}$ in.)

On this plate all the touches are repeated, with the exception of No. 1074. There are twenty-one touches, from 1798 to 1824.

1070. WILLIAM BATHUS; a heart, with a rose above it. (Y., 1797.)

THE TOUCH PLATES

1071. PAUL FISHER; a fisher in a boat. (Y., 1798.)
1072. WILLIAM NETTLEFOLD, LONDON, 1799; a dove with olive-branch, perched on a worm of a still. (Y., 1785.)
1073. THOMAS PHILLIPS; a hand bearing a gillyflower (1800 is scratched on the plate). (Y., 1795; W., 1809, '10, '16; M., '17.)
1074. I. F. in plain ringed oval with two clasped hands.
1075. S. T. in oval, with sun. (? Samuel Turner, Y., 1790.)
1076. W. GROOME; a draw-knife, with a hammer and a compass. (Y., 1798.)
1077. WILL^M GIBBS; a soldier. (Y., 1804.)
1078. ROGER MOSER; b. p. three beehives, nine bees flying. (Y., 1806.)
1079. WILLIAM WALKER; a woolsack. (Y., 1787.)
1080. COCKS, LONDON; device, two cocks facing one another. (Samuel Cocks. Y., 1819. L., 1819.)
1081. JOS^H HENRY GODFREY; a tea-tray with a tea service displayed. (Y., 1807.)
1082. R. STANTON, 37, BLACKMAN ST., BORO; a banner of the royal arms of England. (Y., 1810.)
1083. ASHLEY, MINORIES; Britannia, with ship in the offing.
1084. GEORGE ALDERSON; crest, a lion issuing from a battlemented crown, looking back and holding something. (Y., 1817; W., '21; M., '23.)
1085. RICHARD MISTER, BERMONDSEY STREET. Device, a square and compasses, with 86 in the central space. (Y., 1802; W., '20, '25; M., '27.)
1086. W. M. in oval; a dove with olive-branch, likewise a bee or fly.
1087. MAW in small oval; a camel couchant.
1088. W. C. SWIFT; in square touch, a rose and thistle on the same stalk. (Y., 1809.)
1089. J. STANTON, SHOE LANE; a scallop-shell. (Y., 1805.)
1090. E. J. T. ASHLEY, LONDON; a beehive and a tree. (Date scratched in plate, 1824.) (Y., 1821.)

NOTE

The touches on Touch Plate V have not been reproduced.
Vide note, page 268.

TOUCH PLATES

The Touch Plates I, II, III, IV have been reproduced by special permission of the Worshipful Company of Pewterers, London, from the original Touch Plates in its possession.

These have been redrawn to a uniform scale by Sheila McEwan.

Touch Plate V has not been reproduced as, with the exception of pewter made by S. Cocks, very little of this late ware is met with nowadays.

Marks from Touch Plate Nº I

Marks from Touch Plate N° I

Marks from Touch Plate Nº I

Marks from Touch Plate Nº I

Marks from Touch Plate Nº I

Marks from Touch Plate Nº I

Marks from Touch Plate Nº I

Marks from Touch Plate Nº I

Marks from Touch Plate Nº I

Marks from Touch Plate Nº II

Marks from Touch Plate No. II

Marks from Touch Plate No. II

Marks from Touch Plate No. II

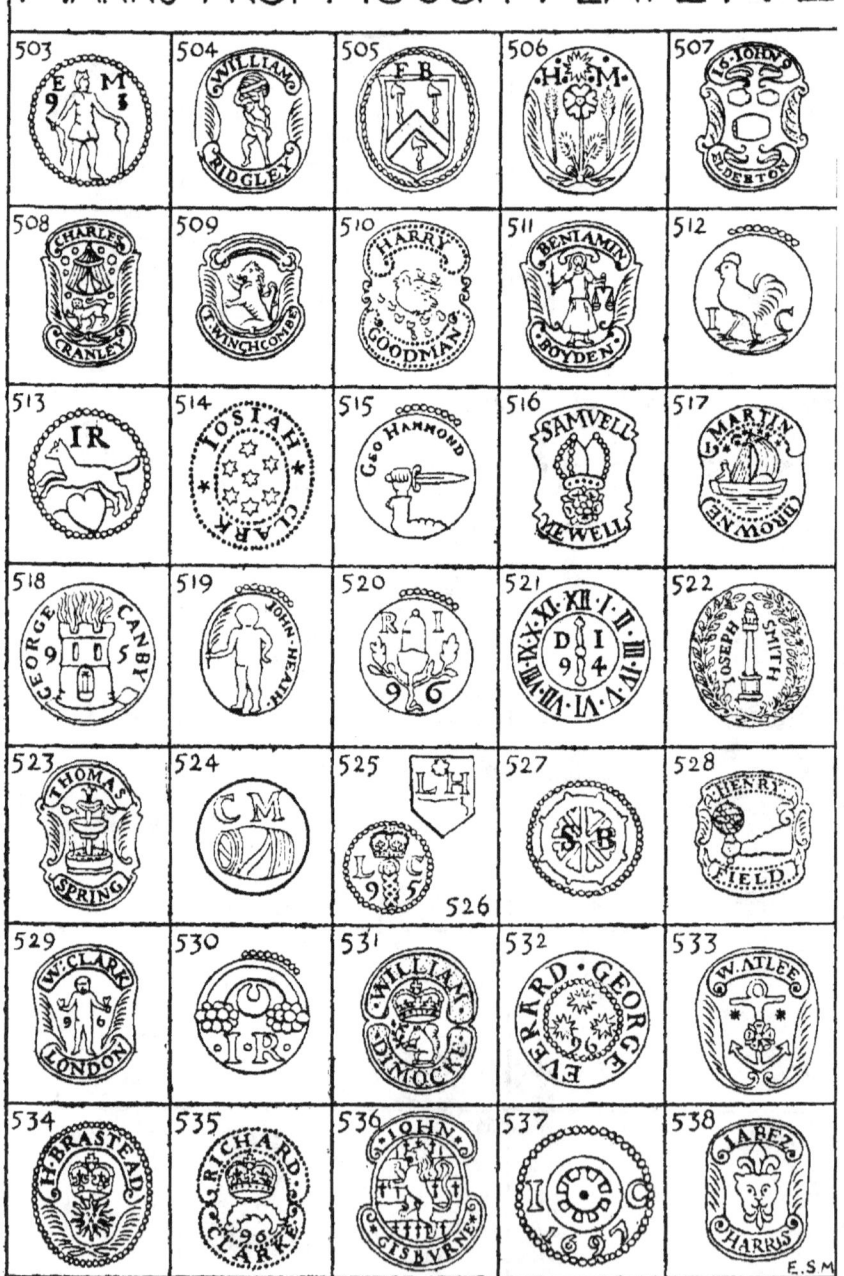

Marks from Touch Plate Nº II

539 GEORGE NORTH	540 WILLIAM ELLWOOD	541 SOLOMON TEMPSON	542 JOSEPH BOWDEN	543 JOHN SUMMERS
544 AW 16 98	545 I T 16 98	546 R W	547 EDWARD STONE 98	548 W P 98
549 THOMAS TILYARD	550 WILLIAM GILLAM	551 W M	552 W S	553 I I 1700
554 JOHN BARLOW	555 ROBERT DAKEN	556 WILLIAM HEYFORD	557 JONAS DURAND	558 RICHARD DYER
559 W R	560 BASIL GRAHAM	561 NICHOLAS SWEATMAN	562 I B 9 9	563 I C
564 T·B 9 9	565 THOMAS COOKE	566 I W 1699	567 P.C. 99	568 REW LEAPIDGE LONDON
569 WILLIAM DIGGES	570 CHARLES RENDER	571 F L	572 CHARLES RANDALL	573 D. BARTON LONDON
574 W H 1709	575 ANT. ROWE	576 T P 1700	577 BERNARD BABB	578 I.E. 86

E S M

Marks from Touch Plate Nº II

MARKS FROM TOUCH PLATE Nº III

Marks from Touch Plate No. III

Marks from Touch Plate Nº III

Marks from Touch Plate Nº III

Marks from Touch Plate Nº III

776 SAMUEL MILES	777 THOMAS JAMES	778 WILLIAM ELLIS	779 JOHN SHAW	780 JAMES MATTHEWS
781 JAMES BISHOP	782 ROWLAND COLE	783 R·M	784 THOMAS PHILLIPS	785 ELLIS OR BRADSTREET
786 MARK CRIPPS	787 HENRY SMITH	788 I. SMITH	789 JOHN PAYNE	790 JOHN HATHAWAY
791 ALEX CLEEVE	792 JOHN CATER LONDON	793 JOHN ROGERS	794 THOMAS GOSLING	795
796 SAMUEL SMITH	797 JOHN BLENMAN	798 JOSEPH 1726 CARTER	799 W M	800 THOMAS PIGGOTT
801 IN·WATTS	802 THOMAS SWINDELL	803 ANN TIDMARSH	804 JOS:PH DONNE	805 R B
806 T·K 1799	807 JOS:PH DONNE	808 SMITH & LEAPIDGE	809 JOSEPH SHERWIN	810 JOSEPH CLARIDGE
811 DANIEL PICKERING	812 W·H	813 SAMUEL COOKE	814 BENJAMIN BROWN	815 WILLIAM NORWOOD

E.S.M

Marks from Touch Plate Nº III

Marks from Touch Plate No. IV

Marks from Touch Plate No. IV

Marks from Touch Plate Nº IV

921 GEORGE BACON	922 JONATHAN LEACH	923 JOHN YVONNE	924 RICHARD PITTS	925 JOHN HARTWELL
926 RICHARD NEWMAN	927 JOSEPH WHITE	928 JOHN TOWNSEND	929 BURFORD GREEN	930 RICHARD POOLE
931 WILLIAM HARRISON	932 JAMES LETHARD	933 GLOVER ANNISON	934 JOHN WINGOD	935 JOHN SELLON
936 I M	937 WILLIAM BAMPTON	938 DANIEL LAWSON	939 GEORGE BEESTON	940 ISAAC READ
941 MATHEW TONKIN	942 DANIEL LAWSON	943 HENRY APPLETON	944 JOHN UBLY	945 WILLIAM PHIPPS
946 JAMES BULLOCK	947 VER ANNISON	948 ROWLAND SMITH	949 WILLIAM PHILLIPS	950 CHARLES MAXEY
951 BOURCHIER CLEEVE	952 LABENTIA BEVIS	953 RICHᴰ PEALE	954 WILLIAM WHITE	955 ROBERT RANDALL

Marks from Touch Plate Nº IV

956 JAMES BOOST	957 JOHN WALKER	958 MATTHEW UNDERWOOD 1752	959 RICHARD ALDERWICK	960 WILLIAM HEALEY
961 JAMES FONTAINE	962 Rᵉ PAWSON	963 JOHN EDWARDS	964 JOHN FASSON	965 JOHN HOME
966 WILLIAM HARRIS	967 BENJAMIN TOWNSEND	968 JAMES TEEVERS	969 THOMAS LANGFORD	970 WILLIAM DE JERSEY
971 JOHN WHITE	972	973 THOMAS BUTTER	974 HENRY BOWLER	975 THOMAS HAWKINS
976 GEORGE GREY	977 WILLIAM	978 THOMAS MUNDAY	979 BENJAMIN BACON	980 ROBERT SCATCHARD
981 CHARLES CLARIDGE	982 JOSEPH SPACKMAN	983 JAMES PULESTON	984 W H 1709	985 JOHN VAUGHAN
986 JOSEPH JEFFERYS	987 W F	988 MARY WILLEY	989 T S	990 THO. JONES
991 BROWNE & SWANSON	992 W M E	993 WILLIAM WIGHTMAN	994 BENNETT CHAPMAN	995 JOHN KING

Marks from Touch Plate No. IV

Marks from Touch Plate Nº IV

CHAPTER XIV

PRICES

THE good old days when any collector, no matter what his bent might be, could hope to light upon a " find," or several of them, when on his holiday, have probably gone never to return. It is partly the collector's own fault in the case of pewter and partly the fault of the pewter.

It is the fault of the pewter because the number of articles that can be collected is limited by their very nature, and by the wanton destruction of all weakened or damaged pieces. A cracked plate could be joined and made fit to handle by an expert; glass could be cemented, so too could lustre and other breakable wares; but pewter was known to have a certain value as metal of a kind, and when once cracked, damaged or apparently beyond use it was withdrawn from the stage.

At the date of my first exhibition of pewter in 1904 it was most interesting to hear the various collectors comparing notes and mentioning the prices they had paid for some of their treasures—in many cases literally a few pence for small things like buckles, snuff-boxes, or a few shillings for spoons in the early days, spice-boxes, mugs and plates.

Plates 9 in. in diameter certainly will never again be bought—if in good condition—for three or four shillings, and 15-in. dishes or larger will run into pounds sterling.

The value of the articles even with tin at its present price, over £300 per ton, a fraction over 2s. 8d. per lb., does not warrant the absurdly high prices realized to-day.

The fault lies with the collectors themselves. In olden days the collector used to collect quietly, without bragging too much, except to one or two special friends; and pewter rarely found its way into the auction room, for it was neither understood nor appreciated.

Auction-room sales have been the undoing and the despair of the small collector, and the employment of agents to bid—with a limit—has had the result of sending up the price to the limit set by the anxious buyer. It could not be otherwise.

Then, again, the keenness of two or more rival collectors has naturally been the cause of an upward trend in prices.

Take at the present time an article such as a tappit-hen. If it is in good condition it may command anything over £20. At that price the coveted article may be knocked down to the wealthy collector who has half a dozen or more of them already in his collection.

At times one is tempted to think that a collector is trying to make a corner in such things, then he ceases to be a collector in the proper acceptation of the term and becomes a collector for profit—a very despicable variety of collector.

Prices in the country have generally averaged about one-third less than in towns, but the country dealers generally know what they can reasonably ask, and they are well equipped with a knowledge of local history that will enable them to sell plates with armorial bearings at enhanced rates.

Tankards, again, to-day may fetch £10 or more, and twenty years ago they were to be bought for, say, 5s. I have seen a William and Mary tankard with the lid loose that was bought for 3s. 6d. To-day it would probably be £12.

The collector to-day will have to make up his mind to pay these inflated prices; if he does not he will lose his chance; but the fact that people will pay them is to be regretted.

Pewter collecting has become a craze and the devotees have lost all sense of shame in their anxiety to collect. It is no longer a hobby for the collector with a slender purse—the more is the pity.

It is perhaps inevitable that prices should have risen. The writer has been told that they began to go up immediately after he had organized the Clifford's Inn Exhibition in 1904, as soon as a genuine interest had been aroused in the ware; but it may honestly be said that they have gone up beyond the bounds of what is reasonable, bearing in mind the small intrinsic worth of the material and the simplicity of the methods of manufacture.

There is no real reason why a pewter spoon—not absolutely in perfect order—should be sold at something above the price of a similar spoon in silver. As long as this kind of thing goes on collecting becomes restricted in its range if not altogether out of the question for the average collector.

It is exactly the same with foreign pewter. A dish that the writer bought in Bruges in 1885 for 5 francs would now probably be cheap at 50 or 60—ten or twelve times the price.

This inflation of prices has been the fault of the collector in England. As soon as it was known abroad that there was a demand for pewter in England the price, even for poor badly made rubbish, went up at a bound.

Tourists came home with dull-looking plates and dishes, with fine clear marks, many of them enriched (?) with repoussé work of modern date, for which they had had to pay fancy prices.

GLOSSARY

Acorn-Knopped. Spoons bearing an acorn at the end of the stem.

Alloy. A mixture of two or more metals.

Ampulla. A small vessel to contain incense or the oil for Extreme Unction.

Apostle Spoons. Spoons with knops representing the Apostles. They are extremely rare in Pewter.

Appliqué. A piece of material cut out and fastened on the surface of another is termed *appliqué*.

Ashberry Metal. A very hard alloy, containing about 25 per cent of antimony. It was used for buckles, snuff-boxes, forks, spoons, teapots, coasters.

Assay. To put to the test.

Badges. Signs worn on their sleeve or breast by beggars, pilgrims, porters and by some servants.

Ball-Knopped. Spoons having a small ball at the top end of the stem.

Baluster-Knops. A type of knops on spoons having a small button on the stem end of the baluster. (Sixteenth century.)

Baluster-Stems. Candlesticks or cups with a swelled boss in the stem or shaft.

Beaker. A drinking-vessel, with sides tapering from the foot outwards.

Bénitiers. Small stoups for holy water.

Billet. Another name for the thumb-piece or purchase.

Bismuth. A metal which is added to pewter to harden it.

Black Metal. An alloy of 60 parts of tin and 40 of lead.

Bleeding-Dishes. } Bowls to hold blood. Sometimes
Blood-Porringer. } graduated.

Booge. The curved part of a plate between the rim and the flat bottom.

Britannia Metal. A varying alloy of tin, antimony, copper, and bismuth.

GLOSSARY

Burettes. Pewter bottles for sacramental wine, or for water. They are in pairs: one marked "A" for aqua (water), and the other "V" for vinum (wine).

Burnisher. A tool for surfacing metal. Burnishers are made of agate, bloodstone, or steel.

Cardinals' Hats. A name given to flat dishes from their resemblance to hats of this shape.

Cassolette. A vessel or box for perfumes, with an elaborately perforated lid so as to allow the dispersion of the perfume.

Chalice. A cup especially for sacramental use.

Chapnet.
Chapnut. } A name applied to a kind of salt-cellar.

Chased. Decoration produced on the surface of metal by fine punches and lining tools. No metal is removed as is the case in engraving.

Chopin. A Scottish measure containing six gills.

Chrismatory. A vessel for the oil for Extreme Unction.

Claw-Ball. A common ornament for the feet of large tankards, beakers, and hanaps.

Coaster. A stand for a decanter.

Coffin. A mould for containing the crust of a meat-pie.

Costrel A harvest or pilgrim's bottle, usually of wood, or earthenware, but sometimes of pewter.

Counterfeits. Another name for porringers.

Cri. The name given to the sound given by tin, and by the best pewter when bent backwards and forwards.

Cruets. Small sacramental vessels on feet, with lids, usually found in pairs, one marked "A" for aqua, and the other "V" for vinum.

Cupping-Dish. *Vide* Bleeding-Dish.

Cup-Foot. A semi-spherical foot used for inkstands.

Danske Pots. In all probability pots of a Danish pattern.

Diamond-Pointed Knop. A name given to an early type of spoon. (Fifteenth century.)

Ear-Dish. A shallow dish with one or two flat projecting handles.

Ecuelles. Bowls and porringers.

Embossed. *V.* Repoussé.

Engraved. Decorated by a design which is cut with a burin or other sharp tool.

Ewer. A jug.

Fashion. The making.

Flagon. The name given to large tankards with flat or domed lids.

GADROON. A geometrical design consisting of curved lines radiating from a centre, the space between them being generally repoussé.

GALENA. A sulphide of lead, sometimes containing traces of silver.

GARNISH. The old name for a complete set of vessels in pewter, consisting of 12 platters, 12 dishes or flat bowls, and 12 saucers, i.e. small flat plates.

GRATER. A tool for scraping pewter.

GUT. Vessels for holding and cooling wine.

HAWKSBILL. A ewer of large size.

HEXAGONAL KNOPS. A common type of knop found on spoons. (Sixteenth century.)

HIND'S FOOT. *V.* Pied-de-biche.

HOLLOW-WARE. The generic name given to large pots, measures, tankards, and flagons.

HORNED HEAD-DRESS. A type of knop found on spoons. (Fifteenth century.)

HORSE-HOOF KNOP. A rare type of knop found on spoons. (Sixteenth century.)

KAYZERZINN. A modern German pewter alloy.

LATTEN. A brass alloy of a pleasant colour, and of good quality.

LAY.
LEA. } Tin mixed with lead so as to be of lower quality.

LAY-MEN.
LEY-MEN. } The name given to men who worked in such metal

LION KNOP. A form of knop in which the lion is sejant, or sitting. (Sixteenth century.)

LOGGERHEADS. Circular inkstands, usually with a flat dish for a base.

MAIDENHEAD. A type of knop found on spoons. (Fifteenth century.)

MONK'S HEAD. A very rare type of knop found on spoons. (Sixteenth century.)

MUTCHKIN. A Scottish measure holding five gills.

PALE. The pewterers' name for solder.

PANE. That part of the hammer with which the pewterer strikes the object that he is making.

PATINA. A form of oxidation.

PEAK. The old pewterers' name for lead.

PECHKRÜGE. Wooden tankards, with pewter work either inlaid or *appliqué*.

PEG-TANKARD. A tankard with pegs on the inside, at regular intervals.

GADROON. A geometrical design consisting of curved lines radiating from a centre, the space between them being generally repoussé.

GALENA. A sulphide of lead, sometimes containing traces of silver.

GARNISH. The old name for a complete set of vessels in pewter, consisting of 12 platters, 12 dishes or flat bowls, and 12 saucers, i.e. small flat plates.

GRATER. A tool for scraping pewter.

GUT. Vessels for holding and cooling wine.

HAWKSBILL. A ewer of large size.

HEXAGONAL KNOPS. A common type of knop found on spoons. (Sixteenth century.)

HIND'S FOOT. *V.* Pied-de-biche.

HOLLOW-WARE. The generic name given to large pots, measures, tankards, and flagons.

HORNED HEAD-DRESS. A type of knop found on spoons. (Fifteenth century.)

HORSE-HOOF KNOP. A rare type of knop found on spoons. (Sixteenth century.)

KAYZERZINN. A modern German pewter alloy.

LATTEN. A brass alloy of a pleasant colour, and of good quality.

LAY. }
LEA. } Tin mixed with lead so as to be of lower quality.

LAY-MEN. } The name given to men who worked in such
LEY-MEN. }   metal

LION KNOP. A form of knop in which the lion is sejant, or sitting. (Sixteenth century.)

LOGGERHEADS. Circular inkstands, usually with a flat dish for a base.

MAIDENHEAD. A type of knop found on spoons. (Fifteenth century.)

MONK'S HEAD. A very rare type of knop found on spoons. (Sixteenth century.)

MUTCHKIN. A Scottish measure holding five gills.

PALE. The pewterers' name for solder.

PANE. That part of the hammer with which the pewterer strikes the object that he is making.

PATINA. A form of oxidation.

PEAK. The old pewterers' name for lead.

PECHKRÜGE. Wooden tankards, with pewter work either inlaid or *appliqué*.

PEG-TANKARD. A tankard with pegs on the inside, at regular intervals.

GLOSSARY

PIED-DE-BICHE. A type of spoon so called because the end is split like a deer's foot.

PITCHER. The old term for any vessel with a handle and an open spout.

PITCH-BLOCK. *V.* Repoussé.

PLANISH. To smooth and harden a plate of metal by means of blows of a special hammer.

PLATE-METAL. Pewter of good quality.

PLATTER. A flat disk of metal with a slightly raised rim.

POINTILLÉ. Ornament produced by stabbing the metal with a pointed tool.

PORRINGER. A porridge dish.

POUNCE-BOX. *V.* Sand-box.

PRICKET. A candlestick with a spike to hold the candle.

PURCHASE. The thumbpiece by means of which a tankard lid is raised.

QUAIGH. A word used of a shallow circular drinking vessel, somewhat like a deep saucer, with two handles.

RAVENSBILL. A ewer.

REPOUSSÉ. A design raised up by repeated blows on the under side of a piece of metal by means of special hammers and raising-tools. The work is fixed to a pitch-block.

SADWARE. The trade name for the heavier articles, e.g. plates, trenchers, dishes, and chargers.

SALER. A saltcellar.

SAND-BOX. A box with a perforated lid, by means of which fine sand was sprinkled on documents to dry the ink.

SCOURING. The proper name for the cleaning of pewter.

SEAL TOPS. A type of knop found on spoons.

SILVORUM. A sham-silver alloy of seventeenth century.

SLIPPED IN THE STALK. A variety of spoons in which the stem is cut (or slipped) on the slant. (Sixteenth century.)

SOLDER. An alloy of low fusing-point used for joining two or more pieces of metal.

SPINNING. Process by which a thin plate of metal in a lathe is forced to take the shape of a solid or built-up wooden core.

STIPPLED. Ornament produced by marking or pricking the surface with small dots.

STUMP-END, OR STUMP-TOP. A rare type of spoon. (Sixteenth century.)

SWAGE. An anvil upon which large dishes were made.

TAPPIT-HENS. The name given to Scottish vessels of various sizes with lids. The capacity varied from $\frac{1}{4}$ gill to $\frac{3}{4}$ gallon.

Temper. The name given to pewter when alloyed with copper.

Thumb-piece. The name given to the lever by which the lid of a jug or tankard is raised. It is often called a purchase.

Tokens. Small pieces of pewter formerly issued in Scotland to intending Communicants. They were sometimes circular, sometimes square, sometimes octagonal.

Touch. A private mark impressed on pewter ware by the pewterer.

Touch-plates. Five plates of pewter preserved at Pewterers' Hall, on which all the touches or private marks of pewterers were supposed to be stamped.

Treen. The old name for wooden bowls, wooden plates.

Trifle. Pewter of common quality is usually called trifle.

Triflers. The trade name given to the men who made spoons, forks, buckles, buttons and toys.

Tundish. A funnel.

Wriggled. A broken-line pattern produced by pushing the tool with a regular rocking from side to side is termed " wriggled."

Writhen-knop. A very rare form of knop found on spoons. (Sixteenth century.)

THE REFERENCE LITERATURE OF PEWTER

IN "Pewter Plate" published in 1904 and in its second edition of 1910, there was a Bibliography, possibly more full than the Collector wants in the ordinary way.

For anyone who wants to study the History of the Pewterers' Company mainly, and who at the same time wishes to possess reproductions of the existing Touch-plates, the "History of the Worshipful Company of Pewterers of the City of London," by Charles Welch, published in 1902, is indispensable. Though the work is mainly, as its title implies, historical, there is a certain amount of technical information contained in the two volumes. There is one feeling of regret which must enter the mind of the reader, and that is that the compiler was not more interested in the Pewterer and his art. The historical interest would not have been diminished at all, but how much more alive it would have been for us to-day.

The five touch-plates—reproduced in collotype—are almost better cut out and framed, though there is not much interest in the fifth of the series. Frequent reference to the plates is bound to cause speedy havoc and decay.

The two Charters which are also given as illustrations, are worth framing.

"Pewter Plate," published by Messrs. Bell & Sons in 1904, and in a second edition in 1910, was the result of over eight years of almost continuous research and investigation of authorities. The book tried to fill the gap that had been left by Mr. Welch and to some extent succeeded. There were bound to be mistakes, errors in facts and errors in judgments, especially in any attempt to decipher the touches on the touch-plates, many of these touches being almost if not quite illegible. Conjectures were made with some amount of confidence, but it was never pretended that they were infallible, and the mistaken readings were never intended to be slavishly copied and without acknowledgment.

In the year following its publication, Mr. L. Ingleby Wood brought out his " Scottish Pewter Ware and Pewterers," a most careful work and worthy of a place of honour in the Collector's library.

The illustrations of the existing Scottish touch plates are particularly valuable.

Another Scottish book—and of great interest to pewter-lovers, is " Old Scottish Communion Plate," by Rev. Thomas Burns (1892). The portion dealing with Communion Tokens is likely to be of most interest to the Pewter Collector.

" Chats on Pewter " (by the Writer of this volume) was published in 1910-11, and being designed to serve as a supplement to " Pewter Plate," contained various special features. It had a list of all the Pewterers who were then known to have existed between the middle of the sixteenth to the beginning of the nineteenth century, and this list contained all the names of Pewterers that were legible in the MS. list of the Yeomanry preserved at Pewterers' Hall. In addition to this were added the names of various Scottish and Irish Pewterers, chiefly obtained from rubbings or drawings sent to me by those interested in the subject, and from Mr. R. C. Hope's MS. notes on " Old English Pewter," an interesting book of considerable value. It was this MS. which led me to number the touches on the touch-plates for greater ease in reference.

My old friend, Mr. A. de Navarro, published his delightful " Causeries on English Pewter " in 1911. It is invaluable as a stimulating influence to the Collector, and moreover is a most thoughtful and suggestive book, enriched with many excellent illustrations.

After each of the Exhibitions of Pewter organized by me in 1904 and 1908 in the Hall of Clifford's Inn, Fleet Street, illustrated catalogues were brought out dealing mainly with the specimens exhibited at those two exhibitions. These were printed by subscription and published by me. The Catalogue of 1904 is now a somewhat rare book, and that of 1908 is becoming scarce.

Shortly before his death, Mr. F. G. Hilton Price (Dir. S.A.) published a monograph called " Old Base Metal Spoons," 1908. It deals with both latten and pewter spoons, and is indispensable to any Collector of spoons and should be studied carefully.

Many articles, some authoritative, some very speculative,

have appeared in periodicals and magazines, but it is not proposed to refer to them here in detail. The files of the magazines, etc., will give the necessary clues.

Of other publications which, as they have been of use to me, may be some help to others, there may be mentioned the various books on the church plate of the various counties. The first and best of these was "Old Church Plate of the Diocese of Carlisle" (1882), by R. S. Ferguson. Others are "Church Plate of Carmarthenshire," "Church Plate of Gloucestershire," Church Plate of Pembrokeshire," "Church Plate of Radnorshire," all by the Rev. J. H. Evans.

Mr. R. C. Hope gave us the "Church Plate of the County of Rutland." Mr. Halliday compiled a similar survey of the Diocese of St. David's and St. Asaph's.

Mr. J. M. Fallow wrote on the "Plate of the East Riding of Yorkshire," the Rev. James E. Nightingale on the "Church Plate of Dorset, the Church Plate of Wilts, and the Church Plate of Norfolk"; the Rev. A. Trollope took in hand the inventory of the church plate of Leicestershire. The Hon. B. S. Stanhope and Mr. H. C. Moffatt wrote "The Church Plate of the County of Hereford."

In all of these books there are scattered references to the pewter-plate once so common in the various dioceses. Often the chronicler can only record that there used to be a pewter flagon, or a paten, or else that the specimens preserved are in a state of neglect or decay. It is something in these days of progress to find that what was once a cherished gift is allowed to remain as rubbish in a disused cupboard.

Anyone who wishes to trace the ubiquity of the pewterers' art must read Germain Bapst's "Études sur l'étain," or, better, the book from which Bapst culled most of his information, "Étude sur l'histoire de la production at du commerce de l'étain," by Hector Dufrène, Paris, 1881. Bapst's own copy of it with his annotations is in my possession.

For the goldsmiths work in pewter that is found in various museums, such as the British Museum, the Victoria and Albert Museum, the Musée Cluny in Paris, the book to study is Demiani's "François Briot, Gaspar Enderlein und das Edelzinn," published at Leipzig in 1897. For those acquainted with German the bibliography will prove of surpassing interest.

For information as to pewter in earlier days in England, reference may be made to Halliwell's "Ancient Inventories," William Harrison's "Elizabethan England," reprinted in the

Walter Scott Library; Havard's "Dictionnaire de l'Ameublement," Vol. II., under "Estaimier" and "Étain," also Jules Labarthe's "Histoire des arts industriels au moyen âge et à l'époque de la renaissance," Paris, 1873, and also to T. H. King's "Orfévrerie et ouvrages en metal du Moyen Âge," published at Bruges in 1852–55.

Viollet-le-duc in his "Dictionnaire du Mobilier français," under the words Bénitier, Assiette, Cuiller, Ecuelle, Fourchette, gives much interesting information.

INDEX

INDEX

Abbreviations explained, 145
— for touch plates, 221
Alloys, 18
Altar candlesticks, 16
Aluminium, 16
American pewter centre, 101
Amphorae, 117
Ampoules (ampullae), 119, 129
Antimony, 17
Arabesque work, 91
Arrangement of pewter, 31-34
Articles made in pewter in 1430, 61
Assay, right of, in London, 59

Badges, 125
— for pilgrims, 125
— for porters, 125
Bateman Collection, 27
Beakers, 19, 109
Beer bowls, 109
— cups, 109
— goblets, 109
— jugs, 109
— mugs, 19
Beggars' badges, 127
Bénitiers, 117, 118
Bismuth, 17
Bleeding dishes, 103
Blood porringers, 103
Boar's head dishes, 27
Bottle-holders, 21
Bowls (bolles), 61
Briot, 98
Britannia metal, composition of, 18
— — Communion Plate, 124
Broad arrow mark, the, 62

Brooches, 127
Buckles, 127
Burettes, 117
Burnishing, 42

Candelabra, 117
Candlesticks, 17-22
Casting pewter, 18
Centres of trade, 63, 73
— — abroad, 73, 74
Chalices, 87, 115
— sepulchral, 116
Chandeliers, 117
Chapnut (chapnet), 117
Chargers, 27, 55, 61, 62
Charles I, pewter, 17, 27, 87, 90
Charles II, pewter, 17, 86
Chasing, 84, 85
Chastleton House, inventory in 1632, 100
Chinese pewter, 91
Chopins, 113
Chrismatories, 119
Church candlesticks, 16, 117
— chalices, 115, 125
— cruets, 55, 117
— dishes, 124
— flagons, 124
— plate, 31, 90, 91
Cimaises, 130, 131
City churches, 90, 119
Clifford's Inn pewter, 95
Cleaning and scouring pewter, 35-40
Cluny Museum, 89
Coffins (for pies), 68
Coins, pewter, 130
Collectors, advice to, 19

311

Communion Plate, 121–123
— tokens, 124
Control by Company, 16
Cotterell, Howard H., vii, 53, 54
Counterfettes (dishes), 99, 103
Counterpayne, 134
Cracks and defects, 46, 47
Craft of the pewterer, 53, 59
Cri, 81
Crooked Lane men, 76

Danske pots, 68, 111
Decline of trade, 16
Display, effective, 31–34
Domestic pewter, 93 sqq.

Eared cups, 103
Eccentricity in pewter, 20, 21
Ecuelles, 103
Edelzinn (by Demiani), quoted, 91
Efflorescence of pewter, 42
Emery, to be used with care, 36
Enamel, 87
Enderlein, 98
Engleheart, Rev. R. G., 27
Engraved pewter, 83, 84
Étain Sonnant, 101
Exhibitions, 27, 306

Fakes, 21
Feast vessels, 97
Fine pewter, 18
Fines, 110
Flagons, 111, 121, 122, 123
Font basins and ewers, 118, 119
Food-bottles (?), 22
Foreign pewterers, 138
— ware, 67, 71, 73, 138
— workmen, 69, 70, 71, 138

Garnish, 74
Gilding pewter, 87, 89, 119
Glossary, 300-304
Gun-metal moulds, 18
Guild-cups, 16, 25
— regulations, 59
Gurney collection, 25

Hall-marks (?), 143 sqq.
Hanaps, 16, 25, 86
Handles, 43, 81
Harrison, quoted, 74, 94, 95, 97, 103, 109
Hawkers, 63
Hawkesbills, 111
Heart cases, 117
Henry VII, pewter, 26
Henry VIII, 71
Hiring of pewter, 97
Hollow-ware men, the, 62

Imitation, keynote to pewterers' art, 16
Inkstands, 23, 131, 132
— loggerheads, 132
Inlaid work in pewter, 26, 85, 90
Irish pewter, 52

Jersey measures, 113
Joggled ornament, 82
John, King, of England, 53
"Journal d'un Voyage à Paris," 98

Knife for testing pewter, 79

Lacquered pewter, 87, 92
Lamps, 101
Lathe work, 25
Laymen, the, 62
Lea (ley), 17
Lead, 17
Lily-pots, 59
Livery or brotherhood, 59
Loggerheads, 132

Marks on pewter, 133 sqq.
— compulsory in 1503, 63
Ménagier de Paris, 97
Mercurial solder, 82
Metropolitan Museum, N.Y., 33
Monstrances, 119
Montpellier standard, 18
Moulds for pewter, 18
Musée Plantin, Antwerp, 89
Mustard pots, 19
Mutchkins, 113

INDEX

Northumberland Household Book, 97
Nürnberg Museum, 33

Ordinances of the Pewterers, 1348, 54, 55, 57, 58
Ornament on pewter, 83 *sqq*.
Oxford, Queen's College, 94

Paraffin, 36, 38
Patens, 31, 90, 91
Peak, 302
Pechkrüge, 85, 113
Pepper cruets, 19
Pewter, alloys, 18
— black-metal, 132
— cleaning, 35–40
— colour of, 89
— hard metal, 18
— plate metal, 18
— tin and temper, 18
Pewterers' Company, vii
Pierced work, 85
Pilgrim bottle, 46
Pilgrim flagons, 46, 127
Plates, 20
Platters, 54
Pointillé ornament, 85, 86
Polishing, 37
— pastes, 37
Porringers, 54, 99, 103
— for bleeding, 103
Posset cups, 19
Pot clips, 95
Pot lids, 110
Pre-Elizabethan ware, 26
Pre-emption rights, 62
Pricked ornament, 85
Punch ladles, 106
Pyxes, 119

Quaighs, 103, 114
Quality mark, 138, 139
Queen's metal, 18

Ravensbills, 111
Repairs, 35–40
Repoussé pewter, 83
Richard II, 60
Rijks Museum, Amsterdam, 86

Rings, 127
Roman pewter, 26, 27, 41, 44
— analysis of, 28
Rose and Crown, 140, 141
Rosewater dishes, 27, 87
Rubbings, 29, 30
Russian pewter, 91

Sadware men, the, 62
Sadware, 102
Salers, 54
Salvers, 102
Saltcellars, 19
Scottish pewter, 52
— pewterers, 54
Scouring of pewter, 36
Scraping, 43
Scratches, 41
Search, right of, 62
Sepulchral chalices, 116
— plaques, 116
Silver marks on pewter, 139
Silver pewter, so called, 51
Silvering pewter, 87
Silvorum ware, 17
Snuff-boxes, 19
Solders and soldering, 45, 46
Spoonracks, 31
Spoons, 23, 31, 105
Squillery officers, 97
Standardized pewter ware, 61, 77
Standing pots, 121
Standish, 132
Staple Inn pewter, 95
Stone-pot lids, 110
Stone-pots, 25, 110
Stoup, 121
Sugar-sifters, 107
Swaythling, Lord, 26

Tankards, 20
Tappit-hens, 113
Teapots, 19, 93
Testing pewter, 79, 81
Thriddendales (thurndells), 68
Tin, 17
— and temper, 18

Tinkers (travelling), 60
Tokens, 124
Touch plates, 221 *sqq.*
Touches, 69
Toys of pewter, 107, 108
Treen or treene, 94
Trifle, 18, 68
Triflers, 62

Vessel, 77

Welch, C., "History of Pewterers' Co.," *passim*
Westropp, M. S. Dudley, vii
William and Mary, 26
Winchester pints, 111

Winchester quarts, 111
Wine flasks, 22
Women pewterers, 75, 76
Wooden spoons, 94, 105
Workmen's rules, 54–58
Wriggled ornamentation, 82

X and Crown, quality mark, 138, 139
Yeates, A. B., 26
Yeomanry, the, 59
York pewterers, 102
Young, Dr., vii

Zinc, 16, 81

BOOK JUNGLE

Bringing Classics to Life

www.bookjungle.com email: sales@bookjungle.com fax: 630-214-0564 mail: Book Jungle PO Box 2226 Champaign, IL 61825

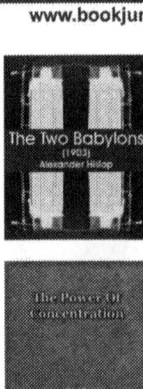

The Two Babylons
Alexander Hislop

You may be surprised to learn that many traditions of Roman Catholicism in fact don't come from Christ's teachings but from an ancient Babylonian "Mystery" religion that was centered on Nimrod, his wife Semiramis, and a child Tammuz. This book shows how this ancient religion transformed itself as it incorporated Christ into its teachings....

Religion/History Pages:358
ISBN: *1-59462-010-5* MSRP $22.95 QTY ☐

The Go-Getter
Kyne B. Peter

The Go Getter is the story of William Peck. He was a war veteran and amputee who will not be refused what he wants. Peck not only fights to find employment but continually proves himself more than competent at the many difficult test that are throw his way in the course of his early days with the Ricks Lumber Company...

Business/Self Help/Inspirational Pages:68
ISBN: *1-59462-186-1* MSRP $8.95 QTY ☐

The Power Of Concentration
Theron Q. Dumont

It is of the utmost value to learn how to concentrate. To make the greatest success of anything you must be able to concentrate your entire thought upon the idea you are working on. The person that is able to concentrate utilizes all constructive thoughts and shuts out all destructive ones...

Self Help/Inspirational Pages:196
ISBN: *1-59462-141-1* MSRP $14.95 ☐

Self Mastery
Emile Coue

Emile Coue came up with novel way to improve the lives of people. He was a pharmacist by trade and often saw ailing people. This lead him to develop autosuggestion, a form of self-hypnosis. At the time his theories weren't popular but over the years evidence is mounting that he was indeed right all along...

New Age/Self Help Pages:98
ISBN: *1-59462-189-6* MSRP $7.95 ☐

Rightly Dividing The Word
Clarence Larkin

The "Fundamental Doctrines" of the Christian Faith are clearly outlined in numerous books on Theology, but they are not available to the average reader and were mainly written for students. The Author has made it the work of his ministry to preach the "Fundamental Doctrines." To this end he has aimed to express them in the simplest and clearest manner.

Religion Pages:352
ISBN: *1-59462-334-1* MSRP $23.45 ☐

The Awful Disclosures Of Maria Monk

"I cannot banish the scenes and characters of this book from my memory. To me it can never appear like an amusing fable, or lose its interest and importance. The story is one which is continually before me, and must return fresh to my mind with painful emotions as long as I live.."

Religion Pages:232
ISBN: *1-59462-160-8* MSRP $17.95 ☐

The Law of Psychic Phenomena
Thomson Jay Hudson

"I do not expect this book to stand upon its literary merits; for if it is unsound in principle, felicity of diction cannot save it, and if sound, homeliness of expression cannot destroy it. My primary object in offering it to the public is to assist in bringing Psychology within the domain of the exact sciences. That this has never been accomplished..."

New Age Pages:420
ISBN: *1-59462-124-1* MSRP $29.95 ☐

As a Man Thinketh
James Allen

"This little volume (the result of meditation and experience) is not intended as an exhaustive treatise on the much-written-upon subject of the power of thought. It is suggestive rather than explanatory, its object being to stimulate men and women to the discovery and perception of the truth that by virtue of the thoughts which they choose and encourage..."

Inspirational/Self Help Pages:80
ISBN: *1-59462-231-0* MSRP $9.45 ☐

Beautiful Joe
Marshall Saunders

When Marshall visited the Moore family in 1892, she discovered Joe, a dog they had nursed back to health from his previous abusive home to live a happy life. So moved was she, that she wrote this classic masterpiece which won accolades and was recognized as a heartwarming symbol for humane animal treatment...

Fiction Pages:256
ISBN: *1-59462-261-2* MSRP $18.45 ☐

The Enchanted April
Elizabeth Von Arnim

It began in a woman's club in London on a February afternoon, an uncomfortable club, and a miserable afternoon when Mrs. Wilkins, who had come down from Hampstead to shop and had lunched at her club, took up The Times from the table in the smoking-room...

Fiction Pages:368
ISBN: *1-59462-150-0* MSRP $23.45 ☐

The Codes Of Hammurabi And Moses - W. W. Davies

The discovery of the Hammurabi Code is one of the greatest achievements of archaeology, and is of paramount interest, not only to the student of the Bible, but also to all those interested in ancient history...

Religion Pages:132
ISBN: *1-59462-338-4* MSRP $12.95 ☐

Holland - The History Of Netherlands
Thomas Colley Grattan

Thomas Grattan was a prestigious writer from Dublin who served as British Consul to the US. Among his works is an authoritative look at the history of Holland. A colorful and interesting look at history....

History/Politics Pages:408
ISBN: *1-59462-137-3* MSRP $26.95 ☐

The Thirty-Six Dramatic Situations
Georges Polti

An incredibly useful guide for aspiring authors and playwrights. This volume categorizes every dramatic situation which could occur in a story and describes them in a list of 36 situations. A great aid to help inspire or formalize the creative writing process...

Self Help/Reference Pages:204
ISBN: *1-59462-134-9* MSRP $15.95 ☐

A Concise Dictionary of Middle English
A. L. Mayhew
Walter W. Skeat

The present work is intended to meet, in some measure, the requirements of those who wish to make some study of Middle-English, and who find a difficulty in obtaining such assistance as will enable them to find out the meanings and etymologies of the words most essential to their purpose...

Reference/History Pages:332
ISBN: *1-59462-119-5* MSRP $29.95 ☐

www.bookjungle.com email: sales@bookjungle.com fax: 630-214-0564 mail: Book Jungle PO Box 2226 Champaign, IL 61825

BOOK JUNGLE

Bringing Classics to Life

www.bookjungle.com email: sales@bookjungle.com fax: 630-214-0564 mail: Book Jungle PO Box 2226 Champaign, IL 61825

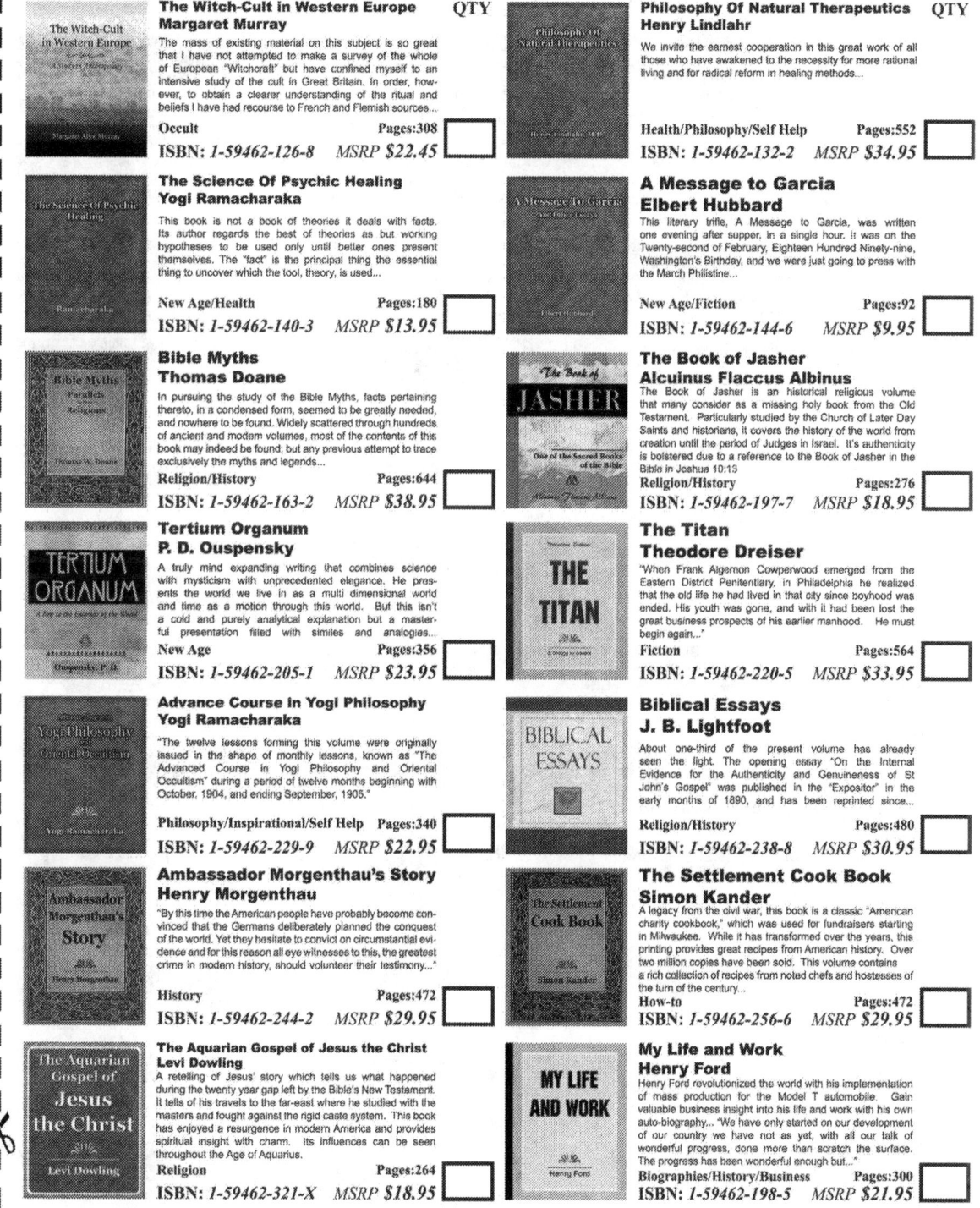

The Witch-Cult in Western Europe
Margaret Murray   QTY

The mass of existing material on this subject is so great that I have not attempted to make a survey of the whole of European "Witchcraft" but have confined myself to an intensive study of the cult in Great Britain. In order, however, to obtain a clearer understanding of the ritual and beliefs I have had recourse to French and Flemish sources...

Occult   Pages: 308
ISBN: 1-59462-126-8   MSRP $22.45

Philosophy Of Natural Therapeutics
Henry Lindlahr   QTY

We invite the earnest cooperation in this great work of all those who have awakened to the necessity for more rational living and for radical reform in healing methods...

Health/Philosophy/Self Help   Pages: 552
ISBN: 1-59462-132-2   MSRP $34.95

The Science Of Psychic Healing
Yogi Ramacharaka

This book is not a book of theories it deals with facts. Its author regards the best of theories as but working hypotheses to be used only until better ones present themselves. The "fact" is the principal thing the essential thing to uncover which the tool, theory, is used...

New Age/Health   Pages: 180
ISBN: 1-59462-140-3   MSRP $13.95

A Message to Garcia
Elbert Hubbard

This literary trifle, A Message to Garcia, was written one evening after supper, in a single hour. it was on the Twenty-second of February, Eighteen Hundred Ninety-nine, Washington's Birthday, and we were just going to press with the March Philistine...

New Age/Fiction   Pages: 92
ISBN: 1-59462-144-6   MSRP $9.95

Bible Myths
Thomas Doane

In pursuing the study of the Bible Myths, facts pertaining thereto, in a condensed form, seemed to be greatly needed, and nowhere to be found. Widely scattered through hundreds of ancient and modern volumes, most of the contents of this book may indeed be found; but any previous attempt to trace exclusively the myths and legends...

Religion/History   Pages: 644
ISBN: 1-59462-163-2   MSRP $38.95

The Book of Jasher
Alcuinus Flaccus Albinus

The Book of Jasher is an historical religious volume that many consider as a missing holy book from the Old Testament. Particularly studied by the Church of Later Day Saints and historians, it covers the history of the world from creation until the period of Judges in Israel. It's authenticity is bolstered due to a reference to the Book of Jasher in the Bible in Joshua 10:13

Religion/History   Pages: 276
ISBN: 1-59462-197-7   MSRP $18.95

Tertium Organum
P. D. Ouspensky

A truly mind expanding writing that combines science with mysticism with unprecedented elegance. He presents the world we live in as a multi dimensional world and time as a motion through this world. But this isn't a cold and purely analytical explanation but a masterful presentation filled with similes and analogies...

New Age   Pages: 356
ISBN: 1-59462-205-1   MSRP $23.95

The Titan
Theodore Dreiser

"When Frank Algernon Cowperwood emerged from the Eastern District Penitentiary, in Philadelphia he realized that the old life he had lived in that city since boyhood was ended. His youth was gone, and with it had been lost the great business prospects of his earlier manhood. He must begin again..."

Fiction   Pages: 564
ISBN: 1-59462-220-5   MSRP $33.95

Advance Course in Yogi Philosophy
Yogi Ramacharaka

"The twelve lessons forming this volume were originally issued in the shape of monthly lessons, known as "The Advanced Course in Yogi Philosophy and Oriental Occultism" during a period of twelve months beginning with October, 1904, and ending September, 1905."

Philosophy/Inspirational/Self Help Pages: 340
ISBN: 1-59462-229-9   MSRP $22.95

Biblical Essays
J. B. Lightfoot

About one-third of the present volume has already seen the light. The opening essay "On the Internal Evidence for the Authenticity and Genuineness of St John's Gospel" was published in the "Expositor" in the early months of 1890, and has been reprinted since...

Religion/History   Pages: 480
ISBN: 1-59462-238-8   MSRP $30.95

Ambassador Morgenthau's Story
Henry Morgenthau

"By this time the American people have probably become convinced that the Germans deliberately planned the conquest of the world. Yet they hesitate to convict on circumstantial evidence and for this reason all eye witnesses to this, the greatest crime in modern history, should volunteer their testimony..."

History   Pages: 472
ISBN: 1-59462-244-2   MSRP $29.95

The Settlement Cook Book
Simon Kander

A legacy from the civil war, this book is a classic "American charity cookbook," which was used for fundraisers starting in Milwaukee. While it has transformed over the years, this printing provides great recipes from American history. Over two million copies have been sold. This volume contains a rich collection of recipes from noted chefs and hostesses of the turn of the century...

How-to   Pages: 472
ISBN: 1-59462-256-6   MSRP $29.95

The Aquarian Gospel of Jesus the Christ
Levi Dowling

A retelling of Jesus' story which tells us what happened during the twenty year gap left by the Bible's New Testament. It tells of his travels to the far-east where he studied with the masters and fought against the rigid caste system. This book has enjoyed a resurgence in modern America and provides spiritual insight with charm. Its influences can be seen throughout the Age of Aquarius.

Religion   Pages: 264
ISBN: 1-59462-321-X   MSRP $18.95

My Life and Work
Henry Ford

Henry Ford revolutionized the world with his implementation of mass production for the Model T automobile. Gain valuable business insight into his life and work with his own auto-biography... "We have only started on our development of our country we have not as yet, with all our talk of wonderful progress, done more than scratch the surface. The progress has been wonderful enough but..."

Biographies/History/Business Pages: 300
ISBN: 1-59462-198-5   MSRP $21.95

www.bookjungle.com email: sales@bookjungle.com fax: 630-214-0564 mail: Book Jungle PO Box 2226 Champaign, IL 61825

BOOK JUNGLE

Bringing Classics to Life

www.bookjungle.com email: sales@bookjungle.com fax: 630-214-0564 mail: Book Jungle PO Box 2226 Champaign, IL 61825

QTY

☐	**The Rosicrucian Cosmo-Conception Mystic Christianity** by *Max Heindel* — The Rosicrucian Cosmo-conception is not dogmatic, neither does it appeal to any other authority than the reason of the student. It is: not controversial, but is: sent forth in the hope that it may help to clear...	ISBN: 1-59462-188-8	$38.95 New Age/Religion Pages 646
☐	**Abandonment To Divine Providence** by *Jean-Pierre de Caussade* — "The Rev. Jean Pierre de Caussade was one of the most remarkable spiritual writers of the Society of Jesus in France in the 18th Century. His death took place at Toulouse in 1751. His works have gone through many editions and have been republished...	ISBN: 1-59462-228-0	$25.95 Inspirational/Religion Pages 400
☐	**Mental Chemistry** by *Charles Haanel* — Mental Chemistry allows the change of material conditions by combining and appropriately utilizing the power of the mind. Much like general chemistry creates something new and unique out of careful combinations of chemicals the mastery of mental chemistry...	ISBN: 1-59462-192-6	$23.95 New Age Pages 354
☐	**The Letters of Robert Browning and Elizabeth Barret Barrett 1845-1846 vol II** by *Robert Browning* and *Elizabeth Barrett*	ISBN: 1-59462-193-4	$35.95 Biographies Pages 596
☐	**Gleanings In Genesis (volume I)** by *Arthur W. Pink* — Appropriately has Genesis been termed "the seed plot of the Bible" for in it we have, in germ form, almost all of the great doctrines which are afterwards fully developed in the books of Scripture which follow...	ISBN: 1-59462-130-6	$27.45 Religion/Inspirational Pages 420
☐	**The Master Key** by *L. W. de Laurence* — In no branch of human knowledge has there been a more lively increase of the spirit of research during the past few years than in the study of Psychology, Concentration and Mental Discipline. The requests for authentic lessons in Thought Control, Mental Discipline and...	ISBN: 1-59462-001-6	$30.95 New Age/Business Pages 422
☐	**The Lesser Key Of Solomon Goetia** by *L. W. de Laurence* — This translation of the first book of the "Lemegton" which is now for the first time made accessible to students of Talismanic Magic was done, after careful collation and edition, from numerous Ancient Manuscripts in Hebrew, Latin, and French...	ISBN: 1-59462-092-X	$9.95 New Age/Occult Pages 92
☐	**Rubaiyat Of Omar Khayyam** by *Edward Fitzgerald* — Edward Fitzgerald, whom the world has already learned, in spite of his own efforts to remain within the shadow of anonymity, to look upon as one of the rarest poets of the century, was born at Bredfield, in Suffolk, on the 31st of March, 1809. He was the third son of John Purcell...	ISBN: 1-59462-332-5	$13.95 Music Pages 172
☐	**Ancient Law** by *Henry Maine* — The chief object of the following pages is to indicate some of the earliest ideas of mankind, as they are reflected in Ancient Law; and to point out the relation of those ideas to modern thought.	ISBN: 1-59462-128-4	$29.95 Religion/History Pages 452
☐	**Far-Away Stories** by *William J. Locke* — "Good wine needs no bush. And a collection of mixed vintages does. And this book is just such a collection. Some of the stories I do not want to remain buried for ever in the museum files of dead magazine-numbers an author's not unpardonable vanity..."	ISBN: 1-59462-129-2	$19.45 Fiction Pages 272
☐	**Life of David Crockett** by *David Crockett* — "Colonel David Crockett was one of the most remarkable men of the times in which he lived. Born in humble life, but gifted with a strong will, an indomitable courage, and unremitting perseverance...	ISBN: 1-59462-250-7	$27.45 Biographies/New Age Pages 424
☐	**Lip-Reading** by *Edward Nitchie* — Edward B. Nitchie, founder of the New York School for the Hard of Hearing, now the Nitchie School of Lip-Reading, Inc, wrote "LIP-READING Principles and Practice". The development and perfecting of this meritorious work on lip-reading was an undertaking...	ISBN: 1-59462-206-X	$25.95 How-to Pages 400
☐	**A Handbook of Suggestive Therapeutics, Applied Hypnotism, Psychic Science** by *Henry Munro*	ISBN: 1-59462-214-0	$24.95 Health/New Age/Health/Self-help Pages 376
☐	**A Doll's House: and Two Other Plays** by *Henrik Ibsen* — Henrik Ibsen created this classic when in revolutionary 1848 Rome. Introducing some striking concepts in playwriting for the realist genre, this play has been studied the world over.	ISBN: 1-59462-112-8	$19.95 Fiction/Classics/Plays 308
☐	**The Light of Asia** by *sir Edwin Arnold* — In this poetic masterpiece, Edwin Arnold describes the life and teachings of Buddha. The man who was to become known as Buddha to the world was born as Prince Gautama of India but he rejected the worldly riches and abandoned the reigns of power when...	ISBN: 1-59462-204-3	$13.95 Religion/History/Biographies Pages 170
☐	**The Complete Works of Guy de Maupassant** by *Guy de Maupassant* — "For days and days, nights and nights, I had dreamed of that first kiss which was to consecrate our engagement, and I knew not on what spot I should put my lips..."	ISBN: 1-59462-157-8	$16.95 Fiction/Classics Pages 240
☐	**The Art of Cross-Examination** by *Francis L. Wellman* — Written by a renowned trial lawyer, Wellman imparts his experience and uses case studies to explain how to use psychology to extract desired information through questioning.	ISBN: 1-59462-309-0	$26.95 How-to/Science/Reference Pages 408
☐	**Answered or Unanswered?** by *Louisa Vaughan* — Miracles of Faith in China	ISBN: 1-59462-248-5	$10.95 Religion Pages 112
☐	**The Edinburgh Lectures on Mental Science (1909)** by *Thomas* — This book contains the substance of a course of lectures recently given by the writer in the Queen Street Hall, Edinburgh. Its purpose is to indicate the Natural Principles governing the relation between Mental Action and Material Conditions...	ISBN: 1-59462-008-3	$11.95 New Age/Psychology Pages 148
☐	**Ayesha** by *H. Rider Haggard* — Verily and indeed it is the unexpected that happens! Probably if there was one person upon the earth from whom the Editor of this, and of a certain previous history, did not expect to hear again...	ISBN: 1-59462-301-5	$24.95 Classics Pages 380
☐	**Ayala's Angel** by *Anthony Trollope* — The two girls were both pretty, but Lucy who was twenty-one who supposed to be simple and comparatively unattractive, whereas Ayala was credited, as her Bambwhal romantic name might show, with poetic charm and a taste for romance. Ayala when her father died was nineteen...	ISBN: 1-59462-352-X	$29.95 Fiction Pages 484
☐	**The American Commonwealth** by *James Bryce* — An interpretation of American democratic political theory. It examines political mechanics and society from the perspective of Scotsman James Bryce	ISBN: 1-59462-286-8	$34.45 Politics Pages 572
☐	**Stories of the Pilgrims** by *Margaret P. Pumphrey* — This book explores pilgrims religious oppression in England as well as their escape to Holland and eventual crossing to America on the Mayflower, and their early days in New England...	ISBN: 1-59462-116-0	$17.95 History Pages 268

www.bookjungle.com email: sales@bookjungle.com fax: 630-214-0564 mail: Book Jungle PO Box 2226 Champaign, IL 61825

BOOK JUNGLE

Bringing Classics to Life

www.bookjungle.com email: sales@bookjungle.com fax: 630-214-0564 mail: Book Jungle PO Box 2226 Champaign, IL 61825

Title	ISBN	Price	QTY
The Fasting Cure by *Sinclair Upton* — In the Cosmopolitan Magazine for May, 1910, and in the Contemporary Review (London) for April, 1910, I published an article dealing with my experiences in fasting. I have written a great many magazine articles, but never one which attracted so much attention... *New Age/Self Help/Health Pages 164*	1-59462-222-1	$13.95	☐
Hebrew Astrology by *Sepharial* — In these days of advanced thinking it is a matter of common observation that we have left many of the old landmarks behind and that we are now pressing forward to greater heights and to a wider horizon than that which represented the mind-content of our progenitors... *Astrology Pages 144*	1-59462-308-2	$13.45	☐
Thought Vibration or The Law of Attraction in the Thought World by *William Walker Atkinson* — *Psychology/Religion Pages 144*	1-59462-127-6	$12.95	☐
Optimism by *Helen Keller* — Helen Keller was blind, deaf, and mute since 19 months old, yet famously learned how to overcome these handicaps, communicate with the world, and spread her lectures promoting optimism. An inspiring read for everyone... *Biographies/Inspirational Pages 84*	1-59462-108-X	$15.95	☐
Sara Crewe by *Frances Burnett* — In the first place, Miss Minchin lived in London. Her home was a large, dull, tall one, in a large, dull square, where all the houses were alike, and all the sparrows were alike, and where all the door-knockers made the same heavy sound... *Childrens/Classic Pages 88*	1-59462-360-0	$9.45	☐
The Autobiography of Benjamin Franklin by *Benjamin Franklin* — The Autobiography of Benjamin Franklin has probably been more extensively read than any other American historical work, and no other book of its kind has had such ups and downs of fortune. Franklin lived for many years in England, where he was agent... *Biographies/History Pages 332*	1-59462-135-7	$24.95	☐

Name	
Email	
Telephone	
Address	
City, State ZIP	

☐ **Credit Card**   ☐ **Check / Money Order**

Credit Card Number	
Expiration Date	
Signature	

Please Mail to: Book Jungle
  PO Box 2226
  Champaign, IL 61825
or Fax to: 630-214-0564

ORDERING INFORMATION

web: www.bookjungle.com
email: sales@bookjungle.com
fax: 630-214-0564
mail: Book Jungle PO Box 2226 Champaign, IL 61825
or PayPal to sales@bookjungle.com

Please contact us for bulk discounts

DIRECT-ORDER TERMS

20% Discount if You Order Two or More Books
Free Domestic Shipping!
Accepted: Master Card, Visa, Discover, American Express

www.ingramcontent.com/pod-product-compliance
Lightning Source LLC
Chambersburg PA
CBHW080238170426
43192CB00014BA/2483